BRAIN QUEST

GRADE 5
WORKBOOK

T0016609

Written by Bridget Heos
Consulting Editor: Kim Tredick

Workman Publishing • New York

This book belongs to:

ISBN 978-1-5235-1739-8

New and updated text by Jen Agresta and Jennifer Szymanski; educational review by Anne Haywood, Peg Keiner, and Jonathan Coor

Illustrations by Matt Rockefeller and Scott Dubar, with cover illustrations by Edison Yan

Workbook series design by Raquel Jaramillo

30th Anniversary Edition Revision produced for Workman by WonderLab Group, LLC, and Fan Works Design, LLC.

Workman books are available at special discounts when purchased in bulk for premiums and sales promotions as well as for fundraising or educational use. Special editions or book excerpts can also be created to specification. For details, please contact special.markets@hbgusa.com.

Workman Publishing Co., Inc., a subsidiary of Hachette Book Group, Inc.
1290 Avenue of the Americas
New York, NY 10104
workman.com • brainquest.com

Distributed in the United Kingdom by Hachette Book Group, UK, Carmelite House, 50 Victoria Embankment, London, EC4Y 0DZ.

Distributed in Europe by Hachette Livre, 58 rue Jean Bleuzen, 92 178 Vanves Cedex, France.

Printed in the USA on responsibly sourced paper.

First printing April 2023
10 9 8 7 6 5 4 3 2 1

Dear Parents and Caregivers,

Learning is an adventure—a quest for knowledge. At Brain Quest, we strive to guide children on that quest, to keep them motivated and curious, and to give them the confidence they need to do well in school and beyond. We're excited to partner with you and your child on this step of their lifelong knowledge quest.

BRAIN QUEST WORKBOOKS are designed to enrich children's understandings in all content areas by reinforcing the basics and previewing future learning. These are not textbooks, but rather true workbooks, and are best used to reinforce curricular concepts learned at school. Each workbook aligns with national and state learning standards and is written in consultation with an award-winning grade-level teacher.

In fifth grade, children continue to strengthen their comprehension and critical thinking skills in preparation for middle school. Fifth graders read and write across all subjects to engage with the world around them and express their ideas. They approach science, technology, engineering, and math (STEM) activities with curiosity and creativity. Brain Quest gives learners a fun and accessible place to practice these foundational skills, while encouraging creative problem-solving.

We're excited that BRAIN QUEST WORKBOOKS will play an integral role in your child's educational adventure. So, let the learning—and the fun—begin!

It's fun to be smart!®

—The editors of Brain Quest

HOW TO USE THIS BOOK

Welcome to the Brain Quest Grade 5 Workbook!

Approach your work in this book with a **growth mindset**, the idea that your abilities can change and grow with effort. With time and practice, you can achieve your goals. Think of mistakes as opportunities, not setbacks. Effort pays off—you can do this!

The **opening page** of each section has a note for parents and caregivers and another note just for kids.

Notes to children give learners a preview of each section.

Notes to parents highlight key skills and give suggestions for helping with each section.

51

READING

Whether we're reading a story or a nonfiction essay, analyzing a chart or a time line, or following a recipe or instructions in a user's guide, our goal is the same: to comprehend (understand) what the text says. Let's sharpen our reading comprehension skills!

PARENTS Reading skills develop by engaging with a variety of content types, including fiction, nonfiction, news articles, maps, charts, and more. In this section, your child will strengthen their thinking skills by analyzing facts and opinions, comparing and contrasting, and considering point of view. Share the range of texts you read each day, from recipe instructions to online articles and sports scores.

For additional resources, visit www.BrainQuest.com/grade5

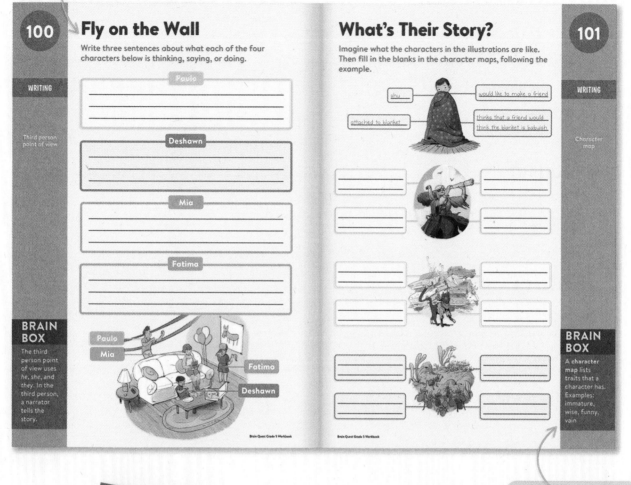

Be sure to read the directions before you begin. Read them twice if you need to!

100 · Fly on the Wall

WRITING

Write three sentences about what each of the four characters below is thinking, saying, or doing.

Paulo

Deshawn

Mia

Fatima

BRAIN BOX

Third person point of view

The third person point of view uses he, she, and they. In the third person, a narrator tells the story.

Paulo
Mia
Fatima
Deshawn

Brain Quest Grade 5 Workbook

101 · What's Their Story?

WRITING

Imagine what the characters in the illustrations are like. Then fill in the blanks in the character maps, following the example.

shy · would like to make a friend

attached to blanket · thinks that a friend would think the blanket is babyish

BRAIN BOX

Character map

A character map lists traits that a character has. Examples: immature, wise, funny, vain

Brain Quest Grade 5 Workbook

Brain Boxes offer friendly explanations of key concepts.

ANSWERS

"Huck Finn rowed down the Mississippi River." (In this sentence river is part of a proper noun.)

$202

(07)

QUESTIONS

ENGLISH — Which is correct? "Huck Finn rowed down the Mississippi river/River."

MATH — The Cub Scouts bought 18 baseball tickets for $11.50 each. How much did they pay in all?

ENGLISH — Rainbow sherbet is the most flavorful sherbet. Fact or opinion?

MATH — What is 56 × 1,000?

BRAIN QUEST

Cut out the Brain Quest Mini-Deck from the back to play and learn on the go!

Be proud of your hard work! Add your name to the certificate when you have completed all the sections. Hang it up on your wall to remind yourself of your effort and success.

CERTIFICATE OF **ACHIEVEMENT**

Earned by

for completing all sections in the

BRAIN QUEST®
GRADE 5 WORKBOOK

CONTENTS

SPELLING AND VOCABULARY

Understanding how words are built—recognizing prefixes and suffixes, Latin and Greek roots, and figurative language—helps you become a stronger reader and a more precise writer. From unusual spellings to hyperbole and jargon, this section will help you become a word wizard. Let's get started!

PARENTS Recognizing and decoding root words, affixes, figurative language, and unusual spellings enriches a reader's understanding of a text and a writer's ability to convey precise information. Encourage your child to use words they learn in this section to enhance their conversations and strengthen their writing.

For additional resources, visit www.BrainQuest.com/grade5

Start at the Beginning

Choose the correct **prefix** from the cards to complete each word.

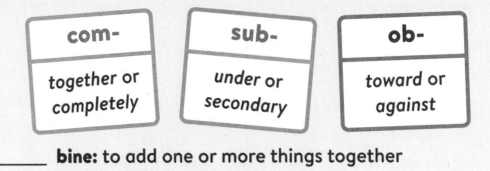

com-	sub-	ob-
together or completely	under or secondary	toward or against

_____ **bine:** to add one or more things together

_____ **long:** to have an elongated shape

_____ **merge:** to put underwater

_____ **heading:** a heading used to divide a chapter

_____ **panion:** a person who spends time with another

_____ **noxious:** offensive or annoying

_____ **rade:** a friend or fellow group member

_____ **struct:** to block or get in the way of

_____ **way:** an underground electric railway

_____ **plot:** a storyline that is secondary to the main story

Write a letter to a restaurant manager, politely asking for your money back because you found a fly in your soup. Use as many of the **com-**, **sub-**, and **ob-** words above as possible.

BRAIN BOX

A **prefix** is a word segment that changes the meaning of a word when added to the word's beginning.

Building Opposites

Add the correct **prefix** from the box to make a new word. Then write the definition of the new word.

un-   dis-   in-

approve	to accept as satisfactory
disapprove	to find not satisfactory

adequate	acceptable

advantage	a situation that gives one an edge over others

accurate	correct or exact

timely	happening at a convenient time

DIS APPROVE

UN CONVENTIONAL

BRAIN BOX

The **prefixes** *un-*, *dis-*, and *in-* can create words that are the opposites of the root words.

A Doable Activity

Word	Word with Suffix	Meaning
do	doable	able to be done
break	breakable	able to be broken

When the root word ends with **e**, drop the **e** before adding **-able**.

Word	Word with Suffix	Meaning
love	lovable	able to be loved
note	notable	worthy of notice

Finish each sentence by adding **-able** to the **highlighted** word and writing the new word in the blank.

Pigeons adapt well to city life. They are _____.

Careful! That porcelain penguin will break easily.
It is _____.

The cozy sweatshirt provides much comfort to Carlos.
It is _____.

The customers desire chocolate fudge sundaes.
The sundaes are _____.

You can distinguish between the fraternal twins.
They are _____.

The lifeboats inflate . They are _____.

Who doesn't love floppy-eared rabbits?
They are absolutely _____.

 Note that detective stories date back to ancient China.
The fact is _____.

Mike hasn't jumped off the high dive before, but his friends
 believe he can do it. It is _____.

Write four additional words ending in **-able**.

_____   _____

_____   _____

BRAIN BOX

A **suffix** is a word segment that changes the meaning of a word when added to the word's ending. The suffix *-able* changes the word to mean *able to be* [the word].

Are You Able or Ible?

Circle the ten words that have incorrect **-able** and **-ible** endings in this letter.

Hey Charlie,

I just heard the horrable news that your cupcakes were stolen. That's terrable! I hope there is tangable evidence pointing to whoever is responsable! I always felt comfortible leaving my food unattended, but not after this unbearible event. I guess none of us is invincable. We are all susceptable to thievery. The sad thing is: The cupcakes probably had incredable frosting.

Sincerely,

Your lovible dog, Junior

P.S. Please excuse the crumbs.

Write the misspelled words correctly.

_____

_____

_____

_____

_____

_____

_____

_____

BRAIN BOX

The suffix *-able* is more common than the suffix *-ible*. The roots of words ending in *-able* are usually complete words. Examples: preferable comfortable

The roots of words ending in *-ible* are less likely to be complete words. Examples: terrible incredible

Fun with Shun

Fill in the blanks with the correct word from the boxes below. Then read the sentences aloud.

| collision | addition | division | nation | revision |
| duration | persuasion | ambition | decision | editions |

Suffixes

The moon was most likely formed by a _____ between Earth and a Mars-size object.

Our _____ guarantees the right to life, liberty, and the pursuit of happiness.

They stayed for the _____ of the dull movie in the hope that it would improve as it went along.

A fraction can also be described as a _____ problem.

To convince her parents to adopt a puppy, Bea would need the power of _____ .

The foreign _____ of the Diary of a Wimpy Kid books are written in various languages, from French to Japanese.

They spent all summer working on a new _____ to the tree house, which included a whole second floor and a ladder.

The poorly written story was in need of _____ before it was published.

The jury could not reach a _____ .

His lifelong _____ was to study penguins in Antarctica and eventually write a book.

BRAIN BOX

The *shun* sound at the end of words is usually spelled -*tion* or -*sion*. Sometimes the two endings sound slightly different, as in *division* and *addition*. Other times, you must memorize the correct ending.

Happy Endings

Write the **-ed** and **-ing** form of each verb by first doubling the consonant. Then find the **-ed** and **-ing** verbs in the word search.

admit _admitted_ _admitting_   refer _____ _____

transfer _____ _____   expel _____ _____

control _____ _____   regret _____ _____

equip _____ _____   tap _____ _____

permit _____ _____   commit _____ _____

Spelling verb endings

H	F	W	U	P	E	R	M	I	T	T	E	D	G	N	I	R	R	E	F	E	R
U	C	A	L	S	A	D	X	R	R	Q	F	A	R	I	B	Z	C	R	Y	P	E
A	O	M	I	Y	S	B	N	G	A	D	M	I	T	T	E	D	X	V	L	D	G
P	N	M	K	B	C	E	H	P	N	Z	Y	H	C	I	Y	R	R	N	V	R	R
E	T	I	T	I	H	C	G	W	S	I	T	A	P	P	I	N	G	X	X	E	E
R	R	F	E	L	R	Z	T	G	F	R	Q	U	E	Y	B	H	W	T	L	E	T
M	O	T	X	M	O	C	Z	S	E	B	V	E	X	P	E	L	L	E	D	Q	T
I	L	E	P	A	L	O	C	U	R	I	O	N	R	V	U	N	T	U	P	U	E
T	L	P	E	X	D	M	C	I	R	E	G	R	E	T	T	I	N	G	P	I	D
T	I	I	L	C	G	M	O	Y	E	K	O	T	N	A	D	I	Y	R	R	P	H
I	N	Y	L	I	I	I	M	N	D	C	O	N	T	R	O	L	L	E	D	P	H
N	G	C	I	K	S	T	M	V	Y	Q	X	C	C	X	R	E	P	K	X	E	O
G	U	Q	N	A	T	T	I	H	E	Q	U	I	P	P	I	N	G	X	E	D	R
E	I	I	G	D	I	I	T	D	U	A	L	D	T	O	E	T	A	O	M	G	O
U	C	I	X	S	D	N	T	R	A	N	S	F	E	R	R	I	N	G	A	X	P
E	I	V	V	O	P	G	E	O	G	L	M	N	A	D	E	P	P	A	T	X	L
R	E	F	E	R	R	E	D	D	V	A	D	M	I	T	T	I	N	G	N	A	A

BRAIN BOX

When adding *-ed* or *-ing* to a verb ending in a consonant, you should double the consonant when the verb ends with one vowel and one consonant, and the stress is at the end of the word.

Example: mop, mop**ped**, mop**ping**

Double or Nothing

Write the **-ing** form of each verb. Decide whether or not to double the consonants.

Double the consonant?

interest	_____	yes	no
forget	_____	yes	no
appear	_____	yes	no
treat	_____	yes	no
stop	_____	yes	no
act	_____	yes	no
explain	_____	yes	no
exit	_____	yes	no
begin	_____	yes	no
edit	_____	yes	no

BRAIN BOX

Do not double the consonant before adding **-ed** or **-ing** when:

• The verb ends with two vowels in a row followed by a consonant.

Examples: peal, pealed, pealing

• The verb ends with two consonants in a row.

Examples: arrest, arrested, arresting

• The verb ends with one vowel and a consonant and the stress is at the beginning of the word.

Examples: target, targeted, targeting

Write four sentences using the **-ing** verbs above.

Surprise Endings

Finish each sentence by choosing the word from the boxes that is an altered form of the **highlighted** word. Then read the sentences aloud, noting how the pronunciation of the word changes.

signaled	circumstantial	criticized	financial	publicity

criminal	electricity	authenticity	residential	influential

Altered sounds

The flashing walk `sign` and the loud beeping _____ that the light would soon turn red.

The restaurant `critic` _____ the food for being too salty.

Though he had committed a `crime` , Robin Hood did not consider himself to be a _____ .

`Electric` cars run on batteries powered by _____ .

After studying `finance` , Michael became a _____ advisor.

The sign said " `authentic` gold," but the ring was so cheap that Delaney questioned its _____ .

Eloise `resided` in a _____ suite at the Plaza Hotel.

The bakery made a `public` apology for selling day-old pastries, but it seemed insincere and resulted in more negative _____ .

The `circumstances` indicated that he was guilty. Unfortunately, the jury was skeptical of the _____ evidence.

The doctor's grandmother `influenced` his early studies. Some say she was the most _____ person in his life.

BRAIN BOX

When the endings of root words change, the pronunciation of the root word may also change. For instance, *define* has a **long i,** but *definition* has a **short i.**

Twin Words

Read the word, definition, and sentence. Circle the ending sound of the word: **it** or **āt**.

Homographs

alternate	to take turns
The altos alternate in singing solos.	

it / āt

associate	a partner or coworker
My associate Bob and I are hard at work on a project.	

it / āt

articulate	able to speak clearly
The toddler was articulate for his age.	

it / āt

graduate	to complete a course of study
My cousin will graduate from college this spring.	

it / āt

separate	divided from each other
Keep the animals in separate compartments.	

it / āt

BRAIN BOX

Homographs are words that are spelled alike, but differ in meaning and sometimes pronunciation. Sometimes the noun or adjective form ends with a **short i** while the verb form ends with a **long a**.

Example: The teacher was an advocate for the poor. (*Advocate*, the noun, ends with an **it** sound.)

We should advocate for more art classes. (*Advocate*, the verb, ends with an **āt** sound.)

Do the highlighted homographs differ in meaning, pronunciation, or both? Circle the answer.

The conductor, who wore a bow tie, turned to bow to the audience.

Meaning   Pronunciation   Both

The circus performer couldn't bear to wrestle another bear.

Meaning   Pronunciation   Both

Park your car on the west side of the park.

Meaning   Pronunciation   Both

We can't waste another minute arguing about minute details.

Meaning   Pronunciation   Both

"I shall contest the results of this pie contest!" roared the baker.

Meaning   Pronunciation   Both

Multiple Meanings

Read the two definitions and the scrambled word.
Then write the word that could be used for both definitions.

Homographs

a player at bat	OR	a mixture for making cakes	tarbet _batter_
a steep slope	OR	a company that keeps money	anbk
new and unusual	OR	a long, fictional book	volen
to mislead	OR	a cliff	bfluf
a shoemaker	OR	a dessert made with fruit and dough	creblob
a weaving machine	OR	to be near and threatening	molo
pieces of ice that fall as precipitation	OR	to greet	hali
a large wading bird	OR	a machine that lifts heavy weights	necra
able to wait calmly	OR	a person receiving medical treatment	tenapit
to look closely	OR	a person who is an equal	eerp

Correct the Comments

Your big sister posted a vacation picture on social media. Some of the commenters have confused the words **its/it's**, **their/they're**, and **your/you're**.

Circle the misspellings. Write the words correctly in the boxes.

Sylvie

I love you're hat. Its so cute!

Chris

I didn't know you went to Silver Beach this summer! Its my favorite place!

Maley

Your so photogenic!

Antonio

Did you ever get ice cream at Mimi's? Its across the street from the beach.

Molly

Where did you're family buy they're great sunglasses?

Kaitlyn

My cousins live in that town. We stayed at they're house last year.

Antonio

Kaitlyn, I played beach volleyball with you're cousins. Their cool.

Chris

Let's all meet up next summer if your around when I am.

BRAIN BOX

Commonly confused words include *its* and *it's*, *their* and *they're*, and *your* and *you're*. *Its*, *their*, and *your* are possessive pronouns. *It's*, *they're*, and *you're* are contractions for *it is*, *they are*, and *you are*.

One Hot Dog

Use the words in the first column to fill in the blanks. Some answers may be used interchangeably.

If you say:	You mean:
However	I am going to contradict my previous thought.
Although	My next thought will contradict this one.
Similarly	This thought will resemble my previous thought.
Moreover	This thought will add to my previous thought.
In addition	This thought will add to my previous thought.
For instance	This example will support my previous thought.
Therefore	This conclusion will be based on my previous statements.

SPELLING AND VOCABULARY

Vocabulary

BRAIN BOX

Words such as *however*, *moreover*, and *for instance* show the logical relationships between thoughts.

Dear Charlie,

_____ I do enjoy hot dogs, I did not eat the hot dog off your plate tonight. _____ , I did not appreciate being blamed for that. I counted three other individuals in the room when the hot dog was eaten. It could have been any one of them. _____ , your dad loves hot dogs, so it might have been him. _____ , your sister said before sitting down to dinner that she was "famished." That means that she was very hungry and might have eaten your hot dog.

I know that your mom said she saw me eat the hot dog. _____ , eyewitness accounts can be very unreliable. _____ , have you ever known me to steal food? I didn't think so. I feel that I have been wrongly accused. Frankly, my feelings are hurt. _____ , I think I deserve an apology. And nothing says "sorry" like a hot dog. Think about it.

Love,

Junior

Journey to Freedom

Read the passage.

Excerpt from "My Escape from Slavery"
By Frederick Douglass (1881)

My free life began on the third of September, 1838. On the morning of the fourth of that month, after an anxious and most perilous but safe journey, I found myself in the big city of New York, a FREE MAN—one more added to the mighty throng which, like the confused waves of the troubled sea, surged to and fro between the lofty walls of Broadway. Though dazzled with the wonders which met me on every hand, my thoughts could not be much withdrawn from my strange situation. For the moment, the dreams of my youth and the hopes of my manhood were completely fulfilled. The bonds that had held me to "old master" were broken. No man now had a right to call me his slave or assert mastery over me. I was in the rough and tumble of an outdoor world, to take my chance with the rest of its busy number. I have often been asked how I felt when first I found myself on free soil. There is scarcely anything in my experience about which I could not give a more satisfactory answer. . . .

It was a time of joyous excitement which words can but tamely describe. In a letter written to a friend soon after reaching New York, I said: "I felt as one might feel upon escape from a den of hungry lions."

BRAIN BOX

You can often determine the meanings of words from clues in the sentence and paragraph. These are called **context clues**.

Circle the correct definition for each word using **context clues** from the passage.

perilous

tasty

risky

long

fulfilled

emptied

achieved

broken

throng

a large crowd

a large noise

a large train

assert

to ask

to demand acceptance of

to refuse

surged

bounced quickly

sank deeply

moved powerfully

scarcely

mostly

barely

definitely

lofty

colorful

tall

strong

satisfactory

unsuitable

acceptable

forbidden

dazzled

surprised by

scared by

amazed by

tamely

completely

without end

without force or power

It's All Greek to Me

Read the meaning of each Greek and Latin prefix and suffix.

Vocabulary

astro
Greek: (astron) a star

photo
Greek: (phot) light

ology
Greek: a field of study

ambi
Latin: both

tele
Greek: far off

aero
Greek: (aer) air

anti
Greek: opposed

phobia
Greek: (phobos) fear

audi
Latin: to hear

meter
Greek: (metron) to measure

amphi
Greek: on both sides

BRAIN BOX

Many English prefixes and suffixes come from Greek and Latin words. Knowing what these suffixes and prefixes mean can help you understand the correct meanings of many words.

Using the Greek and Latin meanings on page 22, fill in the blanks with the correct prefixes and suffixes.

| astro | logy | tele | anti | audi | photo |

| ambi | aero | phobia | meter | amphi |

In the old days, people wanting to send a message to a distant place quickly would send a _____gram.

A device that measures temperature is a thermo_____ .

Plants convert sunlight into energy in a process called _____synthesis.

When a person can use both the right and the left hand with equal skill, they are _____dextrous.

When something is equally suited for water or land, it is _____bious.

The science of air travel is known as _____nautics.

Proteins produced by white blood cells to fight infection are called _____bodies.

If you are able to hear something, it is _____ble.

The study of life is bio_____ , and the study of space is _____nomy.

Arachno_____ is the fear of spiders.

Match the correct word endings and beginnings. Fill in the blanks with three complete words.

| geo | valent | phobia | ambi | logy | claustro |

_____ is the study of the Earth.

_____ is the fear of small spaces.

When you both love and hate something, you are _____ toward it.

Jargon Talk

Read the following sentences. Then on the next page, draw lines to match the highlighted jargon with the correct definitions.

In World War II, the United States, Great Britain, France, the Soviet Union, China, and other countries cooperated to win the war. They were allies.

The Treaty on the Non-Proliferation of Nuclear Weapons was an agreement among 190 nations to stop the buildup of nuclear weapons.

Explorer Ferdinand Magellan set off on a voyage to circumnavigate the globe in 1519.

If you travel around the world at latitude 23 degrees north, you will cross Mexico, northern Africa, Saudi Arabia, India, and southern China.

Following longitude 30 degrees east, you would pass through Europe, Africa, and Antarctica.

The heart is an organ that pumps blood throughout the entire body.

Together, muscle cells known as myocytes form muscle tissue.

The vascular system is the network of arteries, veins, and capillaries that carry blood throughout the body.

Arteries have thick walls that can handle the strong flow of blood as it is pumped out of the heart.

Blood flowing through veins from the feet to the heart must flow against gravity.

BRAIN BOX

Jargon is language that is mainly used in a specific field, like medicine, law, or engineering.

Jargon can be hard to understand at first, but often you can figure out the meaning by context clues.

tissue	an imaginary line around the Earth that is perpendicular to the equator
circumnavigate	an imaginary line around the Earth that is parallel to the equator
vascular	a collection of similar cells that together share a common function
treaty	a thick vessel through which blood from the heart flows to the rest of the body
organ	a formal agreement between two or more parties, usually countries
ally/allies	a vessel through which blood flows from a part of the body back to the heart
longitude	a person or group of people cooperating with another person or group
artery	to travel around something, usually the globe
vein	a part of the body with a specific function
latitude	related to blood vessels

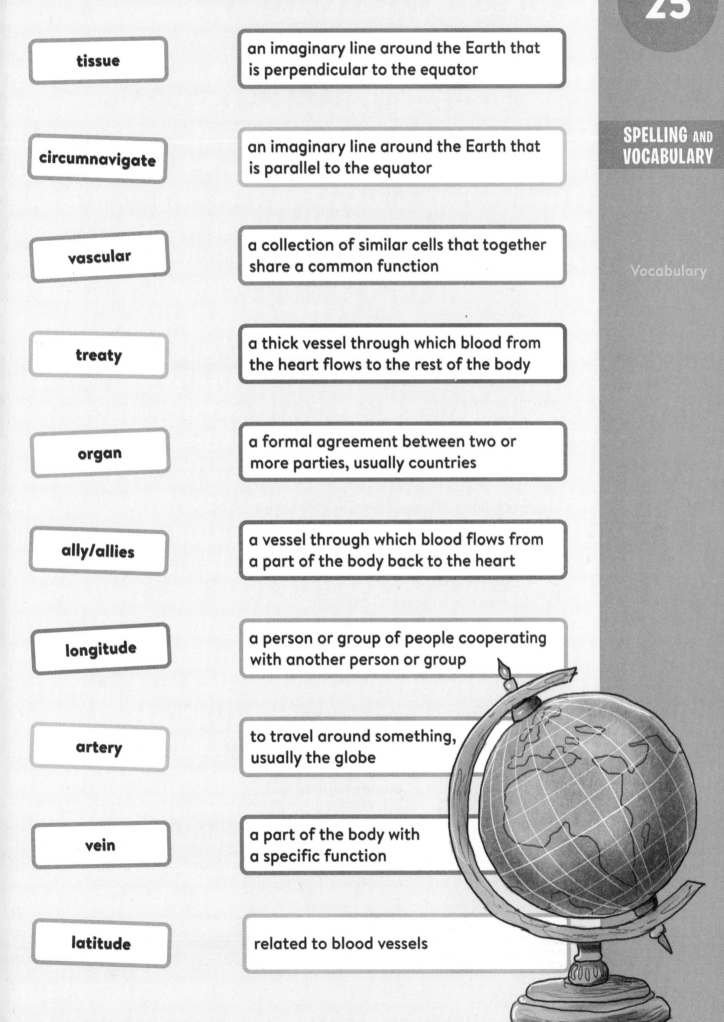

Dictionary skills

Pirate Dictionary

WORD

PRONUNCIATION

pirate ('pī-rət)

DEFINITION

SYNONYM

PART OF
SPEECH

1. *noun* one who robs ships; synonym: raider
2. *verb* to reproduce a work without permission

HOW IT IS USED IN A SENTENCE

Major Steed Bonnet was nicknamed the Gentleman Pirate because he was a wealthy landowner before he began his criminal career on the high seas.

ahoy (ə-'hȯi)

interjection a call used to signal a boat or to say hello

avast (ə-'vast)

interjection (slang) stop

matey ('mā-tē)

noun a friendly form of address; synonym: buddy

pardon ('pär-dᵊn)

1. *verb* to forgive.
2. *noun* an act of forgiveness

parley ('pär-lē)

verb to discuss with an enemy

plank ('plaŋk)

noun a long, thick board

plunder ('plən-dər)

1. *verb* to rob and destroy by force; synonym: pillage
2. *noun* goods taken by force; synonyms: loot, booty

scalawag ('ska-li-,wag)

noun a rascal

Is the first syllable of **matey** pronounced with a long or short a?

_____

Is **scalawag** a noun, a verb, or both?_____

Write a sentence example for **parley**. _____

_____

What is a synonym for the noun **plunder**?

_____

What part of speech is **ahoy**?_____

If someone yells, "**Avast**," what are they telling you to do?

_____

What could be added to the **matey** entry as a synonym?

_____

What part of speech is **plank**? _____

If the word **buccaneer** were added to this dictionary, which word would it follow?

_____

Write definitions for these **p** words. Use a dictionary if you need help, but write the definitions in your own words.

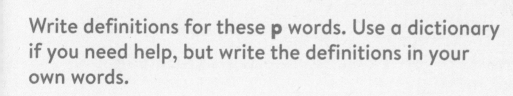

	pasture
	perish
	petrify
	protagonist

BRAIN BOX

A **dictionary** can give you a word's spelling, pronunciation, part of speech (the type of word it is), definition, synonyms, and usage (the way it is used in a sentence).

What's That Supposed to Mean?

Read the **idioms**.

cool as a cucumber calm; not nervous

in a pickle in a bad situation

pie in the sky unrealistic

bee's knees excellent

apple of my eye the one I love

bell the cat to complete an undesirable or impossible task

have a cow be upset

the whole nine yards all of it

dressed to the nines dressed very nicely

piece of cake easy

Fill in the blanks with the correct idioms from above.

When asked if he wanted marshmallows, whipped cream, or sprinkles in his hot cocoa, James said, "I'll take _____."

Although some students were nervous during the spelling bee, Mari was _____ .

"You are the _____ ," said Romeo before kissing Juliet.

Tickets to the concert sold out fast because everybody thought the band was the _____ .

Although not everyone studied, the whole class aced the test because it was such a _____ .

Tommy ran home, knowing that if he was late his parents would _____ .

My four-year-old sister asked for a unicorn for her birthday, which was a _____ request if I ever heard one.

Though she usually wore soccer clothes, Madeline was _____ for the party.

Standing up to the giant was a great idea, but who would _____?

Mickey was babysitting until five p.m. but remembered he was supposed to meet Avery for ice cream at two p.m. He was _____ .

BRAIN BOX

An **idiom** is an expression that means something different from its literal meaning. For instance, *you are the cat's pajamas* means *you are awesome.*

The Party

Circle the **simile**, **metaphor**, or **hyperbole** in each sentence. On the line, write an **s** if it is a simile, an **m** if it is a metaphor, or an **h** if it is hyperbole. Some sentences have multiple answers.

Similes, metaphors, and hyperbole

The Party

Aleia, it is a tragedy that you were out of town for Sierra's birthday party! _____

Sierra lit up the room in her bright pink dress. _____

There were a million kids there from all different schools. _____

We were all dancing like maniacs. _____

Then the lights temporarily went off. We were as blind as bats until they came back on. _____

Afterward, we were as hungry as bears! _____

So the twenty cheese pizzas were a gift from heaven. _____

Then they brought out the cake, and it was as big as a house. _____

Time flew by, and before we knew it, it was time to go home. _____

For party favors, Sierra gave us toy kittens, which were as cute as buttons. _____

BRAIN BOX

A **simile** is a comparison that includes the words *like* or *as*. Example: busy as a bee.

A **metaphor** is a comparison that does not include *like* or *as*. Example: You are my sunshine.

Hyperbole is exaggeration used to make a point. Example: There were a billion people at the zoo today.

Wise Words

Read the following **proverbs**.

A stitch in time saves nine.
Fixing a problem quickly can help prevent it from becoming worse.

Actions speak louder than words.
People's feelings and intentions show more through what they do than what they say.

Don't look a gift horse in the mouth.
Don't complain about gifts or charity.

Fortune favors the bold.
Those who are willing to risk failure are more likely to achieve their goals.

If it ain't broke, don't fix it.
If something is working, changing it unnecessarily may cause it not to work as well.

No man is an island.
People need each other.

Practice makes perfect.
Hard work can lead to improvement.

Rome wasn't built in a day.
Big jobs take time to accomplish.

The early bird gets the worm.
You are more likely to succeed if you start early.

You catch more flies with honey than with vinegar.
A person is more likely to give you what you want if you ask nicely instead of rudely.

BRAIN BOX

A **proverb** is an expression of wisdom that has significance beyond its literal meaning. For instance, *There's no use crying over spilled milk* means *There's no use getting upset about a mistake that's already been made.*

Choose the **proverb** that offers the best advice for each situation.

Alex shot several air balls on his first day of practice. "Forget it," he said. "I'm terrible at basketball."

_____

Mr. Paul planned to fix the leaky toilet later, not knowing that the water would soon damage the ceiling below.

_____

Ava said she was Sophia's best friend, but she completely ignored Sophia when other kids were around.

_____

Brooklyn planned to sell cookies in the neighborhood at ten a.m., but Mia had set her alarm so that she could sell cookies at eight a.m.

_____

Harry was struggling with the pressures of school, sports, and friends, but he refused to ask for help.

_____

Maeve was frustrated that after a day's work, she had completed only one page of the ten-page project.

_____

Ellie made 75 percent of their free throws, but they were thinking about changing their form.

_____

Nick's teacher had marked a test question wrong that should have been correct. He planned to demand angrily that she change his grade immediately.

_____

Audrey's grandparents gave her a sweater for her birthday, but she hated that it was so out of style!

_____

Luke badly wanted to be on the student council but worried that he might flop at giving a campaign speech.

_____

Crossword Puzzle

Read each clue. Write the answer in the crossword puzzle.

Synonyms and
antonyms

Across

2. synonym for annoy
5. antonym for huge
6. synonym for accomplishment
10. antonym for enter
11. antonym for hot
12. antonym for exciting
14. antonym for fast

Down

1. synonym for buy
3. synonym for obvious
4. synonym for sparing
7. antonym for different
8. synonym for avoid
9. antonym for arctic
13. antonym for silence

BRAIN BOX

Synonyms are different words that have the same or nearly the same meaning. **Antonyms** are words that have the opposite meaning.

LANGUAGE ARTS

Wow! Yikes! Hey, guess what? In this section we'll dive into interjections. But what about conjunctions, you ask? We'll look at those too. We'll review how to write titles, when to use quotation marks and commas, and how to avoid feeling tense about tenses!

PARENTS Practice with grammar skills, including punctuation, plurals, possessives, and parts of speech, will strengthen your child's reading, writing, and speaking. Support this learning by sharing examples of grammar mistakes you find in everyday life, like on signs or in text messages. Soon your child will be pointing out mistakes to you!

For additional resources, visit www.BrainQuest.com/grade5

Over Under

Read the common **prepositions** in the colored boxes. Then underline the **prepositional phrase** in each sentence.

above	across	after	against	along	around	at

before	behind	below	beneath	beside	between

during	from	in	into	on	onto	outside	over

past	through	to	toward	under	with

Prepositions

The key is hidden above the door.

We'll settle this at sundown.

The puppy got stuck under the blanket.

The pitch was outside the strike zone.

Follow the man with the eye patch.

The diver swam toward the shipwreck.

I rowed along the shore.

Never try to swim against a rip current.

Behind the mountain, the sun was shining.

During the Little Ice Age, glaciers expanded and destroyed villages.

BRAIN BOX

A **preposition** shows how nouns and pronouns relate to other words in a sentence. They often show where something is or when something happened.

Example:
We skated **on** the icy lake.

Together, a preposition and a noun make up a **prepositional phrase.** Any words used to describe the noun are also part of the phrase.

Example:
We jumped **off the high diving board.**

Where's Furious?

On the line, write a **prepositional phrase** that describes where the guinea pig Furious is. Use prepositions from the boxes to the left.

Underline the prepositional phrases in this verse from the poem "Over the River and Through the Wood" by Lydia Maria Child.

Over the river, and through the wood,

To grandfather's house we go;

The horse knows the way

To carry the sleigh

Through the white and drifted snow.

Uh-Oh! Vampire Bunnies!

Underline the **interjections**.

Wow! It's a vampire bunny.

Uh-oh! It's a hundred vampire bunnies.

Stop, vampire bunnies!

Hey, help me get away from these vampire bunnies!

Oops! I tripped.

Ouch! A vampire bunny bit my arm.

Well, I'm sure I'll be fine.

Yikes, I'm not feeling so well.

Zoinks, I'm a vampire bunny!

Yum. Carrots taste delicious.

Interjections

Write four more sentences that have interjections.

_____

_____

_____

_____

_____

_____

BRAIN BOX

Interjections are words of protest, command, or excitement. They can stand alone as a sentence with a punctuation mark, or they can be followed by a comma in a longer sentence. Examples:

Stop! This isn't the right movie theater.

Oh no, my sandwich is soggy!

The Pizza Shop

Read the **conjunctions**. Fill in each blank with the correct conjunction.

and	but	or	so	yet	if

unless	although	while	because

"I'd like a large pizza with pepperoni, green peppers, _____ black olives, please."

"Would you like any cheesy toast _____ garlic bread with that?"

"No, thank you, _____ maybe next time."

"They are delicious, _____ do keep them in mind for next time."

"Will do. We don't need any tonight _____ we have to save room for birthday cake."

"I'd like to wish you a very happy birthday, _____ it's somebody else's birthday."

"It's actually our cat's birthday. _____ she doesn't eat cake, the rest of us do."

"What do you give the cat, _____ you don't mind my asking?"

"We give the cat anchovies, _____ I wasn't able to find any at the grocery store."

"You're in luck. We have anchovies. I'll put some in a container _____ you wait for your pizza."

Pep Talk

In each sentence, the **correlative conjunction** is missing its matching word. Fill in the blank with the correct matching word.

both . . . and   either . . . or

whether . . . or   not . . . but   neither . . . nor

not only . . . but also   not so much . . . as

Conjunctions

You are both ready _____ able to win this race.

You have trained not only hard _____ smart.

You'll start out in either second _____ third place.

You should pass neither at the start _____ on the curve.

Then it will be not so much a matter of taking the lead _____ a matter of keeping the lead.

Remember, it's not the size of the dog in the fight _____ the size of the fight in the dog.

Whether you win _____ lose, I'll be proud of you.

Rewrite these sayings correctly.

Neither a borrower or a lender be.

_____

_____

Either you are with us nor you are against us.

_____

_____

BRAIN BOX

Correlative conjunctions are words that pair up in a sentence to link words or phrases. For instance, *either* pairs with *or*, and *neither* pairs with *nor*.

Perfect! Just Perfect!

Fill in each blank with the **perfect-tense verbs**.

has been	had entered	has watched	have practiced

had graduated	will have hiked	had suctioned	will have solved

has studied	have volunteered

Verb tense

By the time we reach the summit, we _____ 3 miles.

Hawai'i _____ a state since 1959.

The marine biologist _____ octopuses for eight years.

When her youngest brother was born, she _____ from high school already.

I _____ the ukulele every day this week, and I need a break.

My family _____ this TV show since it first aired nine years ago.

By the time the episode is over, the detective _____ both cases.

The hiker _____ out the rattlesnake venom by the time paramedics arrived.

They rowed as fast as they could, but the thief _____ the cave two minutes earlier.

I _____ at the pet rescue shelter every Saturday since January.

Write three sentences, each containing one of the following perfect-tense verbs:

have swum	had stopped	will have chosen

_____

_____

_____

BRAIN BOX

In the **perfect verb** tenses, the words *have*, *had*, or *will have* come before the main verb.

Present perfect shows that something occurred at an indefinite time or is still occurring. Example: I **have played** volleyball since third grade.

Past perfect shows that something happened before another past action. Example: The movie **had started** by the time we arrived.

Future perfect shows that an action will occur before another action. Example: By the end of the summer, I **will have read** twenty novels.

Leave the Past in the Past

Circle the verbs that are in the incorrect **tense**.

What I Did on My Summer Vacation

This past summer, I worked for my aunt at the Blue Bonnet Café. It is a vegetarian restaurant downtown. My aunt is the chef and owner.

My job was to fill water glasses and clear plates. I also washed dishes. Sometimes I chop vegetables too.

One day, another worker was sick, so I substituted as a server. I wrote orders on a notepad. I have to write neatly so that my aunt knows what to cook. I also have to bring the customers their food quickly. Even though I was in a rush, I don't drop any plates.

Working at the restaurant was fun. I especially liked being a server. I am going to ask my aunt if I can be a server next summer.

BRAIN BOX

When a sentence is about something that happened in the past, the verb should be in the **past tense**. If a sentence is about the present, the verb should be in the **present tense**. A story can have both past and present tense verbs. However, it is important to have a reason for shifting tenses. Example: Sarah went to see *Flowers for Flora*. It is rated PG.

Sarah saw the movie in the past, but the movie is rated PG in the present, so it is correct for the verbs to shift tense.

Hottest, Coldest, Biggest, Tallest

Capitalization

Each of the following sentences has at least one **capitalization** mistake. Draw three lines under letters that should be capitalized. Draw a diagonal line through letters that should not be capitalized.

The longest River in the world is the nile river.

However, the amazon river is the largest river by volume.

From its base, which is far below sea level, to its summit, mauna kea is the tallest mountain in the world.

Measuring from sea level to summit, Mount Everest is the highest Mountain.

With an average temperature of 93°F, the Danakil Desert in ethiopia is the world's hottest Desert.

The highest temperature on earth—134°F—was recorded in Death Valley, california.

The record was set on july 10, 1913.

Only two us states have never surpassed 100°F: Alaska and hawai'i.

The lowest temperature ever—negative 136°F—was recorded in antarctica.

The coldest town in the world is oymyakon, Russia, where the average temperature is negative 58°F.

BRAIN BOX

Proper nouns, such as people, places, and things, should be **capitalized**.

Always capitalize:

- the names of people, buildings, schools, businesses, streets, towns, cities, states, countries, continents, rivers, lakes, oceans, and mountains.

- the titles that come before people's names, as in Dr. Flood or Professor Plum.

- the days of the week and the months of the year.

Never capitalize:

- words such as *school*, *river*, *mountain*, or *doctor* unless they are parts of names.

- the names of animals, plants, or foods unless they have a proper noun in their name. For example, Italian in Italian dressing is a proper noun and, therefore, capitalized.

Comma Drama

Add **commas** to the story. You need to add thirteen commas in all.

Commas

We meet again Marcos.

What an unpleasant surprise Elise!

Hand over the PB&J and don't try any funny business.

I'll give you your PB&J but you have to give me back my chips first.

If you think I'm here to negotiate you are sorely mistaken.

Well if that's how you feel then say goodbye to your sandwich.

Wait what's that noise?

Look it's a bunch of puppies.

It's hard to stay mad while looking at puppies Marcos.

I agree Elise. Should we call a truce?

Yes but where do you think these puppies came from?

I don't know but they are eating your sandwich and my chips.

BRAIN BOX

Use **commas** in a series of three or more words. Example: I'd like a burger, fries, and a drink. Use a comma after an introductory word or group of words. Example: If you like french fries, you'll love sweet potato fries. Use a comma in a compound sentence. Example: I'll search the alley, and you check the fire escape. Use a comma to offset an interjection or to address a person directly. Example: Yes, I'll also search the corridor, Bill.

Lions and Hunters and Commas! Oh, My!

Add commas to the story.

Living with Lions

What if your neighbors were lions? That is true for the San people of the Kalahari Desert. The San are hunters and gatherers. They work play and eat outside. They also share their land with lions. Usually the San are able to avoid the lions. Lions generally hunt at night and the San hunt and gather during the day. The San still sometimes encounter lions by day. In that case the people calmly walk away from the lions. The lions usually walk away too.

At night lions can be heard roaring and they sometimes visit the people's camps. The San tell the lions in a stern voice to go away. If the lions do not leave the people wave flaming branches at the giant cats. This does not hurt the lions but it scares them off. What about when the San are sleeping? They sleep in shelters made of grass and sticks so the lions are unable to attack them from behind. This is the lions' preferred method of attack. Therefore the lions tend to leave the San alone even when they are sleeping.

The San are afraid of lions and it's easy to see why. A lion can easily kill a person. In some situations groups of lions have been known to attack people. The lions that live with the San rarely attack. By avoiding the lions by day confronting them with fire in the evening and sleeping in shelters at night the San have managed to stay safe. As for the lions they have learned not to see people as easy prey. For both the San and the lions being neighbors is a way of life.

44

My Favorite Things

List your five favorites in each category. Underline **titles** of movies, books, and TV shows. Put titles of songs in quotation marks.

my TOP 5

My Top 5 Movies

_____

_____

_____

_____

_____

My Top 5 TV Shows

_____

_____

_____

_____

_____

My Top 5 Books

_____

_____

_____

_____

My Top 5 Songs

_____

_____

_____

_____

Bonus: My Top 2 Plays/Musicals

_____

_____

BRAIN BOX

The **titles** of movies, magazines, TV shows, plays, newspapers, and books should be underlined when handwritten and formatted in italics when typed.
Examples:

The Wonderful Wizard of Oz

The Wonderful Wizard of Oz

Put quotation marks around titles of songs, poems, and articles.

The Flip

Write in the missing **quotation marks** in the story.

Giana and her friend Rose were taking turns going off the high and low diving boards. Giana did a flip off the low dive after Rose did one off the high dive. Now it was Giana's turn to do a flip off the high dive. But she was scared.

Let's both jump instead of doing a flip, said Giana. I'll jump off the high dive, and then you jump off the low.

Why? Are you scared to do a flip off the high dive? asked Rose.

No, said Giana.

It's okay if you're scared, said Rose. I won't make fun of you. I promise.

Okay, said Giana. I'm scared.

What are you afraid of? asked Rose.

I'm afraid of doing a belly flop, said Giana.

How about you jump this time, but while you're in midair, you picture yourself doing a flip? said Rose. Then maybe you'll be ready to do a flip next time.

Giana jumped off the high dive, closed her eyes, and pictured herself doing a flip.

Rose asked, So are you ready to do a flip this time?

I think so, Giana said.

Giana jumped, flipped, and landed on her belly, but it didn't hurt too much.

Now it was Rose's turn to flip off the high dive. She hesitated. Now I'm scared I'm going to land on my belly, she said, backing away from the edge.

BRAIN BOX

Quotation marks can show what a person says. Place quotation marks before the first word and after the ending punctuation of each quotation.

Plural possessives

Whose Shoes?

Write whose items appear in these pictures.

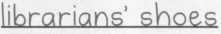
librarians' shoes

_____

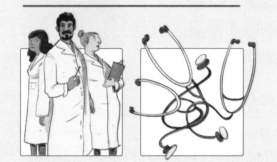

_____

_____

 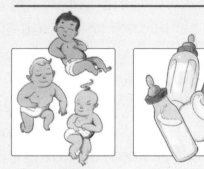

_____

_____

_____   _____

BRAIN BOX

Plural nouns are made **possessive** by adding an **apostrophe** after the **s.**

Example: librarians'

If the plural noun does not end in s, add **apostrophe s.**

Example: women's.

Dear Diary 1876

Write the **paragraph** symbol ¶ where a new paragraph should begin.

Paragraphs

May 10, 1876

Dear Diary, ¶ Today, I went to the Centennial Exposition — the first World's Fair ever to be held in America. And to think, it was held right here in Philadelphia! President Ulysses S. Grant, the emperor of Brazil, and pretty much everybody in Philadelphia were there — not to mention folks who traveled from far and wide. I can't describe all the exhibits, but I'll tell you the highlights. There was tomato ketchup. Very tasty! I also drank root beer made with sixteen roots and berries. Not only was it delicious, the poster said it is also good for your blood. I'm feeling healthier already! Second best to the food and drinks was the telephone. This device allows you to talk to your friend without either of you ever leaving home! It was made by Alexander Graham Bell. Not everything at the World's Fair was American, of course. The Italian exhibition had statues of men, women, and children. They looked so real! As for the British, they brought bicycles. These are machines with two wheels — a giant one in front and a tiny one in back. The man demonstrating how they worked sped downhill and appeared to be flying! When the wheel hit a tree root, he really did go flying through the air, over the bicycle, and onto the grass. I wonder if I will ever be so brave as to ride a bicycle. As I write, my mind is full of possibilities. I feel like the world must be full of such things as bicycles. I hope to see them all!

Another innovation shown at a World's Fair was the hot-air balloon. Write a paragraph to describe a hot-air balloon to someone who has never seen one.

_____

_____

_____

_____

BRAIN BOX

Start a new **paragraph** to begin a new topic, introduce a new speaker, or skip to a new time or place. The details you choose to focus on can change the tone, or the general feeling, of a piece of writing.

All About Animals

Use your own words to rewrite each **incomplete sentence** as a **complete sentence**. Rewrite each **run-on sentence** as either two sentences or a compound sentence.

If a rat can squeeze through a hole the size of a quarter

_____
_____
_____

Did you know dolphins gossip they chat about good places to find food?

_____
_____
_____

BRAIN BOX

A **complete sentence** needs a subject and a verb. Even with a subject and a verb, a dependent clause by itself is an **incomplete sentence**, or **fragment**.

Example: If you study for the test

Two sentences combined without a conjunction make a **run-on sentence**.

Example: We rode our bikes to the movies we got popcorn.

Most monarch butterflies live for only eight weeks the generation that migrates to Mexico each fall lives for eight months.

_____
_____
_____

The bats under the bridge

_____
_____
_____
_____

When ants find crumbs

_____
_____
_____

Peanut Butter and Jelly

Rewrite the sentences as **compound sentences**.

Modern jelly was invented in the Middle Ages. Peanut butter as we know it today wasn't invented until 1895.

Modern jelly was invented in the Middle Ages, but peanut butter as we know it today wasn't invented until 1895.

At first, peanut butter was served at fancy parties. It was served not with jelly, but with other foods, such as pimientos or watercress.

_____

_____

_____

Compound sentences

Then a businessperson began to sell peanut butter in jars. It became affordable for families.

_____

_____

In 1928, presliced bread began being sold. That helped kids make their own sandwiches.

_____

_____

_____

BRAIN BOX

Peanut butter and jelly sandwiches have been popular ever since. Peanut butter also goes with bananas, apples, or bacon on sandwiches.

_____

_____

_____

Short sentences can be combined with a **conjunction** to make **compound sentences.** Examples of conjunctions: and, but, for, nor, or, so, yet

Many children are allergic to peanuts. Some schools do not allow peanut butter in the lunchroom.

_____

_____

You Be the Teacher

Circle the mistakes on the homework. Look for errors involving commas, capital letters, italics/underlining, quotation marks, plural possessives, sentence fragments, and run-on sentences.

Name: Conrad Cates

Homeroom: 5H

Opossum Facts

Opossums are the only marsupials that live in north america. Other marsupials, including Kangaroos and Koalas, live in australia, new zealand, or south america. All marsupials give birth to extremely small babies twenty baby opossums would fit in a single teaspoon. Once born, baby opossums climb into their mothers pouch, where they drink milk. When they are bigger, they ride around on their Mother's back. Opossums eat a variety of foods, including mice insects birds and slugs. They also scavenge in trash cans for this reason, some people think of opossums as pests. However, usually Raccoons, Dogs, or Cats knock over the garbage cans opossums just eat what they find afterward. In fact, opossums are so harmless that they usually play dead. When they feel threatened.

Write a note to Conrad explaining the capitalization rules he needs to use in his writing.

_____

_____

_____

_____

_____

READING

Whether we're reading a story or a nonfiction essay, analyzing a chart or a time line, or following a recipe or instructions in a user's guide, our goal is the same: to comprehend (understand) what the text says. Let's sharpen our reading comprehension skills!

PARENTS Reading skills develop by engaging with a variety of content types, including fiction, nonfiction, news articles, maps, charts, and more. In this section, your child will strengthen their thinking skills by analyzing facts and opinions, comparing and contrasting, and considering point of view. Share the range of texts you read each day, from recipe instructions to online articles and sports scores.

I ♥ Facts

Read the **nonfiction** essay about the heart shape.

The Heartfelt History of Hearts

Did you know that ten-thousand-year-old heart-shaped drawings have been found in prehistoric caves? Archaeologists don't know what the heart shape meant to the Cro-Magnon people living at the time, but an ancient coin offers a clue.

A heart shape appears on a very old coin from the African city-state of Cyrene. In this case, historians know that it represents the heart-shaped silphium seed, which was valued for medicinal purposes.

Beyond the silphium seed, the heart shape is ubiquitous in nature. Heart-shaped leaves grow on many plants, including squashes, rosebud trees, and morning glory vines. There are also heart-shaped flowers called bleeding hearts. So perhaps the Cro-Magnon people were simply drawing something that they saw in nature.

Yet the human heart is the namesake of the heart shape today. Tapered at one end and large and curved at the other, the human heart is somewhat heart-shaped. (A strawberry shape is a more accurate description.) Its job is extremely important but not very romantic. It pumps blood through veins and arteries. But the heart has long been regarded as more than just a physical organ. Ancient Greeks and Aztecs believed that the heart contained the human soul.

In the Middle Ages, the heart also came to represent love. Men during this time period tried to woo ladies by singing songs, reciting poetry, and offering presents. This practice was called courtly love. Tapestries and illustrated manuscripts show men giving women their hearts (in the form of the heart shape).

Today, the heart shape still symbolizes love, and heart-shaped cards and candy are popular gifts on Valentine's Day. Perhaps you have even doodled a heart in the margin of a notebook. In that way, you share something with people who lived ten thousand years ago.

BRAIN BOX

Whether **nonfiction** is read for an assignment or for fun, its purpose is to teach new information.

Write five new facts that you learned from the essay.

_____

_____

_____

_____

_____

The Sami

Read the nonfiction story about the reindeer herders.

The Sami: Reindeer Herders

The Sami live in Norway, Sweden, Finland, and Russia, but they are a culture unto themselves. They have their own language, style of clothing, and specific way of making a living.

The Sami are reindeer herders. They follow the herds across the Arctic tundra as the reindeer migrate from their winter to summer grazing grounds. While on the journey, the Sami sleep in cone-shaped tents that can endure fifty-mile-per-hour Arctic winds. They wear warm wool clothing and hats that are known for their bright colors and intricate designs.

The reindeer are the Sami's livelihood. The Sami have traditionally eaten the meat, made tools and toys with the antlers, and used the skins for clothing. They even used the tendons as thread. Today, the Sami sell the reindeer to butchers, who use only the meat.

The Sami way of life is changing. They now must maintain fences so that their reindeer do not roam onto private property. Many Sami live in towns and have jobs other than reindeer herding. Few speak the traditional Sami language. But some families continue to herd reindeer and to follow the traditions of their ancestors.

Supporting details

Write the **main idea** (MI) and **supporting details** (SD) for each paragraph above. You may need extra paper.

First Paragraph

(MI) _____

(SD) _____

Second Paragraph

(MI) _____

(SD) _____

(SD) _____

Third Paragraph

(MI) _____

(SD) _____

(SD) _____

Fourth Paragraph

(MI) _____

(SD) _____

(SD) _____

BRAIN BOX

A **main idea** is explained and supported by details. Every good paragraph has one or more **supporting details.**

The Louisiana Purchase

This **map** shows the area (in orange) of the 1803 Louisiana Purchase on top of a modern map of the continental United States. Study the map and answer the questions.

Maps

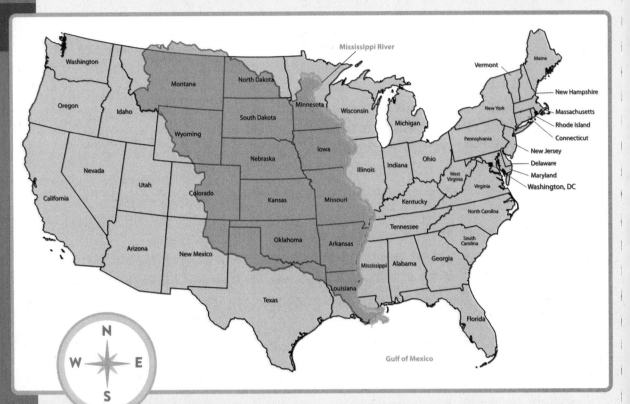

What modern-day states were part of the Louisiana Purchase?

_____

What river marks the eastern boundary of the purchase?

_____

Was the western or eastern half of Colorado part of the purchase?

_____

BRAIN BOX

Maps can show **political territories**, **physical characteristics** (mountains, lakes, etc.), and more, including climate, economics, and resources.

What large body of salt water borders a part of the purchase?

_____

Were any of the Great Lakes part of the Louisiana Purchase?

_____

Coming to the US

Read the **chart** about immigration and population.
Then answer the questions.

YEAR	US POPULATION	NUMBER OF IMMIGRANTS*
1820	9,638,453	143,439
1830	12,860,702	599,125
1840	17,063,353	1,713,251
1850	23,191,876	2,598,214
1860	31,443,321	2,314,825
1870	38,558,371	2,812,191
1880	50,189,209	5,246,613
1890	62,979,766	3,687,564
1900	76,212,168	8,795,386

*The number of immigrants through 1860 does not include captive Africans who were forcibly taken to the US. Although the international slave trade was outlawed in 1808, illegal trading continued and reliable records weren't kept.

Did the population decrease or increase from 1820 to 1830?

_____

How many people lived in the US in 1840?

_____

How many more people lived in the US in 1900 than in 1820?

_____

In what year did the most immigrants arrive?

_____

What important information does the
asterisk tell you about the data?

_____

_____

Phone Storage

Read the **pie chart** and answer the questions about Katie's phone storage.

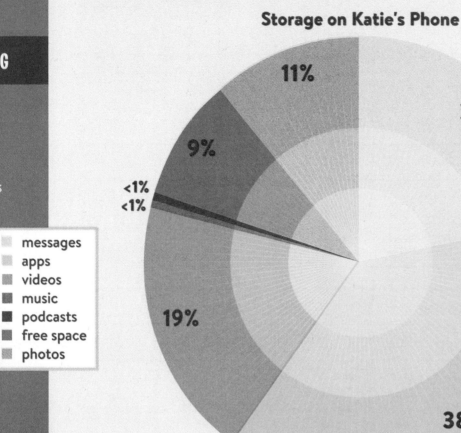

Storage on Katie's Phone

22%

11%

9%

<1%
<1%

19%

38%

- messages
- apps
- videos
- music
- podcasts
- free space
- photos

What uses the most space on Katie's phone?

_____

How much free space does the phone have?

_____

What percentage of storage do photos take up?

_____

What color represents podcasts on the chart?

_____

Apps and messages use a lot of memory! What percentage of the phone's storage do they represent?

_____

Fossil Fuels

Read the **diagram** about how coal forms. Then answer the questions.

How Coal Forms Over Millions of Years

1. In prehistoric swamps, trees and other woody plants die.

2. Through natural processes, the dead plants are buried underground.

3. As bacteria and other organisms eat the dead plants, they decompose.

4. Over time, the decomposed plants are pushed farther underground.

5. Oceans shift and cover the ground under which the plants are buried.

6. The decomposing plants become peat, another form of fuel.

7. Finally after millions of years, they become coal.

8. The oceans shift again so that coal is buried beneath dry land, where it can be mined.

Drawings and diagrams

Circle true or false . If false, write the correct statement on the line. If true, place an **X** on the line.

Coal forms from dinosaur remains.   true   false

_____

The plants are buried through natural processes.   true   false

_____

Bacteria eat the dead plants.   true   false

_____

Coal is formed by desert plants.   true   false

_____

The decomposing plants first become oil, then coal.   true   false

_____

It takes 10–15 years for coal to form.   true   false

_____

BRAIN BOX

Drawings and **diagrams** can show how something works.

Revolutionary Times!

Read the **time line** about the Revolutionary War.

October 14, 1774	The First Continental Congress (twelve delegates from the thirteen colonies) opposes Britain and asserts the rights to "life, liberty, and property."
February 1, 1775	Congress prepares for war.
February 9, 1775	Britain declares Massachusetts to be in a state of rebellion.
March 23, 1775	American politician Patrick Henry gives his famous speech in Virginia, declaring, "Give me liberty or give me death!"
April 18, 1775	Seven hundred British soldiers are deployed to Concord, Massachusetts. Paul Revere warns the colonists.
April 19, 1775	The "shot heard round the world" is fired, beginning the Revolution.
April 23, 1775	Colonial soldiers place Boston under siege.
May 10, 1775	George Washington is named commander-in-chief of the revolutionary army.
June 17, 1775	The Battle of Bunker Hill is the first major battle in the war, with a loss of about one thousand British soldiers and four hundred revolutionary soldiers.
March 4–17, 1776	The British pull out of Boston, ending the nearly yearlong siege.
May 2, 1776	France promises financial support to the Revolutionary War effort.
July 4, 1776	The United States declares its independence from Britain.
August 27–29, 1776	Washington's army is defeated in the Battle of Long Island. A series of defeats follows.
December 25–26, 1776	Washington leads a surprise attack on 1,500 British soldiers, who surrender, turning the tide of the war.
February 27, 1782	The British House of Commons votes to discontinue the war in America.
September 3, 1783	The United States and England sign the Treaty of Paris. The war is officially over.

BRAIN BOX

A **time line** shows a sequence of events.

Answer the questions.

When was the Battle of Long Island?

_____

What happened on May 2, 1776?

_____

What did Patrick Henry say on March 23, 1775?

_____

When was the "shot heard round the world" fired?

_____

Between what two events should the following item go?
July 10, 1778: France declares war against Britain.

_____

How did France first promise to support America in the war?

_____

About how many soldiers were lost in the Battle of Bunker Hill?

_____

Who won the Battle of Long Island?

_____

When was the Treaty of Paris signed?

_____

How long did the siege of Boston last?

_____

Roping the Wind

Read the **article**. Then answer the questions.

Greenville Students Harness the Wind

Students at Greenville Middle School have raised $20,000 to purchase a wind turbine for their school. The turbine will supply up to 20 percent of the school's energy. It will also teach students at the school about renewable energy.

Principal Ana Martin said, "This is going to save the school money on energy sources and will teach the students firsthand about renewable energy sources. And it has already taught students how to accomplish civic goals."

The effort was led by the Green Team, a club made up of 37 seventh- and eighth-grade members. Club president Magda Kita, 14, said, "We thought the biggest impact our club could have would be to help our school switch to clean energy."

To raise money, the Green Team held a recycling drive, collecting used carpeting, clothing, and electronics, which they sold back to various manufacturers. They also sought sponsorships from local businesses, whose names appear on plaques on the wind turbine.

Jack Ahn, who is the owner of Kokoroko Maki House, is one of the ten gold sponsors. He said the Green Team members frequented his restaurant after school. "They are good kids," he said. "They had this big dream and I wanted to support them."

How much money have the students raised for the wind turbine?

What is the name of the club that raised the money?

How did the club raise money?

What are two things the principal likes about the turbine?

What is one direct quote from the article? Who said it?

BRAIN BOX

News articles in print or on the web can tell you what is happening throughout the world.

Holy Guacamole!

Read the **recipe**. Then answer the questions.

Guacamole

INGREDIENTS:
4 avocados
1 tomato
1 onion (optional)
1 lime
1 teaspoon salt
Tortilla chips

DIRECTIONS:

1. Cut the avocados into halves. Peel off the skin. Discard the skin and the pits.

2. In a large bowl, mash the avocados with a fork.

3. Chop the tomato. Add to the avocados.

4. Chop up the onion if using. Add to the avocado mixture.

5. Slice the lime in half and squeeze the juice into the mixture.

6. Add the salt.

7. Stir until all the ingredients are well combined.

8. Serve with chips.

How many avocados are needed?

_____

What step in the directions could you skip and why?

_____

How many bowls will you need to make this dip?

_____

What kitchen tools will you need?

_____

Will you mash or chop the avocado?

_____

How will you get the juice out of the lime?

_____

BRAIN BOX

A **recipe** tells you how to cook or bake a particular food dish.

Step by Step

Read the **instructions**.

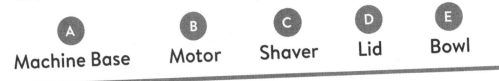

How to Assemble Your Snow Cone Maker

Ⓐ Machine Base   Ⓑ Motor   Ⓒ Shaver   Ⓓ Lid   Ⓔ Bowl

1. Make sure the machine base (A) is unplugged.

2. Place the motor (B) inside the hollow area of the machine base (A). Press down until it clicks into place.

3. Align the shaver (C) with the machine base (A). Turn it until it clicks into place.

4. To make a snow cone, fill the shaver (C) with ice cubes. Put on the shaver lid (D). Put the bowl (E) under the shaver. Press Start. The machine will stop automatically when the ice is shaved.

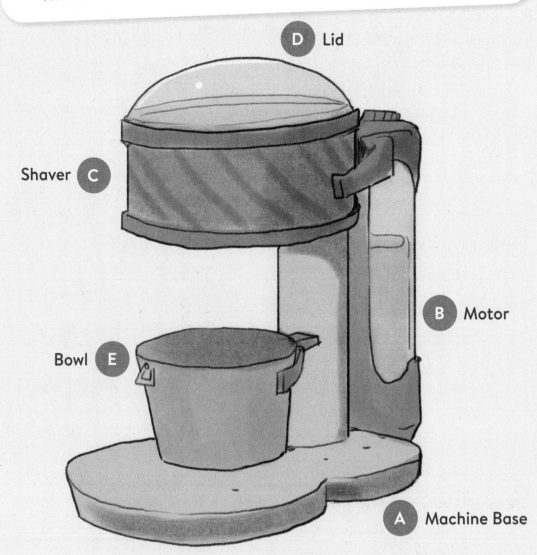

Ⓓ Lid

Shaver Ⓒ

Ⓑ Motor

Bowl Ⓔ

Ⓐ Machine Base

Manuals

BRAIN BOX

Manuals teach you how to do something.

Name the parts of the snow cone machine. Write the number 1 next to the first part you need, then number the other parts in the order you need them to build your snow cone maker.

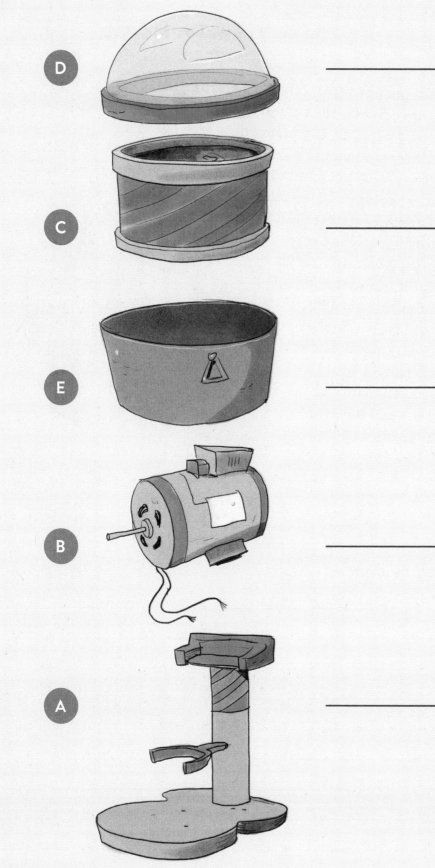

D _____

C _____

E _____

B _____

A _____

Light Bulb Moment!

Read the **persuasive essay**. Then write the author's **opinion** and **supporting evidence**.

Turn Them Off!
by Magda Kita, Green Team President

Our school needs to turn off lights and all electronic devices at night. If you drive by the school at night, you can see lights on in almost every window. In the morning, you can see that the beverage machines in the cafeteria and the computers in the library have been left on overnight. This wastes energy, and wasting energy wastes money. The Seattle School District saved $20,000 just by turning off beverage machine lights at night. If all American workers turned off their computers at night, they would save a total of $2.8 billion. Imagine how much our school could save by shutting off lights, computers, and beverage machine lights at night.

Opinion:

_____

Supporting Evidence:

_____

_____

_____

_____

_____

_____

_____

Pink Lake

Circle Fact if the statement is a fact. Circle Opinion if it's an opinion.

Lake Hillier in Australia is bubble-gum pink.   Fact   Opinion

When scooped up in a clear glass, the water still appears pink.   Fact   Opinion

Pink is a pretty color.   Fact   Opinion

Lake Hillier isn't the only pink lake in Australia.   Fact   Opinion

There is a pink lake called Pink Lake.   Fact   Opinion

Lake Hillier and Pink Lake are salt lakes.   Fact   Opinion

The water is full of salt-loving algae and bacteria.   Fact   Opinion

It is safe to swim in pink lakes.   Fact   Opinion

Salt lakes are better than freshwater lakes.   Fact   Opinion

Every lake should be pink.   Fact   Opinion

READING

Fact and opinion

BRAIN BOX

A **fact** is something that can be proven to be true. An **opinion** states what someone thinks, feels, or believes.

Naked Mole . . . Ants?

Read the short essays. Circle whether they are organized in **chronological order** or by **comparing and contrasting**.

50 States in 50 Weeks

This year, my brothers and I are taking off school to visit every state in the US. We started in Kansas, where we hiked in the Flint Hills. Next, we traveled through Missouri, home of the St. Louis Arch. In Illinois, we toured Chicago's museums. We'll watch a baseball game in Indiana next week. I can't wait to reach the East Coast states next month.

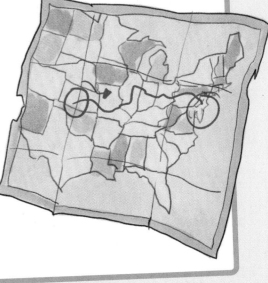

chronological order   comparing and contrasting

BRAIN BOX

There are different ways to organize an essay. For instance, it can be written in **chronological order**, which is the order in which the events occurred. Or it can **compare and contrast** two or more things by showing how they are alike and different.

Swamps and Marshes

Swamps and marshes are both wetlands. However, they are different in that a swamp has trees, such as mangroves and cypresses. A marsh does not have trees but rather has grasses and sedges. Both swamps and marshes can be either saltwater, freshwater, or a mixture. Both serve as nurseries for fish and other wildlife. Whether the vegetation is woody or grassy, it provides lots of places for fish and other baby animals to hide from predators that would eat them easily in other environments.

chronological order   comparing and contrasting

Strange Fossils

Did you know that much of today's dry land was once underwater? One example is the North American Inland Sea. In the early Cretaceous Period, tectonic plates shifted, creating lower land in the center of North America. The sea level was also much higher at the time than it is now because of a warmer climate. By 100 million years ago, the inland sea covered much of Canada and twenty US states. Later in the Cretaceous Period, the land was uplifted. Over time, the seaway shrank and ultimately disappeared. Recently, fossils of giant sea reptiles have been found in states such as Kansas.

chronological order   comparing and contrasting

Naked Mole . . . Ants?

Naked mole rats are mammals, which means they are not related to ants at all. And yet the two animals have surprisingly similar lifestyles. First, they both live in colonies. Like ant colonies, naked mole rat colonies have a single queen. She is the only one in the colony that can have babies. The other naked mole rats are workers that gather food, dig burrows, and take care of the queen. Ant workers perform the same jobs. Naked mole rats and ants also follow trails that colony members mark with their scents. Scientists have discovered other vertebrates that live similarly to ants, but none so similarly as the naked mole rat.

chronological order   comparing and contrasting

Volcano!

Read the **secondhand** and **eyewitness accounts** of the eruption of Mount Vesuvius. Then answer the questions.

Secondhand Account:
Article about Mount Vesuvius

Mount Vesuvius erupted in 79 CE, sending a mushroom cloud of gas, ash, and rock into the sky. The people living nearby hadn't known that Vesuvius was an active volcano and were caught off guard. However, those that fled right away were able to survive. Some people instead chose to take cover and wait out the eruption. For people living in the towns closest to the volcano, Herculaneum and Pompeii, it was a disastrous choice.

Ashes and pumice rained down on their roofs, and some people died when buildings collapsed from the weight. But that wasn't the most dangerous effect of the volcano. The deadliest result of the eruption occurred when the mushroom cloud rising above the volcano collapsed several times, causing 570-degrees-Fahrenheit gases and ash to surge down the mountain. The surge of gases and ash reached Herculaneum and Pompeii, killing everyone who remained in the towns.

Pliny the Younger was a scholar who lived in Misenum. Misenum was farther away from the volcano than Herculaneum and Pompeii, and the townspeople there survived the volcano. Pliny later wrote to a friend describing the events he witnessed during the eruption. His letters have been preserved for thousands of years and have helped historians understand what happened during the eruption.

Eyewitness Account:
Excerpts from the Pliny Letter

Ashes were already falling, not as yet very thickly. I looked round: a dense black cloud was coming up behind us, spreading over the earth like a flood. "Let us leave the road while we can still see," I said, "or we shall be knocked down and trampled underfoot in the dark by the crowd behind."

You could hear the shrieks of women, the wailing of infants, and the shouting of men; some were calling their parents, others their children or their wives, trying to recognize them by their voices. People bewailed their own fate or that of their relatives, and there were some who prayed for death in their terror of dying.

At last the darkness thinned and dispersed into smoke or cloud; then there was genuine daylight, and the sun actually shone out, but yellowish as it is during an eclipse. We were terrified to see everything changed, buried deep in ashes like snowdrifts. We returned to Misenum where we attended to our physical needs as best we could, and then spent an anxious night alternating between hope and fear.

BRAIN BOX

An event can be described from different points of view. An **eyewitness account** is the point of view of a person who witnessed an event. A **secondhand account** is the point of view of a person who was not there but who learned about an event from other sources.

In what year did Mount Vesuvius erupt? _____

Why were the people not prepared for the event?

_____

What is one way that historians have learned about the volcano?

_____

Why did Pliny want to get off the road while fleeing from the volcano?

_____

Circle the details told in the secondhand account.

Those who fled Herculaneum and Pompeii right away survived.

The surges of gases and ash were the deadliest effect of the volcano.

The people were terrified to see their town buried in ashes.

Pliny's letters would survive for thousands of years.

Circle the details told in the eyewitness account.

Men and women were shrieking and yelling.

There was a risk of being trampled as people fled.

A dark cloud spread over the land.

In some places, the temperature during the eruption reached 570°F.

Points of view

Cool Caves!

Read the passage.

Main ideas
and details

Why Mammoth Cave Is an Amazing National Park
By Adjua

Mammoth Cave National Park is in the west-central part of the US state of Kentucky. It has many natural features, creatures, and activities that make it an interesting place to read about and visit.

Mammoth Cave is the longest-known cave system in the world. At least 400 miles of its underground passages have been explored and mapped. Over the years, explorers have found connections to other cave systems in the area. In 1972, a passage was found connecting Mammoth Cave to the nearby Flint Ridge Cave System. About a decade later, a passage between Mammoth Cave and Roppel Cave was discovered.

Mammoth Cave was created by the erosion of limestone by water. Rain and rivers broke down and shaped the limestone into caves over time. Mammoth Cave has icicle-shaped natural features called stalactites and stalagmites. Stalactites form along ceilings and hang downward, whereas stalagmites form upward from the floor.

Animal species in Mammoth Cave have adapted over time to live in the dark, subterranean (below ground) environment. About 130 animal species make their homes in the caves. Some of the most amazing animal adaptations are found in a group of animals called troglobites. Because of the darkness of their home, some are "eyeless"—they developed other senses to identify their prey and their predators.

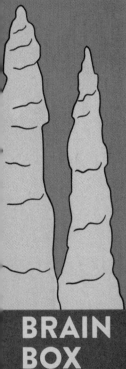

There are many activities for visitors to Mammoth Cave. Tours of varying lengths, distances, and level of difficulty are available. There are accessible modified tours for visitors with limited mobility. Visitors can also fish, hike, camp, and go canoeing in the national park.

BRAIN BOX

The **main idea** of a story is supported by details.

Write the supporting details for the main idea.

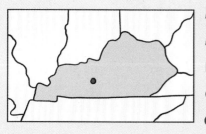

Main idea
Mammoth Cave National Park has many amazing natural features, creatures, and activities that make it an interesting place to visit.

First supporting detail

It is the longest cave system in the world.

Second supporting detail

_____

Third supporting detail

_____

Fourth supporting detail

_____

Fifth supporting detail

_____

Sixth supporting detail

_____

My Father's Dragon

Read the passage.

Illustration

Read the excerpt from *My Father's Dragon*
by Ruth Stiles Gannett

The river was very wide and muddy, and the jungle was very gloomy and dense. The trees grew close to each other, and what room there was between them was taken up by great high ferns with sticky leaves. My father hated to leave the beach, but he decided to start along the riverbank where at least the jungle wasn't quite so thick. He ate three tangerines, making sure to keep all the peels this time, and put on his rubber boots.

My father tried to follow the riverbank but it was very swampy, and as he went farther the swamp became deeper. When it was almost as deep as his boot tops he got stuck in the oozy, mucky mud. My father tugged and tugged, and nearly pulled his boots right off, but at last he managed to wade to a drier place. Here the jungle was so thick that he could hardly see where the river was. He unpacked his compass and figured out the direction he should walk in order to stay near the river. But he didn't know that the river made a very sharp curve away from him just a little way beyond, and so as he walked straight ahead he was getting farther and farther away from the river.

It was very hard to walk in the jungle. The sticky leaves of the ferns caught at my father's hair, and he kept tripping over roots and rotten logs. Sometimes the trees were clumped so closely together that he couldn't squeeze between them and had to walk a long way around.

He began to hear whispery noises, but he couldn't see any animals anywhere. The deeper into the jungle he went the surer he was that something was following him, and then he thought he heard whispery noises on both sides of him as well as behind. He tried to run, but he tripped over more roots, and the noises only came nearer.

BRAIN BOX

An **illustration** is a piece of artwork that is part of a book. Illustrations contribute to the meaning, tone, and beauty of the text.

List details from the story that could be included in an illustration.

_____

_____

_____

_____

What Happens Next?

Read each paragraph. Circle the correct **inference** or **inferences.**

Inferences

Ahmed is planning to write his book report on the archaeological site of Chichén Itzá (CHEE-chen EET-suh), located on the Yucatan Peninsula in Mexico. He wants to draw a colorful map to include in his report, but he doesn't have any markers. Miguel, Ahmed's classmate, notices that Ahmed seems upset.

"Are you OK?" Miguel asks.

"I've been better," replies Ahmed, and he tells Miguel about his dilemma.

"I think," Miguel says with a smile as he reaches inside his desk, "I might be able to help."

A Miguel is going to tell Ahmed not to include a map.

B Miguel is going to offer to share his lunch with Ahmed.

C Miguel has markers he's going to loan to Ahmed.

D Miguel is going to loan Ahmed a book about Chichén Itzá.

Romy had been working on her invention for weeks: a solar-powered robot that would move around the house and turn off lights in empty rooms. She was so excited! She had designed it as an entry in her class science fair, but if it worked, this could be a way for people to conserve energy and make their households greener.

The day before the science fair, Romy was so busy she forgot to leave her robot outside to charge in the sun. Oh no! Now it was the big day, but she wouldn't have time to charge the robot before she left for school. She was so disappointed! Her father watched as she boarded the school bus, sad and empty-handed.

When it came time for the science fair, Romy walked around admiring all the projects. She couldn't help but think of the robot she had worked so hard to build. Suddenly, she saw her father carrying something familiar into the fair. "I can't believe it!" she exclaimed happily as she ran toward him.

A Romy's father charged the robot and brought it to school.

B Romy's father was home from a long trip.

C Romy was excited to see a friend she hadn't seen in a while.

D Romy was happy to have a ride home from school.

BRAIN BOX

An **inference** is a logical conclusion. You can make an inference by combining what you already know with what the author has told you.

Jimmy and Kate

Read the story about a family living in New York in the late 1890s.

Though the sun was not yet up, Jimmy's shirt already stuck to him with sweat. His sister, Kate, was still asleep on the floor. She had kicked off her thin blanket, which was for comfort—not warmth—on this sweltering summer night. Though they always had blankets and food enough to fill their bellies, they'd never owned beds. Those were for rich people!

Jimmy recounted the money in his pockets. Two dollars. Actually, he was rich! For today, anyway. He tiptoed to the door. Opening it, he winced at the creaking noise.

"Jimmy?" Kate said groggily.

Jimmy paused. "Go back to sleep, Kate," he said.

"But I'm coming with you."

He shook his head. "Not today. Mom needs your help."

Jimmy frowned as he left the apartment. He had wanted to wish his sister a happy birthday, but he was afraid it would ruin the surprise. He ran past the corner where he usually sold apples. He needed to make his way downtown.

Meanwhile, back at the apartment, Kate made porridge for her mother, who had been working late the night before, and herself. Her mother woke up to the smell.

"Happy birthday," her mother said. "I should be making breakfast for you."

"Very well, then. I'd like a nice ham. And some bread and your finest marmalade, please."

"Coming right up!" her mother said. They laughed. Ham and marmalade were only on the menu in the fancy restaurants and large mansions uptown.

"So what are we making today?" Kate asked.

"A dress," her mother said. She was a seamstress who usually sewed loads and loads of boring shirts. A dress was a bit more fun. Time flew by as Kate and her mother sewed. They didn't talk much, but sometimes one sang a few lines from a song and the other joined in. Soon it was nearly nightfall.

The sun finally sank beneath the buildings, and the heat let up. Just then, Jimmy opened the door.

"How was your day?" their mother asked.

He shook his head. "I didn't sell a single apple."

"Not one?" Kate asked. No wonder he'd forgotten her birthday. He was always so worried about selling apples because of bad days like this.

Then, from behind his back, Jimmy took a doll. "I went downtown instead!" he said. "Happy birthday! From Mom and me."

Kate wiped a tear from her eye. It was her first doll. She was beautiful.

Circle the word from each pair that more accurately describes the three **characters** in this story.

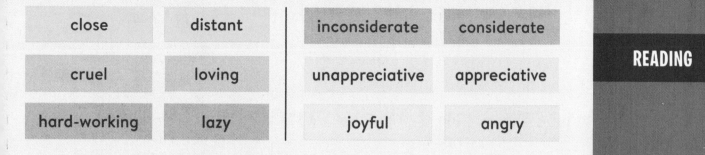

close	distant	inconsiderate	considerate
cruel	loving	unappreciative	appreciative
hard-working	lazy	joyful	angry

Characters

Why does Jimmy wince at the noise from the creaking door?

_____

Why does Jimmy frown after leaving the apartment?

_____

How do we know that Kate and her mother enjoy each other's company?

_____

Give two examples that show us how the family has financial struggles.

_____

_____

When Kate thinks, "No wonder he'd forgotten her birthday," is she upset with her brother or understanding of why he might have forgotten?

_____

_____

How did Kate feel when Jimmy gave her the doll?

_____

_____

_____

A Different Side of the Story

Read the story. Then answer the questions.

Points of view

The Pea and the Princess

Once upon a time, a beautiful pea lived in a garden. The pea dreamed of being left alone in its pod. In the castle beside the garden, there lived a prince. He dreamed of finding a real princess. But that should have nothing to do with the pea. Right? Am I an expert at knowing who is a real princess? No, I'm not. See, I'm the pea.

The prince had searched high and low for a real princess, and apparently all he could find were fake princesses. Then one day, a woman came to the castle claiming to be a princess.

"Really?" said the queen. "You're a princess?"

"Yes," said the princess.

But the queen didn't take the princess's word for it. I think a reasonable course of action would have been to send a message to the princess's alleged kingdom asking if she was a real princess there.

But the queen had a different idea. Some might say she had a pea-brained idea. "I know," thought the queen, "let's drag Pea into this mess and make its life miserable!"

So the queen plucked me from the vine and from my pod.

Then she covered me with ten mattresses. Ten! And on top of all of them, the princess lay down.

"We'll see if the so-called princess can feel that!" the queen said as she walked out.

Well, I don't know about the princess, but I can tell you who did feel it. Me. Pea. Pea felt it!

The next morning, the queen knocked on the door. "Good morning, princess," the queen said. "How did you sleep?"

"Terrible!" I blurted out. "I am bruised and in a great deal of pain."

"Wonderful!" the queen said, thinking it was the princess who had spoken.

When the queen burst in the door, the princess, who had been dozing away, woke up.

"You passed the test," the queen said. "You're a real princess!"

But was she really a real princess? Don't ask me. As I said, I'm not an expert on princesses. I'm just a pea. A smashed pea.

BRAIN BOX

In a story, **point of view** refers to who is telling the story. Point of view can affect how a story is told.

What does Pea want?

_____

What does the prince want?

_____

From whose point of view is this story told?

_____

How does Pea think the queen should determine whether or not the princess is a real princess?

_____

What does Pea say the queen is thinking when she decides to pick Pea?

_____

What mix-up occurs in this story that leads the queen to believe the princess passed the test?

_____

Draw an illustration to go with the story, perhaps from Pea's point of view.

Points of view

What Kind of Story?

Read the description of the different genres and then circle the correct genre.

Realistic Fiction

Setting: the present

Plot: events that could happen in real life

Historical Fiction

Setting: the past

Plot: the way events in real life could have happend

Mystery

Setting: usually the past or present

Plot: the solving of a puzzle, usually a crime

Fantasy

Setting: usually a world that is full of magic

Plot: often involves a quest or a battle between forces of good and evil

Science Fiction

Setting: usually the future or an outer space world

Plot: often involves a quest or battle with elements based on scientific theories

As soon as the teacher turned her back, Lily stared out the window again. There were the usual flowering trees, the dog that was always left outside, and the squirrels raiding the compost pile. But now Lily also saw a man carrying a large duffel bag. And now she saw that there was a hole dug in his yard. He lowered the bag into the hole. Then he disappeared for a moment and came back with a tree for planting. He placed that in the hole too. Lily thought that he must be pretending that the hole was for the tree when really it was for the bag. But what was in the bag? "Lily!" the teacher said.

realistic fiction	historical fiction	mystery	fantasy	science fiction

BRAIN BOX

A **genre** is a category or type of artistic work with a particular style, form, or content.

Blake stared straight ahead as he made his way down the hall. He wondered if the other students could tell he was different. He hadn't been different at his old school. But this school was in Verona Hills, and that meant the students were rich, which meant their parents had designed them to be genetically perfect or as perfect as possible. (Scientists were still learning about genes that made people tall, good-looking, smart, and athletic.)

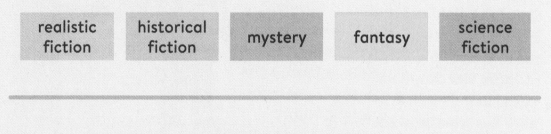

| realistic fiction | historical fiction | mystery | fantasy | science fiction |

Where Liana was from, the mermaids had tails in every color, just like the other creatures that lived in the coral reef. But here, the ocean colors were icy blue and white. The mermaids' tails were all white too. They wore coats that made them look like polar bears.

| realistic fiction | historical fiction | mystery | fantasy | science fiction |

Lottie awoke choking on dirt. The sod ceiling had partially collapsed again. Well, better dirt than mud, which is what they slept in when it rained. She had heard that along riversides, people were building big log cabins. But here in the sea of grass, there wasn't a single tree to be chopped down for shelter.

| realistic fiction | historical fiction | mystery | fantasy | science fiction |

BRAIN BOX

Fiction genres can include: realistic fiction, historical fiction, mystery, fantasy, and science fiction. Books within each genre share characteristics. Some books overlap genres.

Miguel had studied all night for the math test. He'd hardly slept a wink. As he walked to school that morning, past the suburban homes and falling autumn leaves, an idea popped into his head. What if he simply pretended to be sick today? Then he'd have the entire day to study for the test. He'd take the exam tomorrow and ace it, but would he feel guilty about lying?

| realistic fiction | historical fiction | mystery | fantasy | science fiction |

Words and Actions

Read the paragraphs. Then circle the highlighted word that completes each sentence correctly.

Sybil and Noor were friends who competed on opposing soccer teams. The day of the district semifinals, the girls wished each other luck before the game, then ran out onto the field. A few minutes in, Sybil saw one of her teammates, Lena, push Noor over to get the ball. The referee blew her whistle at Lena, and Noor remained on the ground with a sad look on her face. "Hey! That's not OK!" Sybil yelled at her teammate.

Noor shows how she feels about having been fouled through her words actions .

Sybil shows that she is unhappy about what has happened through her words actions .

The referee acknowledges that a foul was made through her words actions .

Noor sat on the ground for a few more minutes while her coach checked to make sure she was OK. When she stood up, she saw Sybil looking at her with concern on her face. Noor smiled, gave Sybil a nod, and yelled, "I'm fine!" Both girls then looked over at Lena, who had been sent to the bench. She was sitting with her head in her hands, looking down at the ground.

Noor indicates to Sybil that she is fine and unhurt through her words actions both .

Sybil communicates her concern for Noor's well-being through her words actions both .

Lena's posture while seated on the bench most likely means she is happy regretful for fouling Noor.

After five minutes, Lena returned to the field. But she kept her distance from the other players as much as she could for the remainder of the match. And she didn't look anyone in the eye as the game ended and the teams went back to their sides to pack up their equipment. Sybil noticed that Lena seemed upset. And because Lena had never pushed anyone before, she wondered if there was something bothering Lena today. Gathering her courage, Sybil slowly walked up to Lena.

Characters

In this paragraph, Sybil shows that she is a person who cares about others through her words actions .

Lena seemed bothered unbothered by having been given a time-out. We know this through her words actions after she returned to the field.

"You don't seem like yourself today, Lena," Sybil said. "It's not like you to push another player."

"I feel so badly about that," Lena replied. "I had a really stressful day. And because of that, I was distracted during the game."

"Oh, Lena," Sybil sighed, "everyone has tough days. Would you like to hang out after the game to talk about it?"

Lena's mood totally changed. "I'd love that!" she said excitedly.

Sybil smiled at Lena. "We all have those days. But talking things through with a friend can really help."

"You're right," replied Lena. "But before I do anything else, I have something I want to say to Noor."

Lena tells us why she was upset during the game through her words actions .

Once Sybil understood why Lena was upset, this helped didn't help her be a friend to Lena.

The "something" Lena wants to say to Noor is probably "I'm sorry for pushing you" "See you in the math study group."

Summer Crush

Read the **poem** by William Shakespeare. Then answer the questions.

Sonnet 18

Shall I compare thee to a summer's day?   Quatrain 1
Thou art more lovely and more temperate.
Rough winds do shake the darling buds of May,
And summer's lease hath all too short a date.

Sometime too hot the eye of heaven shines,   Quatrain 2
And often is his gold complexion dimm'd;
And every fair from fair sometime declines,
By chance, or nature's changing course, untrimm'd;

But thy eternal summer shall not fade   Quatrain 3
Nor lose possession of that fair thou ow'st;
Nor shall Death brag thou wander'st in his shade,
When in eternal lines to time thou grow'st;

So long as men can breathe or eyes can see,   Couplet
So long lives this, and this gives life to thee.

BRAIN BOX

Stanzas, meter, and rhyme provide the structure of poems.

A **stanza** consists of lines in a poem that are grouped together. In an **English sonnet**, there are always three four-line **stanzas** called **quatrains** followed by a two-line couplet.

Meter is the rhythm of the poem. A sonnet is written in **iambic pentameter**, meaning that each line has ten syllables. Syllables 2, 4, 6, 8, and 10 are stressed.

Rhyme is the repetition of the ending sounds of words, often occurring at the end of a line. Rhymed words commonly share all sounds following the word's last stressed **syllable**.

What is the first quatrain about?
Ⓐ comparing the loved one to a summer's day
Ⓑ the fun of summer
Ⓒ the windiness of May

In the first quatrain, which two pairs of syllables rhyme?
Ⓐ *day* and *-rate*, *May* and *date*
Ⓑ *shall* and *rough*, *thou* and *and*
Ⓒ *day* and *May*, *-rate* and *date*

How could the second quatrain be paraphrased?
Ⓐ Gold is a valuable metal.
Ⓑ The beauty of some things fades with time.
Ⓒ It can get extremely hot during summer.

What is the theme of this poem?
Ⓐ Nature isn't as beautiful as most people think.
Ⓑ Beauty in nature fades, but the beauty of the loved one never will.
Ⓒ Everything is beautiful in its own way.

No! Vember

Read the **poem**. Then complete the sentences.

Poetry

"November" by Thomas Hood
   No sun—no moon!
   No morn—no noon—
   No dawn—no dusk—no proper time of day.
   No warmth, no cheerfulness, no healthful ease,
   No comfortable feel in any member—
   No shade, no shine, no butterflies, no bees,
   No fruits, no flowers, no leaves, no birds!
   November!

Moon rhymes with _____.

Ease rhymes with _____.

Member rhymes with _____.

Dawn and *dusk*, *shade* and *shine*, and *fruits* and *flowers* are examples of _____.

Write three more lines for this poem, using at least one **sound effect**.

No_____

_____

No_____

_____

No_____

_____

BRAIN BOX

Poets use **sound effects** to reinforce meaning.

Alliteration: words that start with the same letter or sound close together

Internal rhyme: rhyme that occurs within one line of a poem

Onomatopoeia: words that mimic sounds

Rhyme scheme: the pattern of rhyming in the last sounds of the lines

Crossword Puzzle

Across

1. A _____ consists of lines in a poem that are grouped together.

4. An _____ is a piece of artwork that is part of a book.

6. A _____ presents organized data.

9. Persuasive arguments need _____ to support them.

10. _____ refers to words that mimic sounds.

12. An _____ expresses what someone thinks, feels, or believes.

13. _____ is the rhythm of the poem.

Down

2. The use of groups of words beginning with the same letter or sound is called _____ .

3. A _____ is something that can be proven to be true.

5. One main purpose of _____ is to teach new information.

7. An _____ is a logical conclusion.

8. A main idea is supported by _____ .

11. _____ of view refers to who is telling the story.

WRITING

Like any process, writing has steps. We brainstorm, research, outline, write, get feedback, and revise. We use these steps for all kinds of writing: personal essays, narratives, parodies, poems, and more. Let's learn more about how to craft a spectacular piece of writing.

PARENTS In this section, your child will review stages of the writing process and practice writing parts of personal and persuasive essays, stories, letters, and more. They'll learn to plan their writing effectively and how to add details, descriptions, and dialogue to multiple writing types. Talk about the writing styles you use as an adult and how and why your writing differs by purpose.

For additional resources, visit www.BrainQuest.com/grade5

What's Your Point?

Circle the main **purpose** of each summary of a piece of writing or speech.

A defense attorney gives a closing argument stating that his client is not guilty.

informs   entertains

persuades   connects to the human experience

A comedian tells jokes.

informs   entertains

persuades   connects to the human experience

A travel writer details the smells and sights of the foods that street vendors are selling.

informs   entertains

persuades   connects to the human experience

A science writer gives a report on the migration of monarch butterflies.

informs   entertains

persuades   connects to the human experience

A novelist writes about a character who loses a friend.

informs   entertains

persuades   connects to the human experience

BRAIN BOX

The **purpose** of a piece of writing can be to inform, entertain, persuade, or connect people to the human experience. The human experience includes feelings such as love, loss, longing, anger, fear, compassion, and courage.

Step by Step

Fill in the blanks with the correct step in the **writing process.**

| brainstorm | research | plan | write | revise | proofread |

Joey is trying to write a story, but he feels disorganized.
He should _____ how the story will go.

Julie needs to write a story about her life, but she doesn't
know what to write about. She should _____.

Saskia has a story in mind and a plan for telling it.
They should _____ the story.

Lena wants to write a story set in a bakery. But she doesn't
know what bakers do all day. She should _____.

Darcy has written a rough draft of her story.
She should _____ it.

There may be some spelling and grammar mistakes in
Dwight's second draft. He should _____ it.

BRAIN BOX

The **writing process** is the series of steps that allow you to transform an idea into a piece of writing to share. The process includes the following steps: **brainstorming, researching, planning, writing, revising,** and **proofreading.**

Did I Ever Tell You About the Time . . .

Fill in the blanks, and use these writing prompts to think of a topic for a **personal essay**.

A problem I have had to overcome is . . .

_____

Nothing went as planned the day I . . .

_____

A big misunderstanding occurred when I . . .

_____

A long time ago, my friend and I got in trouble when we . . .

_____

I got to know _____ much better when . . .

_____

I've never been so surprised as when . . .

_____

_____

I knew I had a true friend when . . .

_____

_____

I've never been so scared as when . . .

_____

_____

BRAIN BOX

A **personal essay** tells a true story from the author's point of view. Funny or serious, it often has a universal theme that allows people to relate to the story even if they have never experienced the exact same thing.

I Remember Like It Was Yesterday

Choose one of the writing prompts from page 88. Write down as many details as you can remember about the memory using the prompts from the cards below.

Where were you?

Who was with you?

How did you feel?

Do you recall any distinct sounds or smells?

What did the place look like?

How old were you?

What were some of the things you and other people said?

Why do you think you remember this event?

Brainstorming

BRAIN BOX

Brainstorming is thinking of ideas. While brainstorming, you should write down everything that comes to mind. Don't worry about whether it is important.

Planning Your Story

Fill in the **story map** to plan how you will write your personal essay.

Paragraph 1: Introduction
(State the situation or problem. Try to "hook," or interest, the reader right away.)

_____

_____

_____

Paragraph 2: Important Event Number 1

_____

_____

_____

Paragraph 3: Important Event Number 2

_____

_____

_____

Paragraph 4: Important Event Number 3

_____

_____

_____

Paragraph 5: Summary/Conclusion
(Reflect on what this event meant to you or how it changed you.)

_____

_____

_____

BRAIN BOX

A **story map** can help you organize your writing. It should include the most important events that happen in the story.

BEGINNING MIDDLE END

Writing . . . and Rewriting

Using your story map from page 90 and the details you brainstormed on page 89, write your personal essay. It should be five paragraphs long. Each paragraph should have a topic sentence and two to four supporting sentences. You may need extra paper.

Have someone read your personal essay. Ask the person to tell you two things they like about the essay, two things that could be better, and whether they have any questions. Revise your essay using this feedback.

WRITING

Writing

BRAIN BOX

Feedback is input that people provide in response to something you have done. You can use feedback to make the next draft better.

Interview with the Protagonist

Think of a topic for a fictional story. Get to know the **main character** in your story by pretending that you are the **protagonist** and you are being interviewed. Answer the questions using *I*, *me*, and *my*.

Where do you live?

_____

What is your home like?

_____

Is your world like our own—that is, present-day Earth? If not, what is it like?

_____

_____

What do you do all day?

_____

_____

Who are your friends?

_____

Do you have any enemies? If so, who?

_____

What do others think about you?

_____

_____

What is your biggest flaw or weakness?

_____

_____

What do you want more than anything else?

_____

What is happening right now that will change your life?

_____

_____

What do you eat for dinner? Who do you eat with?

_____

What worries keep you up at night?

_____

What else should we know about you?

_____

_____

Your story should begin on an important day in your main character's life. Draw a picture of what happens on the day your story begins.

WRITING

Character development

BRAIN BOX

A **protagonist** is the **main character** in a story. They must overcome an important problem by taking action.

World Building

Draw a map of the **setting** for your story. Label at least five important places on the map.

Setting

BRAIN BOX

The **setting** of a story is the time and place in which it occurs. Drawing a map of your story's setting can help you to get to know your character's world. It can be a map of a small area, like a school or neighborhood, or of a larger area, like a group of planets on which a science fiction story takes place.

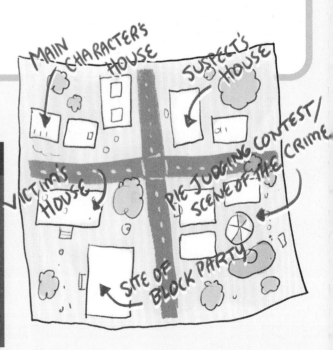

The Five Senses

Imagine you are in the setting shown in the picture. Complete the statements about the setting by using your senses.

Setting

I see _____

I hear _____

I smell _____

The weather is _____

For food, I am going to eat _____

I see _____

I hear _____

I smell _____

The weather is _____

For food, I am going to eat _____

I see _____

I hear _____

I smell _____

The weather is _____

For food, I am going to eat _____

BRAIN BOX

Every setting has distinct sights, sounds, smells, weather, wildlife, people, and foods. For instance, a forest may be shadowy and cool, whereas a meadow may be warm and bright.

I see _____

I hear _____

I smell _____

The weather is _____

For food, I am going to eat _____

Starting at the Beginning

Write the first page of your story. Use the **first person** point of view. In other words, write as if you are the main character.

First person point of view

BRAIN BOX

Stories are usually told from the **first person** or **third person** point of view. The first person uses *I* and *we*. If you write in the first person, your main character is usually the *I* in the story.

Say What?

Write three lines of **dialogue** for each set of characters in the illustrations. Remember to use quotation marks and to write who said what.

Dialogue

"Do you have homework?" asked Mom.

"Yes, and I started," said Bella.

"Great. I'll order pizza," said Mom.

BRAIN BOX

Dialogue is what characters say. It can be used to show what characters are like. Do they speak kindly? Do they use a lot of words or just a few? It can also be used to show how characters relate to one another. Do they get along well? Do they argue? Do they know each other very well?

Day in the Life

Circle one character. Write a diary entry about the day from that character's **point of view**.

Points of view

Dear Diary,
Signed,

BRAIN BOX

Different characters have different **points of view**. That means they see the world differently from one another.

Fractured Fairy Tale

Choose one of the fairy tale characters from the cards.
Write the fairy tale from that character's point of view.

An evil stepsister
in "Cinderella"

The wolf in
"Red Riding Hood"

Rapunzel's hair
in "Rapunzel"

The giant in "Jack
and the Beanstalk"

Points
of view

Once upon a time...

BRAIN BOX

A fractured
fairy tale is
a traditional
fairy tale
told in an
unexpected
way. For
instance,
the setting,
plot, or point
of view can
be different
from the
original.

Fly on the Wall

Write three sentences about what each of the four characters below is thinking, saying, or doing.

Third person point of view

Paulo

_____

_____

_____

Deshawn

_____

_____

_____

Mia

_____

_____

_____

Fatima

_____

_____

_____

BRAIN BOX

The third person point of view uses *he*, *she*, and *they*. In the third person, a narrator tells the story.

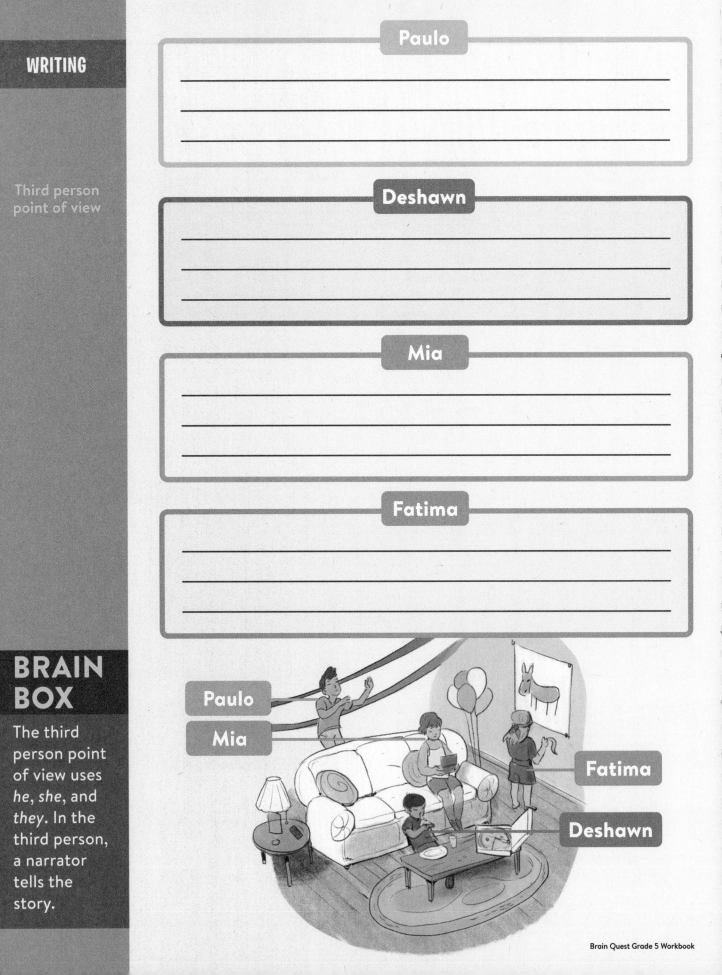

What's Their Story?

Imagine what the characters in the illustrations are like. Then fill in the blanks in the character maps, following the example.

shy

would like to make a friend

attached to blanket

thinks that a friend would think the blanket is babyish

BRAIN BOX

A **character map** lists traits that a character has. Examples: immature, wise, funny, vain

The Five Ws

Read the article. Then answer the five "W" questions that ask about the article.

The Nazca Lines (also spelled "Nasca Lines") are large prehistoric land drawings etched into the ground near the city of Nazca, located in southern Peru. The drawings, called geoglyphs, stretch for almost 190 square miles.

First seen by modern peoples in 1927, these lines date back more than two thousand years. Many were created by the people of the Nazca culture, who lived from around 200 BCE to around 600 CE. Some were drawn by the people of the Paracas culture, who lived from around 900 BCE to around 400 CE.

What are the subjects of these super-size drawings, some of which can measure up to 1,200 feet long? Among the dozens of images are many types of animals, including a variety of birds, a spider, a whale, a duck, a lizard, a two-headed snake, and a monkey the length of a football field. Others show plants, including trees and flowers, as well as shapes, including spirals and triangles. There are even depictions of human figures wearing headdresses.

Why did the Nazca peoples create this large-scale Earth art? What story were they trying to tell? Over the years, archaeologists and historians have had different theories. Some believe the images are meant to depict constellations. Recent research theorizes that the lines may have been related to the need for water, as a ritual to ask the gods to bring rain. Others believe the purpose of the drawings may have changed over time.

Who is this article about?

_____

_____

What is this article about?

_____

_____

Where did the Nazca peoples live?

_____

When did the Nazca peoples live?

_____

Why did the Nazca peoples make the Nazca Lines?

_____

_____

Fortunately, Unfortunately

Finish the "Fortunately, Unfortunately" story. Then write your own by using the given starter sentence. The "Fortunately" lines should tell something good that happens to the character. The "Unfortunately" lines should tell something bad that happens.

Plot

Evie went swimming in a pond.

Unfortunately, a snapping turtle bit her toe.

Fortunately, the turtle only clipped Evie's toenail.

Unfortunately, that made the turtle mad and he _____

_____

Fortunately, _____

Unfortunately, _____

Fortunately, _____

_____

_____

Christopher built a snowman in the woods.

Unfortunately, _____

Fortunately, _____

Unfortunately, _____

Fortunately, _____

Unfortunately, _____

Fortunately, _____

_____

_____

BRAIN BOX

The **plot** consists of the main events of a story. The ups and downs that the characters experience contribute to the plot.

What Next?

Complete the story prompts and write what happens next.

While on a field trip to a science lab, you accidently drink a scientific formula instead of your water and turn into a _____ . What happens next?

_____

_____

In New York City, a skyscraper comes to life as a robot. What happens next?

_____

_____

You discover a tiny village made of acorn houses and groves of dandelions. _____ live there.

What happens next?

_____

_____

You awake to a crash against your window. You go outside and see that a _____ has fallen from the sky. What happens next?

_____

_____

New to a small town, you meet your next-door neighbor George, who is your age. But when you start asking around, no one has ever heard of George. What happens next?

_____

_____

Judging a Book by Its Cover

Look at **book covers** in your home or local library. Think about which covers you like. Then design a cover for a book you want to write. Include the title, the author's name, and an illustration.

Visual elements

BRAIN BOX

A **book cover** should show the reader what kind of book it is and make the reader want to read it.

This I Love

Brainstorm people, places, and things you love.

Read the sonnet on page 82. Then write a sonnet of your own by writing fourteen lines with ten syllables in each line.

Title: _____

1. _____
2. _____
3. _____
4. _____
5. _____
6. _____
7. _____
8. _____
9. _____
10. _____
11. _____
12. _____
13. _____
14. _____

Shall I Compare Thee to a Piece of Cheese?

Write three possible opening lines to **parody** Shakespeare's Sonnet 18.

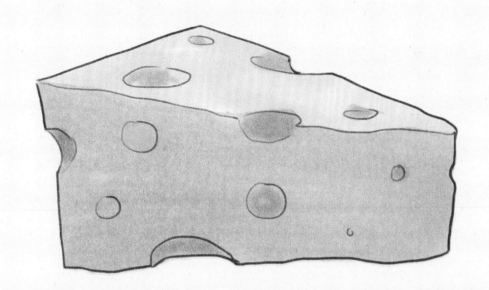

Shall I compare thee to a <u>piece of cheese?</u> _____?

Thou art more <u>square, more smelly, and more cheesy</u>.

Shall I compare thee to a _____?

Thou art more _____.

Shall I compare thee to a _____?

Thou art more _____.

Shall I compare thee to a _____?

Thou art more _____.

BRAIN BOX

A **parody** imitates a poem, story, or other work in a funny way.

Sound effects

A Day at the Beach

Write two to three lines about each picture using one of the **sound effects** below. Write the sound effect you used.

alliteration
a series of words that start with the same sound

internal rhyme
rhyming that occurs within one line of a poem

onomatopoeia
words that mimic sounds, such as *drip* and *drop*

rhyme scheme
the pattern of rhyming that occurs at the end of each line of a poem or song

Crunch drip drip

Nothing beats a

Chip after a dip

Sound effects used:

onomatopoeia and internal rhyme

BRAIN BOX

You can use **sound effects** to add meaning, beauty, or humor to a poem or other composition.

_____
_____
_____
_____
_____

Sound effect used: _____

Sound effects

_____
_____
_____
_____
_____

Sound effect used: _____

_____
_____
_____
_____
_____

Sound effect used: _____

_____
_____
_____
_____
_____

Sound effect used: _____

What Should I Write About?

Brainstorm topics for an **informal email** to a grandparent or other older relative. Then write the email and send it.

Something funny that has happened in the last few weeks is

_____.

Something interesting that happened is

_____.

Something exciting that happened is

_____.

Something new I've tried is _____

_____.

Lately I've been enjoying _____

_____.

A challenge I've had lately is _____

_____.

I thought of you recently when _____

_____.

I remember when you _____

_____

_____

_____.

A question I have is _____

_____

_____

_____.

BRAIN BOX

An informal **letter** or an **email** is written to someone you know well. Both can include thoughts, stories, and questions.

Brain Quest Grade 5 Workbook

Now That's a Sweet Tooth!

Read the **opinion piece**. Then answer the questions.

Narwhals are a species of whale that lives in the frigid waters of the Arctic Ocean. They are the most interesting animals on Earth! One reason is the amazing spiral "tusk" that extends out of their heads—an attribute that has earned these super swimmers the nickname "unicorns of the sea." This "horn" is actually a giant tooth that grows through their upper lips. Most (but not all) of the time, it is male narwhals who have this tooth, which can grow up to ten feet long. Narwhals can live up to fifty years, and they change color as they get older: from blue-gray as newborns, to spotty gray as adults, to almost totally white in their old age.

What is the author's opinion?

_____

_____

What are four facts that support the author's opinion?

1 _____

2 _____

3 _____

4 _____

BRAIN BOX

An **opinion** piece states an opinion and supports the opinion, or backs it up, with logical arguments and facts.

Finding Reliable Sources

Read about **reliable sources**. Then answer the questions.

When you perform research for an essay or a school project, you should choose reliable sources. Reliable sources are also called trusted, or credible, sources. These include books and encyclopedias, both print and online. They also include print and electronic articles published in major newspapers, magazines, or journals.

Reliable online sources include the websites of colleges and universities. They also include government agencies (think NASA!) and museums (natural history museums, for example). You can recognize these because their URLs end with .edu, .org, and .gov. If you need help deciding what a reliable source is, ask yourself, "Is the author knowledgeable about this information?" An interview with a subject-matter expert is also a reliable source.

Unreliable sources include sites that allow anyone to answer questions or that do not have a clear or widely known author. Web pages that have a biased point of view, such as a company selling a product, can also be unreliable.

It's a good idea to use at least three to five different sources for a research project. That way, you can make sure your information is accurate and up-to-date. Always double- and triple-check your facts. Make sure your project or paper is objective by removing any statements of your opinion about your subject.

BRAIN BOX

It's important to use **reliable sources** when doing internet research. Reliable sources include: websites of museums, universities, and professional associations; articles published in major newspapers, magazines, or professional journals, blogs, or web pages.

Unreliable sources may include: sites that allow anyone to answer questions or web pages that have a biased point of view.

Marco is writing a report about the history and culture of Mongolia. Below are some sources he's considering using. Put an R next to the sources that seem reliable and a U next to sources that seem unreliable.

An online encyclopedia article called "Mongolia" _____

A social media post about visiting Mongolia _____

A book in your school library called *Cultures of the World: Mongolia* _____

A travel company that sells a tour around Mongolia _____

A newspaper article featuring a time line of Mongolian history _____

An interview with a scholar of Mongolian history _____

1 Pick a topic to research. For example, if you are interested in writing about space, your research question could be, "What is a black hole?"
2 Look for books, magazines, encyclopedias, and online sources to help you answer your question.
3 With the help of a grown-up, find three reliable sources and note them on the cards below. On each, write the name of the source, the URL (if found online), and the date you accessed the site (if it's an online source).

Source #1

Source #2

Source #3

Taking Good Notes

Lucia is writing a report on black holes. She found a book called *Encyclopedia of Space* that has a lot of information, but she took more notes than she needs. Read her notes below. Put a check mark ✓ next to the notes that are specifically related to her research on black holes and an ✗ next to the notes that aren't.

Taking notes

How are black holes different from other regions of space?

☐ Black holes are areas in space where a large amount of matter is compressed into a small area.

☐ Neptune is the planet in our solar system with the fastest winds.

☐ The gravitational field around a black hole is so strong that not even light can get out.

☐ Gravity on Mars is about one-third as strong as gravity on Earth.

☐ Like most galaxies, the Milky Way has a supermassive black hole at its center.

☐ NASA uses tools like telescopes and satellites to gather information about black holes.

☐ The average surface temperature on Venus is about 900 degrees Fahrenheit.

BRAIN BOX

As you read each source, look for factual information that answers your research question. (A research question is a question that a research project aims to answer.) The key to note-taking is to figure out which details are important enough to write down and include in your report. Ask yourself, "Will this information help someone who doesn't know anything about my research topic understand it?"

Citing Sources

You must cite all the sources you use in your research. You must include specific information for each **citation**. Here is how to cite a book, an article, a website, and an interview:

Book

Author's last name, author's first name. *Title of book.* Name of publisher, date of publication.

Hawking, Stephen. *A Brief History of Time.* Bantam Books, 1989.

Article

Author's last name, author's first name. "Title of article." *Name of publication,* date.

Overbye, Dennis. "Is There a Black Hole in Our Backyard?" *New York Times,* 11 Sept. 2020.

Website

Author's Last Name, First Name. "Title of Web Page." *Title of Website,* website publisher (if different from website name), date published, URL.

Young, Lauren J. "The Very First Image Of A Black Hole." *Science Friday,* WNYC Studios, 10 Apr. 2019, https://www.sciencefriday.com/articles/breaking-first-image-black-hole/.

Personal Interview

Last name of person interviewed, first name of person interviewed. The words "Personal interview." Date of interview.

Smith, Allison. Personal interview. 29 July, 2022.

When creating your **bibliography**, list your sources in alphabetical order by the author's last name. Use the lines below to write a bibliography for the sources you found on page 113. You may need extra paper.

_____
_____
_____
_____
_____

BRAIN BOX

A **citation** gives credit to an author or publication for the information or ideas used in your research. All the sources are compiled into a **bibliography,** an alphabetical list of citations.

What Do You Want to Know?

List **topics** that interest you in each category.

People	Places	Things
Wangari Maathai	The Andaman Islands	Volcanoes

Plants/Animals	Books/Movies	Historical Times
Capybaras	Back to the Future	The Revolutionary War

Circle the topics that
interest you the most.

Be More Specific

Research your topic by using either a book or a website. Then jot down possible narrower topics.

Volcanoes

underwater volcanoes   volcano eruptions in history   volcano monitoring

Circle the narrower topic that you want to write about.

Topic: _____

Narrower Topics

- _____
- _____
- _____
- _____
- _____
- _____
- _____
- _____
- _____
- _____
- _____
- _____
- _____
- _____

BRAIN BOX

When writing about a topic, you can widen or narrow the scope. **Widening the scope** means enlarging the area or subject matter that you write about. **Narrowing the scope** means shrinking the subject matter. When widening the scope of a story on capybaras, you might include other large rodents. When narrowing the scope, you might write about a specific herd of capybaras.

Get Organized!

Read the notes about honeybees.

The queen's only job is to lay eggs.

When the bee stings someone, the venom sac detaches from the bee and kills the bee.

Honeybees live in a hive.

Female bees known as workers find food, build the hive, clean, care for the baby bees, and make honey.

Drones (male bees) mate with the queen.

Bees drink nectar from flowers.

Back in the hive, the bees regurgitate the nectar into the honeycomb.

The water in the nectar evaporates. Honey is left behind.

Hives are usually in hollow trees.

Eighty thousand bees can live in a hive.

Bees sting to defend themselves or the hive.

Their stingers are barbed.

The stinger is attached to a venom sac inside the bee.

Bees eat honey in the winter when there are no flowers.

The sting hurts because of the venom.

BRAIN BOX

An **outline** can help you organize your **notes** in the order in which they will appear in your report.

Fill in the **outline** with the facts from the notes.

Organizing notes

A The hive

1. _____

2. _____

3. _____

B Workers, queens, and drones

1. _____

2. _____

3. _____

C How and why bees make honey

1. _____

   2. _____

     3. _____

       4. _____

D Bee stings

1. _____

2. _____

3. _____

4. _____

5. _____

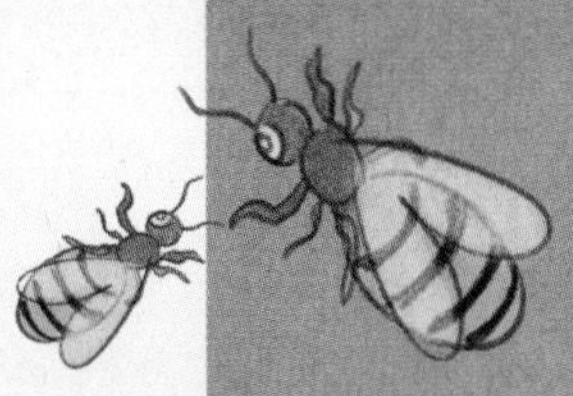

You Be the Editor

Proofreading Marks		**Examples**
Capitalize	≡	The white House
Lowercase	/	The Library is closed
Insert word or letter	∧	The zoo is open
Delete	ℐ	Call me me after the party.
Change order	∽	Today Thursday is.
Spell out	⑤P	There are ⑦ days in a week. ⑤P
Add comma	∧	You look great Tom.
Add period	⊙	This is the end⊙
New paragraph	¶	"Are you done with your sandwich?" he asked. ¶ "No, I'm still eating," I said.

Correct the article using the proofreading marks.

Capybaras

Capybaras are the world's largest Rodents. They live in the rain forests and savannas of central america and south america. Weighing 75 to 100 pounds, they are the size of a large dog. The giant rodents are are semiaquatic. They cool off in the water, graze on aquatic plants, and also use water for protection predators include jaguars anacondas and caimans. If a predator threatens a, it dives underwater. A capybara can hold its breath underwater for 5 minutes!

Capybarras live in groups of 3 to 30. Together, they their defend territory. Capybaras communicate through scent and sound. They bark to warn each other of trouble A male's scent indicates his social status and whether whether he is ready to mate.

The closest rellatives to capybaras are guinea pigs. Like guinea pigs, capybaras are easily domesticated. In some places, they are now raised on ranches. Some people even keep them as pets

BRAIN BOX

Proofreading marks show mistakes in writing and how to correct them.

MATH SKILLS

Time to show off your math skills! In this section, we'll review expanded and standard notation, place value, and prime numbers. Let's do math!

PARENTS In this section, your child will explore place value, standard and expanded notation, prime numbers, and factors. Students will build on this knowledge as they practice their computational skills in subsequent sections. Encourage your child to use a *growth mindset* as they work and to recognize that effort makes them stronger learners.

For additional resources, visit www.BrainQuest.com/grade5

Number Machine

Write the words as numerals.

three thousand two hundred seventy-five
_____

eight hundred million four hundred thousand two hundred
_____

nine hundred ninety-nine billion nine hundred ninety-nine million nine hundred ninety-nine thousand nine hundred ninety-nine
_____

forty-five million four hundred fifty-three thousand eight hundred ninety-two
_____

seven hundred three
_____

seventy-seven thousand seven hundred seventy-seven
_____

nine hundred twenty-two thousand three
_____

five hundred thousand two hundred twenty-three
_____

two hundred two million two
_____

thirty-three thousand
_____

Put the numbers in order from smallest to largest.

_____
_____
_____
_____
_____
_____
_____
_____
_____
_____

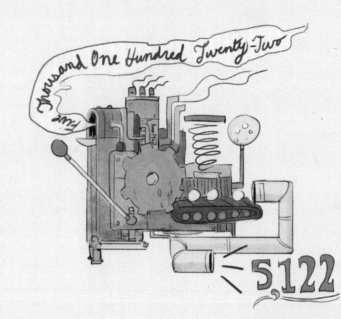

5,122

Figure Eights

Circle the **8** in each number. Write its **place value**.

(8)432 _thousands_

468 _____

585 _____

832 _____

1,278 _____

489 _____

873,322 _____

5,810 _____

80,100 _____

Write a number with an 8 in the given place value.

Ones _____468_____

Tens _____

Hundreds _____

Thousands _____

Ten thousands _____

Hundred thousands _____

BRAIN BOX

The **place value** of a digit in a number is determined by where it appears in the number.

Example: 643,987

Hundred thousands	Ten thousands	Thousands	Hundreds	Tens	Ones
6	4	3	9	8	7

Expand on That

Write out the **expanded notation** for each number.

	Thousands	Hundreds	Tens	Ones

1,246 = _____ + _____ + _____ + _____

2,357 = _____ + _____ + _____ + _____

3,467 = _____ + _____ + _____ + _____

4,578 = _____ + _____ + _____ + _____

5,689 = _____ + _____ + _____ + _____

6,790 = _____ + _____ + _____ + _____

4,219 = _____ + _____ + _____ + _____

3,652 = _____ + _____ + _____ + _____

5,342 = _____ + _____ + _____ + _____

9,243 = _____ + _____ + _____ + _____

Expanded notation

BRAIN BOX

The **standard notation** for a number is the way it is typically written.

Example: 3,579

The **expanded notation** shows how much each digit in the number is worth based on its place value.

Example:
3,579 = 3,000 + 500 + 70 + 9

The 3 is worth 3,000, the 5 is worth 500, the 7 is worth 70, and the 9 is worth 9.

Write the **standard notation** for each expanded notation below.

Ten Thousands		Thousands		Hundreds		Tens		Ones	
90,000	+	1,000	+	800	+	30	+	7 =	_____
40,000	+	6,000	+	500	+	40	+	6 =	_____
70,000	+	4,000	+	300	+	50	+	9 =	_____
80,000	+	8,000	+	200	+	00	+	1 =	_____
20,000	+	9,000	+	800	+	10	+	2 =	_____
30,000	+	2,000	+	700	+	80	+	4 =	_____
20,000	+	3,000	+	100	+	90	+	5 =	_____

Balloon Math

Write the missing number that makes the balloon bigger.

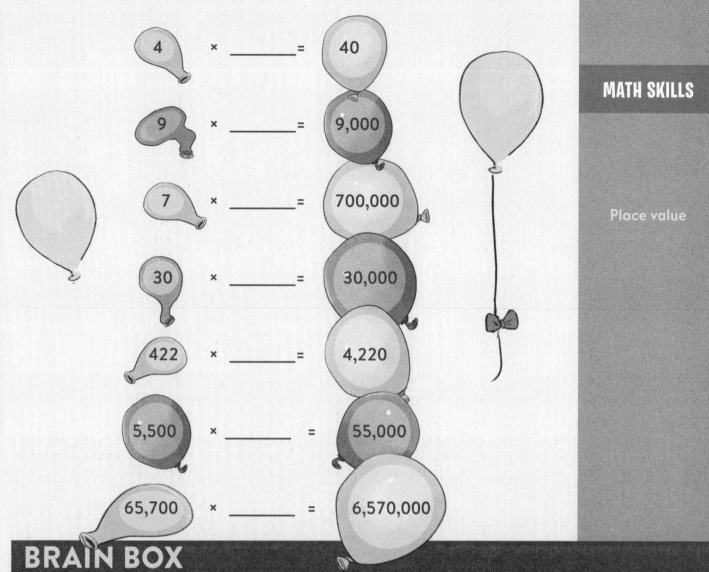

$4 \times \underline{\hspace{2cm}} = 40$

$9 \times \underline{\hspace{2cm}} = 9{,}000$

$7 \times \underline{\hspace{2cm}} = 700{,}000$

$30 \times \underline{\hspace{2cm}} = 30{,}000$

$422 \times \underline{\hspace{2cm}} = 4{,}220$

$5{,}500 \times \underline{\hspace{2cm}} = 55{,}000$

$65{,}700 \times \underline{\hspace{2cm}} = 6{,}570{,}000$

BRAIN BOX

When **multiplying** a whole number by 10, the value of that number increases ten times and the digits of that number move one place to the left to indicate that increase.

So, when multiplying 32 x 10, the value of 32 increases ten times. The digits move one place to the left on the place value chart.

Hundreds	Tens	Ones
	3	2
3	2	0

Digits move one place to the left when multiplying by 10. Insert a 0 in the ones place.

The number of zeroes indicates the amount of places to the left the digits must move.

So, when multiplying a whole number by 100, the value of that number increases one hundred times and the digits of that number move two places to the left on a place value chart.

So, when multiplying 32 x 100, the digits move two places to the left on the place value chart.

Thousands	Hundreds	Tens	Ones
		3	2
3	2	0	0

Digits move two places to the left. Insert 0 in the tens and ones places.

This pattern continues for all multiples of ten.

Balloon Math II

Write the missing number that makes the balloon smaller.

Place value

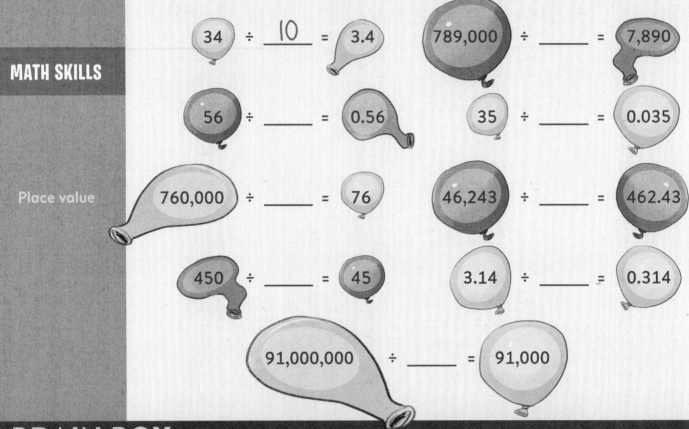

$34 \div \underline{10} = 3.4$

$789,000 \div \underline{} = 7,890$

$56 \div \underline{} = 0.56$

$35 \div \underline{} = 0.035$

$760,000 \div \underline{} = 76$

$46,243 \div \underline{} = 462.43$

$450 \div \underline{} = 45$

$3.14 \div \underline{} = 0.314$

$91,000,000 \div \underline{} = 91,000$

BRAIN BOX

When **dividing** a number by 10, the value of that number decreases ten times. To indicate that decrease, the digits of that number move one place to the right in the place value chart.

First put a decimal point at the end of the number if it does not already have one.

Example: 76 = 76.0

When dividing 76.0 ÷ 10, the value of 76.0 decreases ten times. The digits move one place to the right on the place value chart.

76 ÷ 10 = 7.6

Tens	Ones	Tenths
7	6	.0
	7	.6

The number of zeroes in the divisor indicates the number of places to the right the digits must move.

When dividing a whole number by 100, the value of that number decreases one hundred times. To indicate that decrease, the digits of that number move two places to the right on the place value chart.

76.0 ÷ 100 = .76

Tens	Ones	Tenths	Hundredths
7	6	.0	0
		.7	6

When dividing by 1,000, move the digits in the dividend three places to the right on the place value chart. Insert zeroes as the decimal moves farther to the left.

76.0 ÷ 1000 = .076

Tens	Ones	Tenths	Hundredths
7	6	.0	0
	.0	7	6

The Twenty-Five

Place an **X** over the non-prime numbers with help from the clues. Remember, the number 1 isn't prime! Then color the twenty-five boxes that contain **prime numbers**.

Prime numbers

1	2	3	4	5	6	7	8	9	10
11	12	13	14	15	16	17	18	19	20
21	22	23	24	25	26	27	28	29	30
31	32	33	34	35	36	37	38	39	40
41	42	43	44	45	46	47	48	49	50
51	52	53	54	55	56	57	58	59	60
61	62	63	64	65	66	67	68	69	70
71	72	73	74	75	76	77	78	79	80
81	82	83	84	85	86	87	88	89	90
91	92	93	94	95	96	97	98	99	100

A prime number is always greater than 1. Cross out 1.

All even numbers have the **factor** 2. There is only one even prime number, which is 2. The number 2 can only be divided evenly by itself and 1. Place an X over all other even numbers.

Numbers ending with 5 and 0 have 5 as a factor. (The exception is 5, which is a prime number for the same reason that 2 is a prime number.) Cross out those numbers.

Cross out numbers that have 3 as a factor (other than 3, which is a prime number).
(Hint: When the digits in a multi-digit number add up to a number divisible by 3, such as 6, 9, 12, 15, or 18, that multi-digit number is divisible by 3. Example: 39 is divisible by 3 because 3 + 9 = 12 and 12 is divisible by 3.)

Place an X over the three remaining numbers with 7 as a factor: 49, 77, 91 (7 itself is a prime number.)

BRAIN BOX

The two numbers in a multiplication problem are called **factors**. A **prime number** is a number greater than 1 that can be divided evenly only by 1 or itself. For instance, the number 7 is a prime number because its only factors are 7 and 1. The number 6 is not a prime number because it has four factors: 6, 1, 3, and 2. There are twenty-five prime numbers from 1 to 100.

Factor Trees

Fill in the circles to make a **factor tree** for each number. Circle the prime numbers. Then multiply the prime numbers to get the original number.

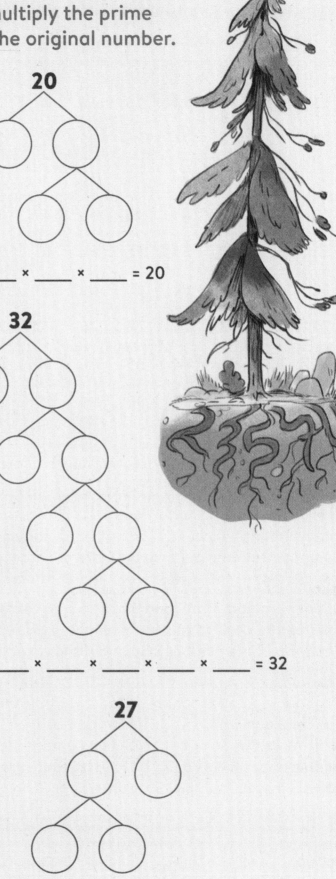

20

_____ × _____ × _____ = 20

32

_____ × _____ × _____ × _____ × _____ = 32

27

_____ × _____ × _____ = 27

BRAIN BOX

A **factor tree** is a diagram used to break down a number into its prime number factors. To make a factor tree, start by writing the largest factor and its counterpart underneath the number.

Do the same thing with any factors that are still not prime numbers.

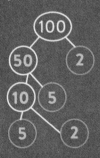

If you multiply the prime number factors, the **product** is the original number:

5 × 2 × 5 × 2 = **100**

The answer to a multiplication problem is the **product**.

MULTIPLICATION AND DIVISION

Learning multiplication and division facts has brought you to this next challenge: multi-digit multiplication and division. The more you practice, the more your skills—and confidence—will multiply!

PARENTS Your child will practice multiplying and dividing multi-digit numbers, using regrouping where needed. This work develops your child's precision and improves their mental math skills. Provide extra paper and encourage your child to show the steps of each problem. When they finish, have them check their work using a different strategy and/or a calculator. Use mistakes as opportunities for improvement.

Ocean Life

Fill in the missing numbers to **multiply** each set.

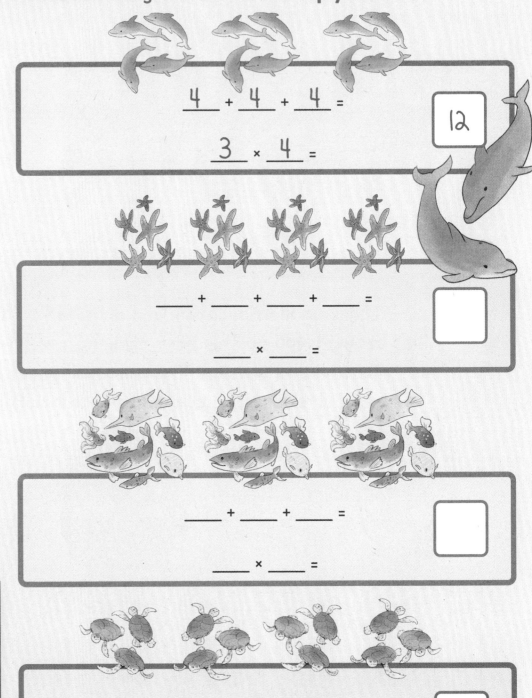

_4_ + _4_ + _4_ = $\boxed{12}$

_3_ × _4_ =

___ + ___ + ___ + ___ = $\boxed{}$

___ × ___ =

___ + ___ + ___ = $\boxed{}$

___ × ___ =

___ + ___ + ___ + ___ = $\boxed{}$

___ × ___ =

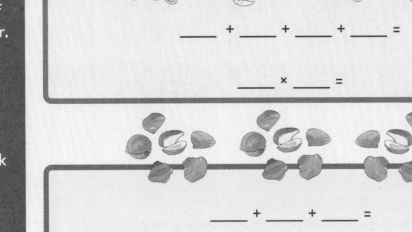

___ + ___ + ___ = $\boxed{}$

___ × ___ =

MULTIPLICATION
AND DIVISION

Multiplication

BRAIN BOX

Multiplication is adding groups of the same number.

Example:
2 + 2 + 2 = 6
3 × 2 = 6

We can also think of 3 × 2 as three groups of two in each group.

Break It Down

Write all the possible sets of **factors** for each **number**.

10

| $1 \times 10 = 10$ | $2 \times 5 = 10$ |

Factors and products

12

14

15

16

18

BRAIN BOX

A number can have multiple sets of **factors**.

Example: factors of 4

$2 \times 2 = 4$

$1 \times 4 = 4$

Fruitilicious

Write out the multiplication problems needed to find the number of seeds in each basket of fruit. Solve the problems.

Multiplication

5 × 5 = 25

Multiplication

Multiply Using Place Value

Multiply using **partial product multiplication**.
Show your work.

Multiplication

$$\begin{array}{r} 258 \\ \times\ 3 \\ \hline \end{array}$$

$$\begin{array}{r} 582 \\ \times\ 6 \\ \hline \end{array}$$

$$\begin{array}{r} 814 \\ \times\ 9 \\ \hline \end{array}$$

$$\begin{array}{r} 147 \\ \times\ 2 \\ \hline \end{array}$$

$$\begin{array}{r} 693 \\ \times\ 7 \\ \hline \end{array}$$

$$\begin{array}{r} 936 \\ \times\ 2 \\ \hline \end{array}$$

$$\begin{array}{r} 369 \\ \times\ 4 \\ \hline \end{array}$$

$$\begin{array}{r} 701 \\ \times\ 8 \\ \hline \end{array}$$

$$\begin{array}{r} 347 \\ \times\ 8 \\ \hline \end{array}$$

$$\begin{array}{r} 479 \\ \times\ 5 \\ \hline \end{array}$$

$$\begin{array}{r} 132 \\ \times\ 9 \\ \hline 18 \\ 270 \\ 900 \\ \hline 1{,}188 \end{array}$$

BRAIN BOX

One method of multiplying is called **partial product multiplication**.

Each place is multiplied separately and the addition of the partial products is the last step.

Step 1: Multiply the numbers in the ones columns. 9 times 2 equals 18. Write that product below the line.

Step 2: Now multiply the 9 times the digit in the tens place in 132. Remember that the 3 is really worth 30. 9 times 30 equals 270. Write that number below the line.

Step 3: Finally, multiply the 9 by the digit in the hundreds place in 132. Remember that the 1 is really worth 100. 9 times 100 equals 900. Write that product below the line.

Step 4: Add up all the products.

Example:
$$\begin{array}{r} 132 \\ \times\ 9 \\ \hline 18 \\ 270 \\ +900 \\ \hline 1{,}188 \end{array}$$

Move On

Multiply. **Regroup** as needed. Show your work.

```
  105
×   3
─────
```

```
  418
×   6
─────
```

```
  817
×   3
─────
```

Multiplying multi-digit numbers

```
  620
×   2
─────
```

```
  729
×   7
─────
```

```
  916
×   8
─────
```

```
  903
×   4
─────
```

```
  821
×   7
─────
```

```
  619
×   6
─────
```

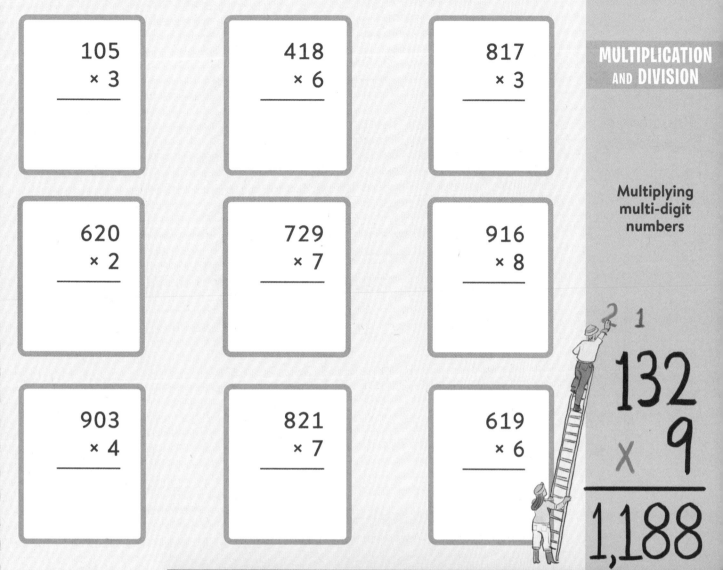

```
  2  1
  132
×   9
─────
1,188
```

```
  928
×   5
─────
```

BRAIN BOX

Another method of multiplying is the **traditional algorithm.**

Step 1: Multiply the numbers in the ones column. 9 times 2 is 18, so write the 8 in the ones place below the line and regroup the 1 above the tens column.

Step 2: Multiply the 9 by the 3 in the tens column. 9 times 3 equals 27, plus add the one ten regrouped from the last step.

27 plus 1 equals 28. Write the 8 below the line and regroup the 2 above the hundreds column.

Step 3: Multiple 9 by the 1 in the hundreds column. 9 times 1 equals 9, and add the 2 tens regrouped from the last step. 9 + 2 equals 11. Write that below the line.

Example:
```
   21
  132
×   9
─────
1,188
```

Big Numbers

Multiply. Show your work.

Multiplying
multi-digit
numbers

$$\begin{array}{r} 675 \\ \times\ 84 \\ \hline \end{array}$$

$$\begin{array}{r} 392 \\ \times\ 57 \\ \hline \end{array}$$

$$\begin{array}{r} 584 \\ \times\ 39 \\ \hline \end{array}$$

$$\begin{array}{r} 294 \\ \times\ 45 \\ \hline \end{array}$$

$$\begin{array}{r} 386 \\ \times\ 63 \\ \hline \end{array}$$

BRAIN BOX

One way to multiply multi-digit numbers uses the **traditional algorithm**. With this method, you multiply the whole first number by the ones and then the tens in separate steps.

Step 1: Multiply the top number by the ones digit of the bottom number (332 times 8). Write the numbers you regroup above the top number.

Step 2: Put a zero below the ones column to indicate that you are multiplying in the tens place. Cross out the regrouped numbers you already added.

Step 3: Multiply the top number by the tens digit of the bottom number (332 times 4). Write the numbers you regroup above the crossed-out numbers.

Step 4: Add the products.

$$\begin{array}{r} 1 \\ 21 \\ 332 \\ \times\ 48 \\ \hline 2{,}656 \\ 13{,}280 \\ \hline 15{,}936 \end{array}$$

Multiplying multi-digit numbers

985
× 74
———

736
× 28
———

293
× 89
———

851
× 62
———

375
× 26
———

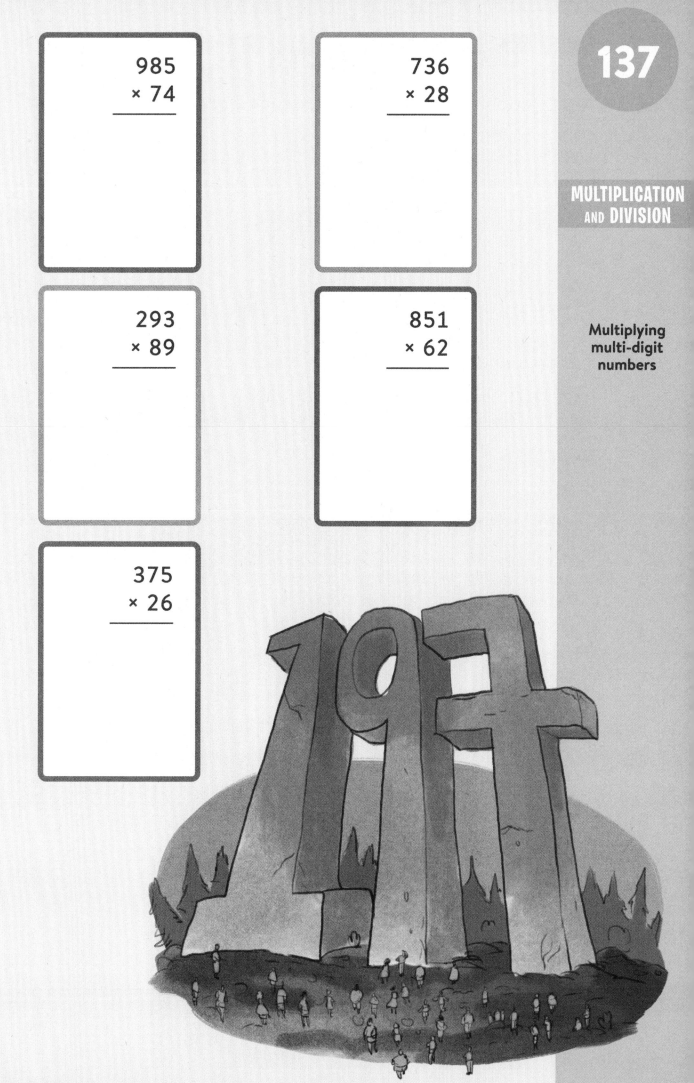

Big Numbers II

Multiply using **partial product multiplication.**
Show your work.

Multiplying
multi-digit
numbers

589	485	936	873
× 29	× 19	× 87	× 39

854
× 67

BRAIN BOX

Another way to multiply two multi-digit numbers uses **partial product multiplication.** In this method, each place value is multiplied separately. Then all the partial products are added together.

Step 1: Multiply the top number by the ones digit (332 times 8). Instead of regrouping numbers, multiply each digit in 332 by 8 according to its place value: 2 × 8 = 16, 30 × 8 = 240, and 300 × 8 = 2400.

Example:
```
   332
 ×  48
 ─────
    16
   240
 2,400
```

Step 2: Now multiply the top number by the tens digit (332 times 4). But remember, the 4 is in the tens place and has a value of 40. So: 40 × 2 = 80, 40 × 30 = 1,200, and 40 × 300 = 12,000.

Example:
```
    332
  ×  48
  ─────
     16
    240
  2,400
     80
  1,200
 12,000
 ──────
```

Step 3: Add the products.

Example:
```
     332
   ×  48
   ─────
      16
     240
   2,400
      80
   1,200
 +12,000
 ───────
  15,936
```

$$\begin{array}{r} 648 \\ \times\ 56 \\ \hline \end{array}$$

$$\begin{array}{r} 346 \\ \times\ 92 \\ \hline \end{array}$$

$$\begin{array}{r} 783 \\ \times\ 47 \\ \hline \end{array}$$

$$\begin{array}{r} 242 \\ \times\ 99 \\ \hline \end{array}$$

Multiplying multi-digit numbers

$$\begin{array}{r} 978 \\ \times\ 43 \\ \hline \end{array}$$

Teamwork

Divide the players into even teams. Circle the groups. Write the equation underneath.

Division

Divide 12 soccer players into 3 teams of 4.

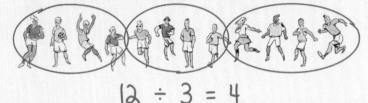

$$12 \div 3 = 4$$

Divide 20 basketball players into 4 teams of 5.

_____

Divide 9 lacrosse players into 3 teams of 3.

_____

Divide 28 gymnasts into 7 teams of 4.

_____

Divide 24 wrestlers into 6 teams of 4.

_____

Divide 18 soccer players into 6 teams of 3.

_____

Divide 32 football players into 4 teams of 8.

_____

Divide and Conquer

Write out the problem. Then solve it. Circle the **quotient**.

The divisor is 8. The dividend is 57.

$$57 \div 8 = \boxed{7\ r1}$$

The dividend is 121. The divisor is 11.

The dividend is 56. The divisor is 7.

The dividend is 43. The divisor is 6.

Divisor and dividend

The divisor is 9. The dividend is 63.

The dividend is 66. The divisor is 8.

The dividend is 81. The divisor is 9.

BRAIN BOX

The number being divided is called the **dividend**. The number being divided into it is called the **divisor**. The answer to a division problem is called the quotient. The quotient may include a **remainder**.

The dividend is 49. The divisor is 7.

Step by Step

Divide. The answer may or may not include a remainder.

Long division

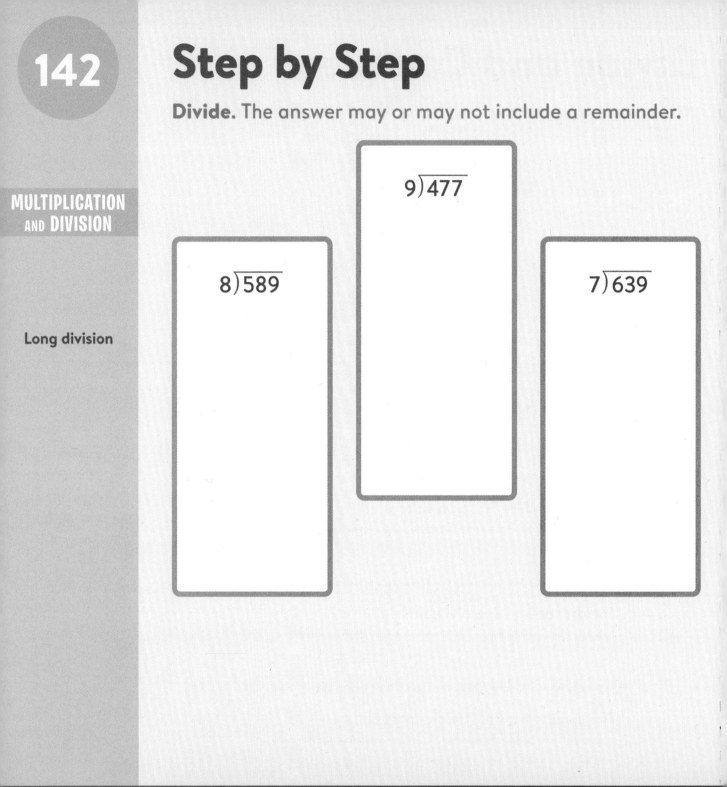

$$9\overline{)477}$$

$$8\overline{)589}$$

$$7\overline{)639}$$

BRAIN BOX

One way to divide a single-digit number into a larger number uses the **traditional division algorithm.**

Step 1: Divide the first digit of the dividend by the divisor (8 divided by 7). Write the result in the quotient, or answer.

Step 2: Multiply the result by the divisor ($1 \times 7 = 7$). Write the result below the digit used in the dividend, then subtract ($8 - 7 = 1$).

Step 3: Bring down the next digit of the dividend next to the result, then divide that number by the divisor (19 divided by 7).

Long division

4)326

6)282

3)741

Step 4: Multiply the result by the divisor (2 × 7 = 14). Write the result below the last digit used from the dividend, then subtract (19 – 14 = 5).

Step 5: Bring down the next digit of the dividend next to the result, then divide that number by the divisor (57 divided by 7).

Step 6: Multiply the result by the divisor (8 × 7 = 56), write it below the last digit used from the dividend, then subtract (57 – 56 = 1). If there is a remainder, write it at the end of the quotient.

Example:

```
         128r1  ← quotient
divisor → 7) 897   — dividend
         -7
         ─────
          19
         -14
         ─────
          57
         -56
         ─────
           1
```

Two Are Better Than One

Divide.

**Dividing
multi-digit
numbers**

$22\overline{)4,686}$

$36\overline{)7,884}$

$84\overline{)2,352}$

BRAIN BOX

One way to divide a two-digit number into a larger number uses the **traditional
division algorithm.**

Step 1: Divide the first two digits of the dividend by the divisor. If that's not
possible, divide the first three digits (124 divided by 26).

Step 2: Multiply the result by the divisor (4 x 26 = 104). Write the result below the
smallest digit used from the dividend, then subtract (124 – 104 = 20).

Dividing multi-digit numbers

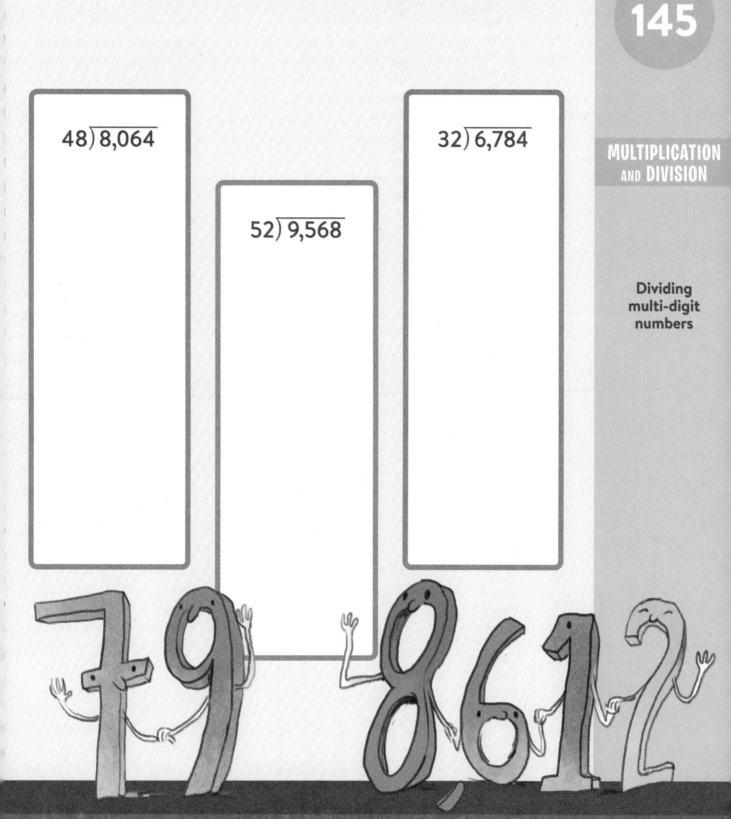

$48\overline{)8,064}$

$52\overline{)9,568}$

$32\overline{)6,784}$

Step 3: Bring down the next digit of the dividend. Then divide that number by the divisor (208 divided by 26).

Step 4: Multiply the result by the divisor (8 x 26 = 208), write it below the smallest digit used from the dividend, then subtract again (208 – 208 = 0).

Step 5: If there is a remainder, write it at the end of the quotient.

divisor →

Example:

$$
\begin{array}{r}
48 \quad \leftarrow \text{quotient} \\
26\overline{)1,248} \quad \leftarrow \text{dividend} \\
-104 \\
\hline
208 \\
-208 \\
\hline
0
\end{array}
$$

Check It

Divide. Then check your answer by multiplying.

Checking your answer

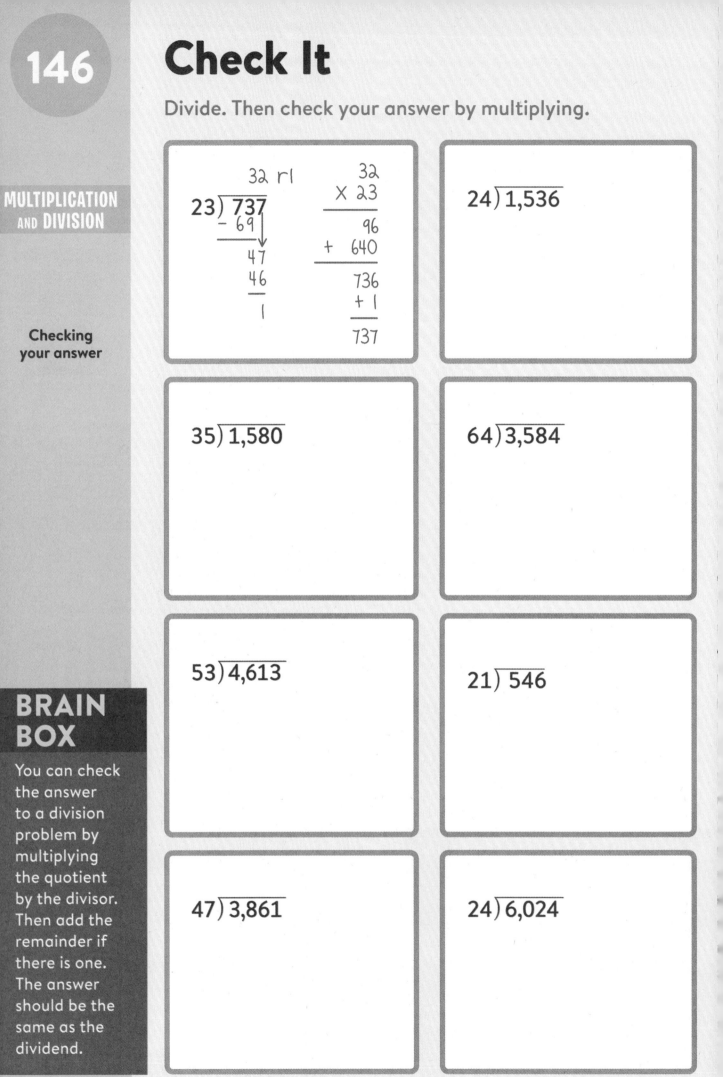

$$\begin{array}{r} 32\ r1 \\ 23\overline{)737} \\ -69\downarrow \\ \hline 47 \\ 46 \\ \hline 1 \end{array} \qquad \begin{array}{r} 32 \\ \times\ 23 \\ \hline 96 \\ +\ 640 \\ \hline 736 \\ +\ 1 \\ \hline 737 \end{array}$$

$24\overline{)1,536}$

$35\overline{)1,580}$

$64\overline{)3,584}$

$53\overline{)4,613}$

$21\overline{)546}$

$47\overline{)3,861}$

$24\overline{)6,024}$

BRAIN BOX

You can check the answer to a division problem by multiplying the quotient by the divisor. Then add the remainder if there is one. The answer should be the same as the dividend.

Practice Makes Perfect

Divide. Show your work.

Long division

$18\overline{)8,442}$

$13\overline{)4,953}$

$47\overline{)7,191}$

$28\overline{)4,116}$

$36\overline{)7,596}$

$42\overline{)6,972}$

$56\overline{)7,392}$

$66\overline{)7,128}$

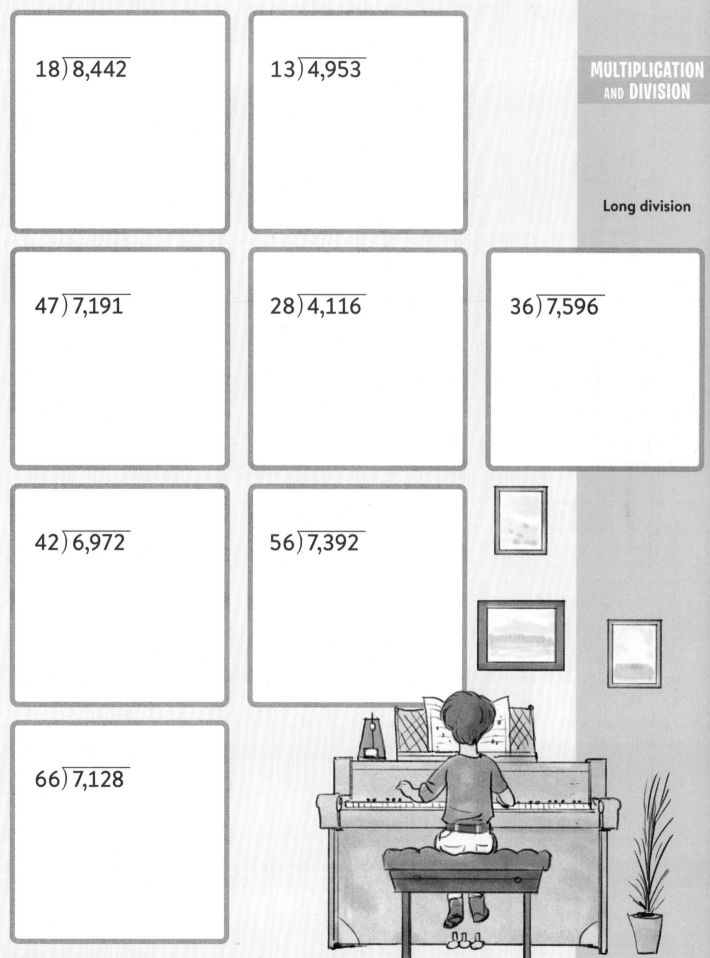

Best Guess

Estimate the product by rounding each factor to the nearest ten and multiplying.

Estimating

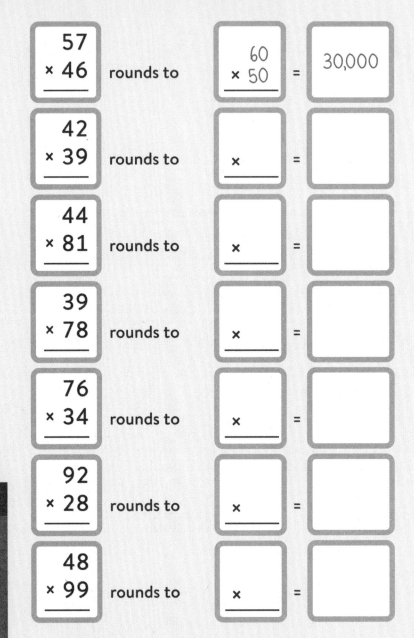

57 × 46	rounds to	60 × 50 = 30,000
42 × 39	rounds to	× =
44 × 81	rounds to	× =
39 × 78	rounds to	× =
76 × 34	rounds to	× =
92 × 28	rounds to	× =
48 × 99	rounds to	× =

BRAIN BOX

An **estimate** is an approximation. To estimate a product, round the factors up or down as necessary.

Example:
43 × 28 rounds to
40 × 30 = 1,200

To estimate a quotient, round the dividend and the divisor as necessary.

Example:
1,204 ÷ 43 rounds to
1,200 ÷ 40 = 30

Estimate the quotient by rounding the divisor to the nearest hundred and the dividend to the nearest ten and then dividing.

6,784 ÷ 23	8,756 ÷ 42

FRACTIONS AND DECIMALS

What fraction of your day do you spend thinking about fractions and decimals? Probably a lot more than you think! Whether you're measuring to bake brownies, counting change at the store, or deciding how to share something with your friend, fractions and decimals are a big part of our lives.

PARENTS In this section, practice with fractions and decimals starts with pictures before moving to numeric calculations. While changing fractions to decimals and vice versa, your child will see the relationship between these two ways of representing numbers. Move through this section sequentially, as the skills build in complexity.

For additional resources, visit www.BrainQuest.com/grade5

Pizza Party

Write the **numerator** and **denominator** that show how much of a whole pizza is left.

Numerator and denominator

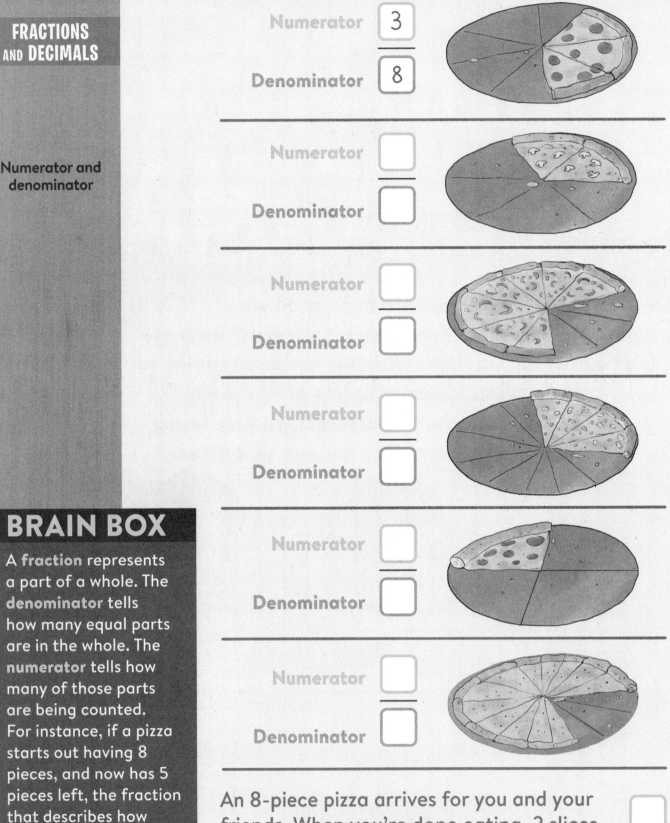

Numerator   3

Denominator 8

Numerator

Denominator

Numerator

Denominator

Numerator

Denominator

Numerator

Denominator

Numerator

Denominator

BRAIN BOX

A **fraction** represents a part of a whole. The **denominator** tells how many equal parts are in the whole. The **numerator** tells how many of those parts are being counted. For instance, if a pizza starts out having 8 pieces, and now has 5 pieces left, the fraction that describes how much pizza is left is $\frac{5}{8}$. 8 is the denominator, and 5 is the numerator.

An 8-piece pizza arrives for you and your friends. When you're done eating, 2 slices remain. Write a fraction that describes how much of the whole pizza is left.

Nice and Simple

Simplify the **fraction**. Shade in the correct amount.

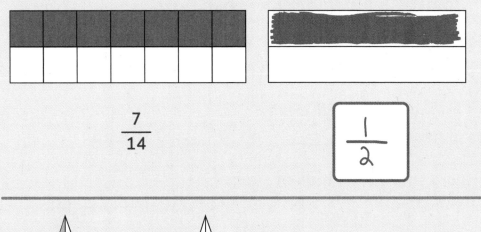

$$\frac{7}{14}$$

$$\boxed{\frac{1}{2}}$$

Simplifying fractions

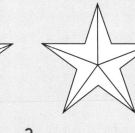

$$\frac{2}{10}$$

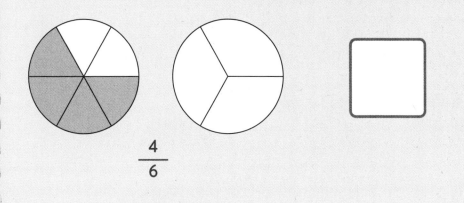

$$\frac{4}{6}$$

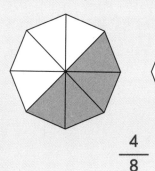

$$\frac{4}{8}$$

BRAIN BOX

When the numerator and denominator share a common factor, the fraction can be simplified.

Example:

$$\frac{6}{8} = \boxed{}$$

The 6 and 8 can both be divided by 2.

$6 \div 2 = 3$

$8 \div 2 = 4$

The simplified fraction is $\frac{3}{4}$.

As you can see, the two fractions represent equal amounts.

$$\frac{6}{8} = \frac{3}{4}$$

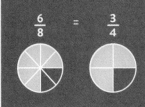

Sharing Is Caring

Fill in the blanks with fractions to solve each word problem. Simplify the fractions.

6 sisters share 2 calzones.
Each sister gets ___$\frac{2}{6}$___ or ___$\frac{1}{3}$___ of a calzone.

64 band members share 8 pizzas.
Each band member gets _____ or _____ of a pizza.

81 neighbors share 9 pounds of sugar.
Each neighbor gets _____ or _____ of a pound of sugar.

36 students share 4 packs of paper.
Each student gets _____ or _____ of a pack of paper.

12 soccer players share 6 oranges.
Each player gets _____ or _____ of an orange.

45 teachers share 9 gallons of glue.
Each teacher gets _____ or _____ of a gallon.

BRAIN BOX

A division problem can be written as a fraction.

Example:
3 divided by 4 can be written as $\frac{3}{4}$.

This means that if 4 people share 3 chocolate bars equally, they should each get $\frac{3}{4}$ of a bar.

Draw a picture to help solve the problem.

24 chefs share 6 sticks of butter.
Each chef gets _____ or _____ of a stick of butter.

Mixed Results

Find the correct **mixed number** for each word problem.
Simplify fractions if necessary.

9 cooks share 50 pounds of butter.
How many pounds of butter does each cook get? _____ $5\frac{5}{9}$

7 mice share 68 pieces of popcorn.
How many pieces of popcorn does each mouse get? _____

12 kids share 40 pieces of paper.
How many pieces of paper does each kid get? _____

Fractions
and dividing

11 crafters share 115 glue sticks.
How many glue sticks does each crafter get? _____

8 ants share 62 crumbs.
How many crumbs does each ant get? _____

22 students share 46 packs of crayons.
How many packs does each student get? _____

Draw a picture to help solve the problem.

4 smoothie stands share 26 pounds of bananas. How many
pounds of bananas does each smoothie stand receive?

BRAIN BOX

When a quotient has a remainder,
the quotient can be written as a
mixed number, which is a whole
number plus a fraction.

Example:
If you evenly divide 13 cookies
among 4 people, each person
would get $3\frac{1}{4}$ cookies.

$$4\overline{)13}\ \ ^{3\ r1}$$

Turn the remainder into a fraction
by placing it over the divisor.
$3\frac{1}{4}$ is a mixed number.

The Pluses and Minuses of Fractions

Add or subtract the **fractions**. Simplify if needed.

Adding and subtracting fractions

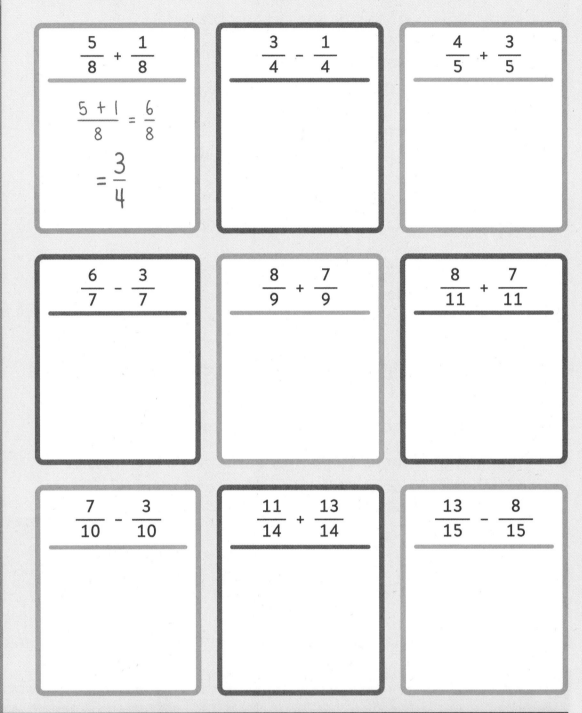

$$\frac{5}{8} + \frac{1}{8}$$

$$\frac{5 + 1}{8} = \frac{6}{8}$$

$$= \frac{3}{4}$$

$$\frac{3}{4} - \frac{1}{4}$$

$$\frac{4}{5} + \frac{3}{5}$$

$$\frac{6}{7} - \frac{3}{7}$$

$$\frac{8}{9} + \frac{7}{9}$$

$$\frac{8}{11} + \frac{7}{11}$$

$$\frac{7}{10} - \frac{3}{10}$$

$$\frac{11}{14} + \frac{13}{14}$$

$$\frac{13}{15} - \frac{8}{15}$$

BRAIN BOX

Adding **fractions** is adding more parts to the whole. Subtracting fractions is subtracting parts from the whole. Fractions with the same denominator can be added or subtracted by adding or subtracting their numerators. The denominator stays the same.

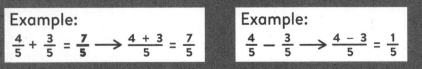

Example:

$$\frac{4}{5} + \frac{3}{5} = \frac{7}{5} \longrightarrow \frac{4 + 3}{5} = \frac{7}{5}$$

Example:

$$\frac{4}{5} - \frac{3}{5} \longrightarrow \frac{4 - 3}{5} = \frac{1}{5}$$

Matchy, Matchy

Draw a line between the equations and the matching pictures.

Adding and subtracting fractions

$\dfrac{1}{3} + \dfrac{2}{3}$

$\dfrac{4}{8} - \dfrac{1}{8}$

$\dfrac{4}{5} + \dfrac{3}{5}$

$\dfrac{3}{4} + \dfrac{1}{4}$

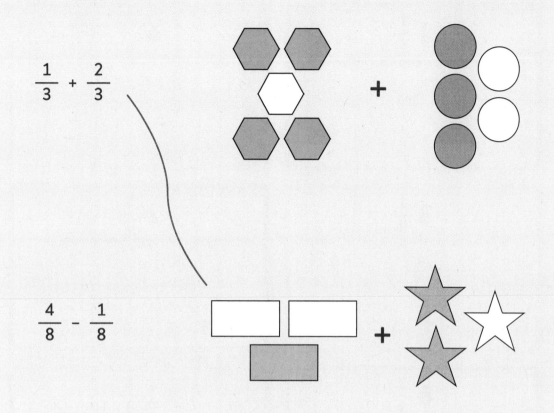

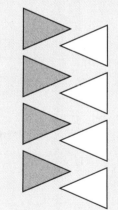

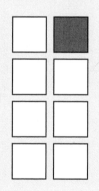

Bigger Products

Convert the mixed number into an improper fraction.

$2\frac{1}{4}$

2 × 4 = 8
8 + 1 = 9 $\frac{9}{4}$

$4\frac{7}{8}$

$3\frac{1}{8}$

$2\frac{5}{6}$

$8\frac{1}{3}$

$1\frac{7}{8}$

$3\frac{2}{5}$

$6\frac{1}{2}$

BRAIN BOX

To convert a mixed number into an **improper fraction**, follow these steps:

$2\frac{1}{4}$

Step 1: Multiply the whole number by the denominator. ⟶ 2 × 4 = 8

Step 2: Add that product to the numerator. ⟶ 8 + 1 = 9

Step 3: Write that sum above the denominator. $\frac{9}{4}$

Less and Less

Multiply. Show your work. Simplify all fractions.

Multiplying fractions

$\frac{3}{8} \times \frac{7}{10}$

3 X 7 = 21 $\frac{21}{80}$
8 X 10 = 80

$\frac{7}{8} \times \frac{4}{5}$

$\frac{1}{2} \times \frac{3}{5}$

$\frac{1}{3} \times \frac{3}{4}$

$\frac{4}{5} \times \frac{2}{3}$

$\frac{5}{8} \times \frac{2}{3}$

$\frac{9}{10} \times \frac{3}{4}$

$\frac{3}{8} \times \frac{7}{8}$

$\frac{6}{7} \times \frac{1}{2}$

$\frac{1}{2} \times \frac{2}{3}$

BRAIN BOX

When multiplying fractions, multiply the numerators. Then multiply the denominators.

Let's compare those fractions.

As you can see, the product is less than the factors. That's because you are multiplying two fractions that are less than 1. That means you are finding a part of a part. In this case, you are finding $\frac{3}{4}$ of $\frac{2}{3}$.

Example:

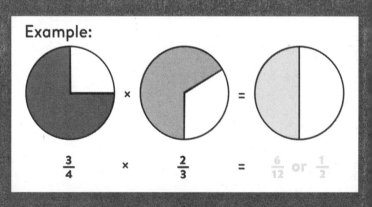

$\frac{3}{4}$ × $\frac{2}{3}$ = $\frac{6}{12}$ or $\frac{1}{2}$

Shortcut

Multiply. Simplify as you solve by **cross-canceling**.

Multiplying
fractions

$$\frac{3}{5} \times \frac{5}{6}$$

$$\frac{3}{1} \times \frac{1}{6} = \frac{1}{1} \times \frac{1}{2}$$

$$1 \times 1 = 1$$

$$1 \times 2 = 2$$

$$= \frac{1}{2}$$

$$\frac{5}{8} \times \frac{4}{5}$$

$$\frac{2}{5} \times \frac{3}{4}$$

$$\frac{2}{3} \times \frac{1}{2}$$

$$\frac{3}{11} \times \frac{5}{12}$$

$$\frac{7}{10} \times \frac{5}{8}$$

$$\frac{4}{5} \times \frac{5}{16}$$

$$\frac{3}{4} \times \frac{4}{5}$$

BRAIN BOX

You can multiply fractions more easily by **cross-canceling**, which reduces the numbers in the multiplication so that the product is stated in lowest terms.

Example:

$\frac{3}{4} \times \frac{4}{5}$ can also be written as $\frac{3 \times 4}{4 \times 5}$.

When a numerator and denominator are the same, you can cross-cancel them.

$\frac{3}{\cancel{4}} \times \frac{\cancel{4}^{1}}{5}$

Crossing out the 4s doesn't change the answer because $\frac{4}{4}$ equals 1. Anything multiplied by 1 is itself; it remains the same.

The new equation is $\frac{3}{1} \times \frac{1}{5} = \frac{3}{5}$

When a numerator and denominator being multiplied share a common factor (in this case 4), they can also be cross-canceled.

Example:

$\frac{3}{\textcircled{8}} \times \textcircled{4}{5}$ Identify the numerator and denominator that share a common factor.

$\frac{3}{\cancel{8}_{2}} \times \frac{\cancel{4}^{1}}{5}$ Cross out 4 and 8, and divide both numbers by the greatest common factor, which is 4.

The new equation is $\frac{3}{2} \times \frac{1}{5} = \frac{3}{10}$

Flip It

Divide. Simplify as you solve.

$$\frac{3}{8} \div \frac{6}{7} \rightarrow \frac{\cancel{3}}{8} \times \frac{7}{\cancel{6}_2}$$
$$\frac{1}{8} \times \frac{7}{2} = \frac{1 \times 7}{8 \times 2} = \frac{7}{16}$$

$$\frac{1}{4} \div \frac{1}{2}$$

$$\frac{1}{2} \div \frac{3}{5}$$

$$\frac{6}{7} \div \frac{1}{2}$$

Dividing fractions

$$\frac{4}{5} \div \frac{2}{3}$$

$$\frac{3}{8} \div \frac{7}{10}$$

$$\frac{2}{5} \div \frac{4}{9}$$

$$\frac{9}{10} \div \frac{3}{4}$$

$$\frac{1}{3} \div \frac{5}{8}$$

$$\frac{7}{8} \div \frac{4}{5}$$

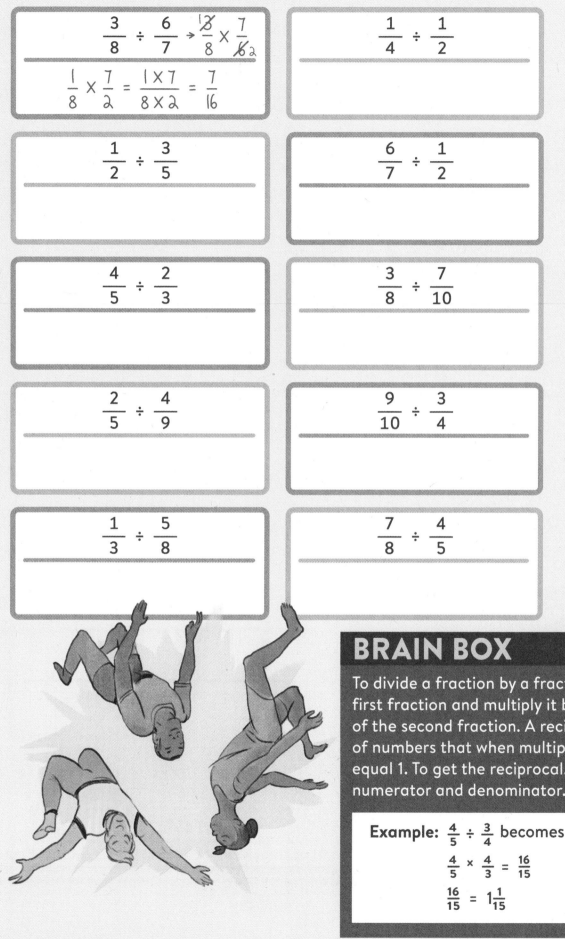

BRAIN BOX

To divide a fraction by a fraction, take the first fraction and multiply it by the **reciprocal** of the second fraction. A reciprocal is a pair of numbers that when multiplied together equal 1. To get the reciprocal, flip (invert) the numerator and denominator.

Example: $\frac{4}{5} \div \frac{3}{4}$ becomes $\frac{4}{5} \times \frac{4}{3}$

$$\frac{4}{5} \times \frac{4}{3} = \frac{16}{15}$$

$$\frac{16}{15} = 1\frac{1}{15}$$

High Divide

Divide. Simplify.

Dividing fractions

$$4 \div \frac{6}{7}$$

$$\frac{4}{1} \times \frac{7}{6} = \frac{2}{1} \times \frac{7}{3} = \frac{2 \times 7}{3 \times 1} \quad \frac{14}{3} = 4\frac{2}{3}$$

$$6 \div \frac{5}{8}$$

$$\frac{1}{2} \div 3$$

$$\frac{1}{4} \div 8$$

$$7 \div \frac{2}{3}$$

$$\frac{6}{7} \div 5$$

$$12 \div \frac{4}{9}$$

$$9 \div \frac{7}{10}$$

$$\frac{9}{10} \div 2$$

$$3 \div \frac{4}{5}$$

BRAIN BOX

When dividing a fraction by a whole number (or vice versa), first insert 1 as the denominator for the whole number (this doesn't change the number because any number divided by 1 is itself). Then flip the second fraction and multiply the fractions.

Example:

$$\frac{4}{5} \div 3$$

$$\frac{4}{5} \div \frac{3}{1}$$

$$\frac{4}{5} \times \frac{1}{3} = \frac{4}{15}$$

Example:

$$3 \div \frac{4}{5}$$

$$\frac{3}{1} \div \frac{4}{5}$$

$$\frac{3}{1} \times \frac{5}{4} = \frac{15}{4}$$

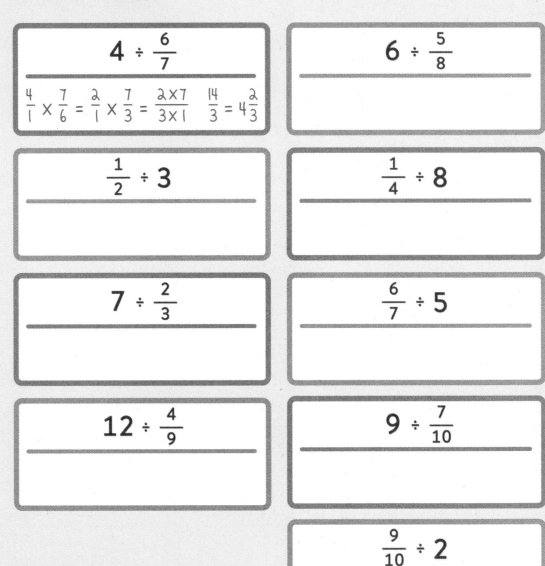

The Great Divide

Divide the shape into smaller parts based on the equation. Solve the problem.

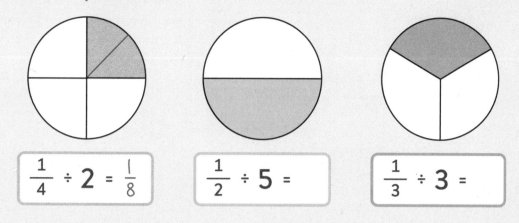

$$\frac{1}{4} \div 2 = \frac{1}{8}$$

$$\frac{1}{2} \div 5 =$$

$$\frac{1}{3} \div 3 =$$

Dividing fractions

Divide the shapes into more parts based on the equation. Solve the problem.

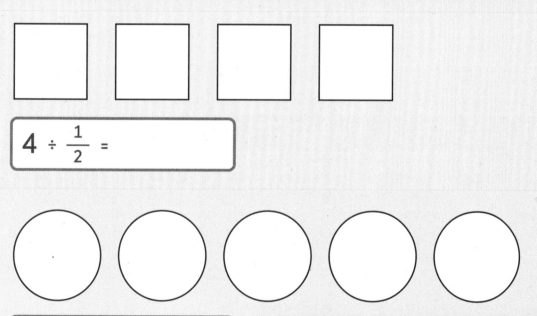

$$4 \div \frac{1}{2} =$$

$$5 \div \frac{1}{3} =$$

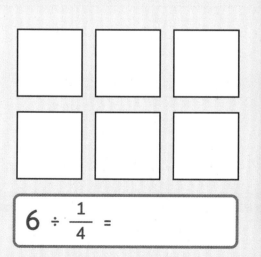

$$6 \div \frac{1}{4} =$$

BRAIN BOX

When you are dividing a fraction by a whole number, you are dividing a part of a whole into smaller parts. So the fraction gets smaller.

Example:

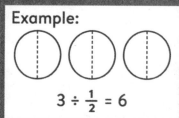

$$\frac{1}{2} \div 3 = \frac{1}{6}$$

When dividing a whole number by a fraction, you are dividing a whole number by a part of a whole. So the number gets bigger.

Example:

$$3 \div \frac{1}{2} = 6$$

Something in Common

Add by finding the **lowest common denominator.**
Simplify if necessary.

Common
denominators

$$\frac{5}{6} + \frac{1}{3} = \boxed{\frac{5}{6} + \frac{2}{6} = \frac{7}{6} = 1\frac{1}{6}}$$

$$\frac{5}{6} + \frac{2}{3} = \boxed{}$$

$$\frac{5}{8} + \frac{1}{4} = \boxed{}$$

$$\frac{3}{7} + \frac{1}{2} = \boxed{}$$

$$\frac{1}{2} + \frac{2}{5} = \boxed{}$$

$$\frac{2}{3} + \frac{8}{9} = \boxed{}$$

$$\frac{3}{16} + \frac{1}{4} = \boxed{}$$

$$\frac{5}{12} + \frac{5}{6} = \boxed{}$$

$$\frac{9}{10} + \frac{1}{5} = \boxed{}$$

$$\frac{7}{12} + \frac{3}{4} = \boxed{}$$

BRAIN BOX

To add or subtract fractions with different denominators, find the **lowest common denominator**, or **least common multiple** of the denominators, to make the denominators equal:

$$\frac{1}{6} + \frac{2}{3}$$

Step 1: What is the least common multiple of both denominators? The 3 can be changed to a 6 by multiplying it by 2.

Step 2: What is done to the denominator also must be done to the numerator.

$$\frac{2}{3} \times \frac{2}{2} = \frac{4}{6}$$

Step 3: Add the new fractions.

$$\frac{1}{6} + \frac{4}{6} = \frac{5}{6}$$

Sometimes both denominators must be changed. Follow the same steps.

$$\frac{2}{3} + \frac{3}{4}$$

The least common multiple of both denominators is 12.
So multiply both fractions to get the denominator.

$$\frac{2}{3} \times \frac{4}{4} = \frac{8}{12} \qquad \frac{3}{4} \times \frac{3}{3} = \frac{9}{12} \qquad \frac{8}{12} + \frac{9}{12} = \frac{17}{12} = 1\frac{5}{12}$$

Long-Lost Twins

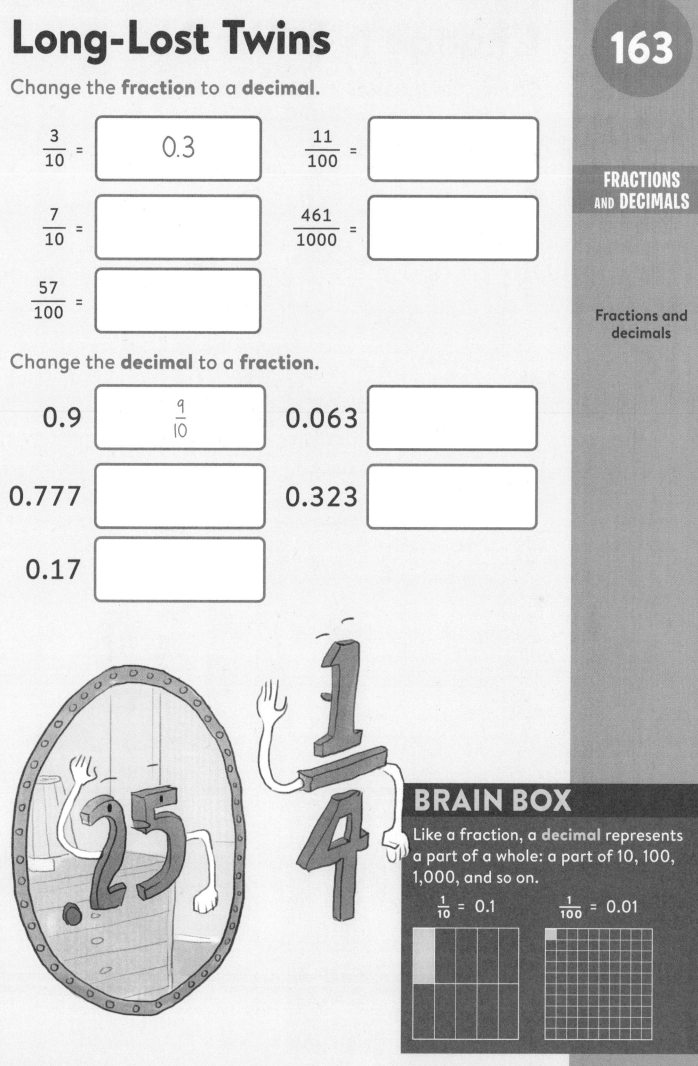

Change the **fraction** to a **decimal**.

$\frac{3}{10}$ = 0.3

$\frac{11}{100}$ =

$\frac{7}{10}$ =

$\frac{461}{1000}$ =

$\frac{57}{100}$ =

Change the **decimal** to a **fraction**.

0.9 $\frac{9}{10}$

0.063

0.777

0.323

0.17

BRAIN BOX

Like a fraction, a **decimal** represents a part of a whole: a part of 10, 100, 1,000, and so on.

$\frac{1}{10}$ = 0.1 $\frac{1}{100}$ = 0.01

Change Is in the Air

Change the **fractions** to **decimals** by changing the denominators to 10, 100, or 1,000.

$\frac{3}{4}$ $\boxed{\frac{3}{4} \times \frac{25}{25} = \frac{75}{100} = 0.75}$ $\frac{7}{25}$ [ ]

$\frac{1}{2}$ [ ] $\frac{29}{50}$ [ ]

$\frac{13}{20}$ [ ] $\frac{4}{5}$ [ ]

$\frac{3}{25}$ [ ]

$\frac{17}{50}$ [ ]

$\frac{3}{5}$ [ ]

BRAIN BOX

To convert a fraction to a decimal, you may need to first change the fraction's denominator to 10, 100, or 1,000.

Find a number you can multiply by the denominator to make it 10, 100, or 1,000. Then multiply both the denominator and the numerator by that number.

Example:
$\frac{2}{5} \times \frac{2}{2} = \frac{4}{10} = 0.4$

Smallest to Biggest

Order the decimals from smallest to largest.

0.42, 0.04, 0.7 _0.04, 0.42, 0.7_

0.78, 0.312, 0.1 _____

0.095, 0.856, 0.006 _____

0.613, 0.5, 0.32 _____

0.18, 0.54, 0.454 _____

0.62, 0.41, 0.19 _____

0.37, 0.4, 0.13 _____

0.11, 0.42, 0.014 _____

0.867, 0.53, 0.09 _____

0.523, 0.02, 0.29 _____

Ordering decimals

BRAIN BOX

In **decimals**, the tenths place is worth ten times more than the hundredths place.

Example:
0.2 is worth $\frac{2}{10}$

0.02 is worth $\frac{2}{100}$

If there is no number in the hundredths or thousandths place, then the value of that place is 0.

Example:
0.7 = 0.70

The Greatest

Compare the fractions and decimals below, using >, <, or =.

Comparing
decimals and
fractions

$\dfrac{3}{4}$ ___<___ 0.85

$\dfrac{7}{10}$ _____ 0.7

$\dfrac{1}{25}$ _____ 0.25

$\dfrac{7}{50}$ _____ 0.89

$\dfrac{3}{20}$ _____ 0.15

$\dfrac{3}{5}$ _____ 0.49

$\dfrac{17}{25}$ _____ 0.36

$\dfrac{41}{50}$ _____ 0.41

$\dfrac{2}{5}$ _____ 0.25

$\dfrac{1}{2}$ _____ 0.30

BRAIN BOX

To compare decimals and
fractions, change all the
decimals to fractions and
find a common denominator.

Example:
$\dfrac{1}{5}$, 0.25

$0.25 = \dfrac{25}{100}$

$\dfrac{1}{5} \times \dfrac{20}{20} = \dfrac{20}{100}$

$\dfrac{20}{100} < \dfrac{25}{100}$

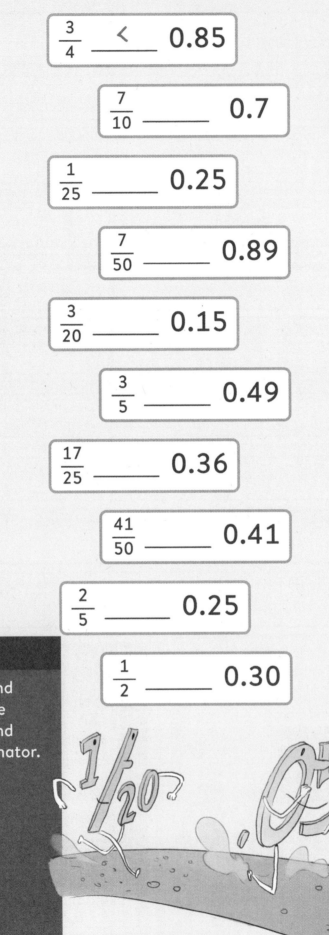

Dot to Dot

Add the decimals.

Adding decimals

$$
\begin{array}{r}
0.180 \\
+\ 0.051 \\
\hline
0.231
\end{array}
$$

$$
\begin{array}{r}
3.28 \\
+\ 37.451 \\
\hline
\end{array}
$$

$$
\begin{array}{r}
747.02 \\
+\ 73.1888 \\
\hline
\end{array}
$$

$$
\begin{array}{r}
10.75 \\
+\ 2.25 \\
\hline
\end{array}
$$

$$
\begin{array}{r}
17.014 \\
+\ 129.54 \\
\hline
\end{array}
$$

$$
\begin{array}{r}
0.0022 \\
+\ 0.8896 \\
\hline
\end{array}
$$

$$
\begin{array}{r}
3.74 \\
+\ 11.4 \\
\hline
\end{array}
$$

$$
\begin{array}{r}
152.3 \\
+\ 31.96 \\
\hline
\end{array}
$$

$$
\begin{array}{r}
7.139 \\
+\ 6.264 \\
\hline
\end{array}
$$

$$
\begin{array}{r}
85.45 \\
+\ 90.53 \\
\hline
\end{array}
$$

BRAIN BOX

To add decimals, make sure the decimal points are lined up. Then add the decimals just like any other number. Move down the decimal point.

Example:
$$
\begin{array}{r}
100.47 \\
+\ 2.4 \\
\hline
102.87
\end{array}
$$

Cha-ching Ch-change

Add the US coins and write the sum as a decimal.
Be sure to include the dollar sign, $.

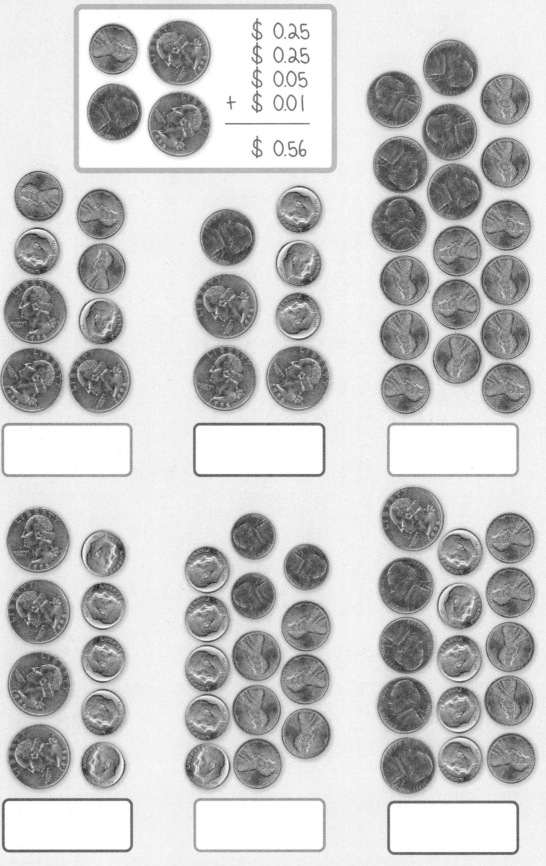

$ 0.25
$ 0.25
$ 0.05
+ $ 0.01
_____
$ 0.56

A candy bar costs $1. Circle the collections of coins that
would be enough to buy the candy bar.

Move It

Multiply.

Multiplying decimals

$$5.61 \text{ (2 decimal places)}$$
$$\times 0.78 \text{ (2 decimal places)}$$

```
        8
      480
     4000
       70
     4200
    35000
  ─────────
    4.3758
```

0.328
× 0.79
_____

1.25
× 0.81
_____

32.4
× 0.76
_____

44.12
× 0.312
_____

98.1
× 7.2
_____

88.32
× 67.1
_____

4.48
× 0.03
_____

82.97
× 0.456
_____

5.8
× 0.3
_____

32.48
× 3.77
_____

BRAIN BOX

Multiply decimals like any other numbers. Then count the number of digits to the right of all the decimals points. Move the decimal point that many places to the left.

Review

Mixed Bag

Solve the fraction and decimal problems.

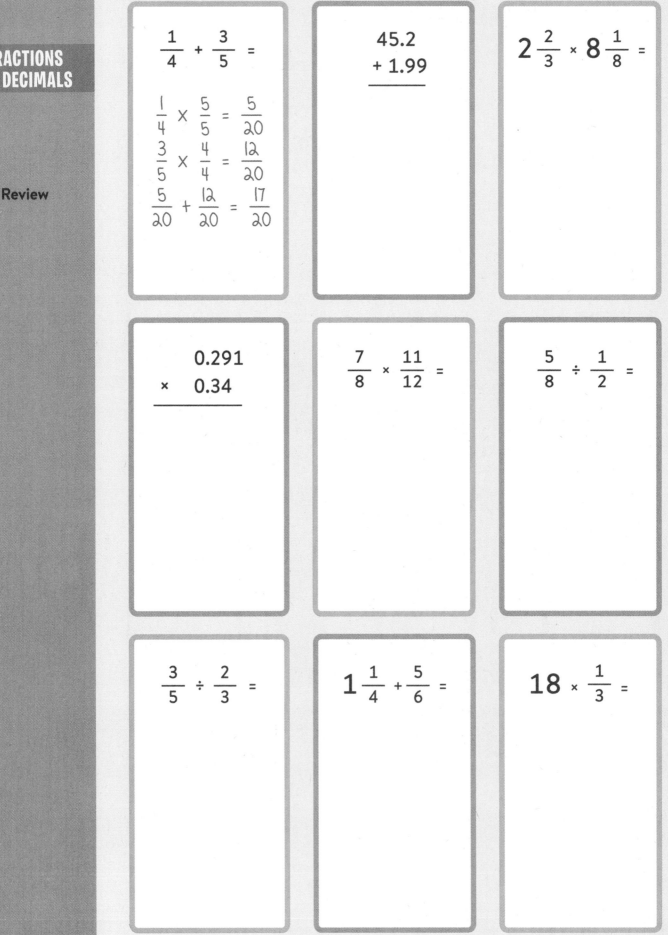

$\dfrac{1}{4} + \dfrac{3}{5} =$

$\dfrac{1}{4} \times \dfrac{5}{5} = \dfrac{5}{20}$

$\dfrac{3}{5} \times \dfrac{4}{4} = \dfrac{12}{20}$

$\dfrac{5}{20} + \dfrac{12}{20} = \dfrac{17}{20}$

$\begin{array}{r} 45.2 \\ + 1.99 \\ \hline \end{array}$

$2\dfrac{2}{3} \times 8\dfrac{1}{8} =$

$\begin{array}{r} 0.291 \\ \times \quad 0.34 \\ \hline \end{array}$

$\dfrac{7}{8} \times \dfrac{11}{12} =$

$\dfrac{5}{8} \div \dfrac{1}{2} =$

$\dfrac{3}{5} \div \dfrac{2}{3} =$

$1\dfrac{1}{4} + \dfrac{5}{6} =$

$18 \times \dfrac{1}{3} =$

GEOMETRY AND MEASUREMENT

Measuring helps us understand and describe the world around us. It allows scientists to accurately conduct experiments, engineers to design bridges and buildings, and farmers to use their land effectively to grow crops. Its use is . . . immeasurable!

PARENTS In this section your child will calculate volume, weight, temperature, and time. They'll work with lines, shapes, and angles, building their understanding of properties of two- and three-dimensional shapes. Point out other real-world examples as you encounter them to help your child connect what they're learning to their life.

For additional resources, visit www.BrainQuest.com/grade5

Perfect 10

Circle which unit should be used to measure the length of the following:

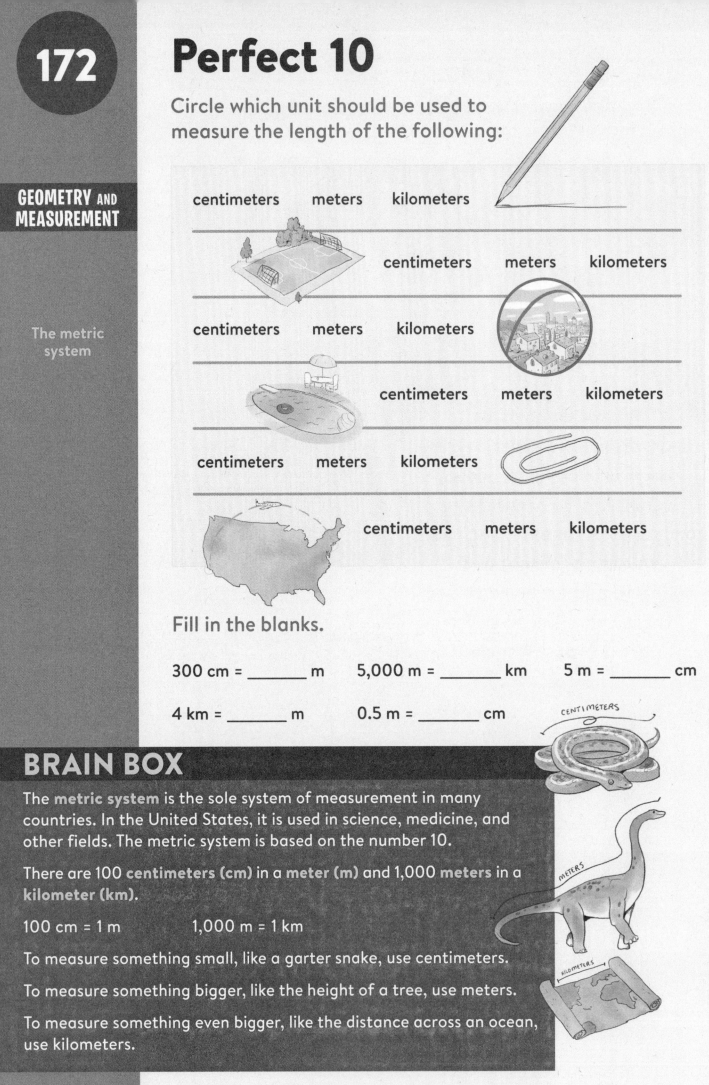

centimeters   meters   kilometers

centimeters   meters   kilometers

centimeters   meters   kilometers

centimeters   meters   kilometers

centimeters   meters   kilometers

centimeters   meters   kilometers

GEOMETRY AND MEASUREMENT

The metric system

Fill in the blanks.

300 cm = _____ m   5,000 m = _____ km   5 m = _____ cm

4 km = _____ m   0.5 m = _____ cm

BRAIN BOX

The **metric system** is the sole system of measurement in many countries. In the United States, it is used in science, medicine, and other fields. The metric system is based on the number 10.

There are 100 **centimeters (cm)** in a **meter (m)** and 1,000 **meters** in a **kilometer (km)**.

100 cm = 1 m   1,000 m = 1 km

To measure something small, like a garter snake, use centimeters.

To measure something bigger, like the height of a tree, use meters.

To measure something even bigger, like the distance across an ocean, use kilometers.

Inch by Inch

Circle which unit should be used to measure the length of the following:

inches   feet/yards   miles

inches   feet/yards   miles

inches   feet/yards   miles

inches   feet/yards   miles

inches   feet/yards   miles

inches   feet/yards   miles

GEOMETRY AND MEASUREMENT

The US customary system

Fill in the blanks.

2 ft = _____ in   2 mi = _____ yd

48 in = _____ ft   3,520 yd = _____ mi   100 yd = _____ ft

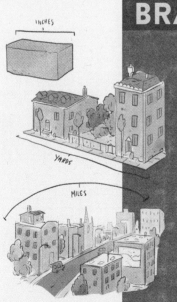

BRAIN BOX

The **US customary system** of measurement is also used in the United States. This system is based on everyday objects that people used long ago to measure things. For instance, people measured short distances with their own feet.

There are 12 **inches (in)** in a **foot (ft)**, 3 **feet** in a **yard (yd)**, and 1,760 **yards** in a **mile (mi)**.

12 in = 1 ft   3 ft = 1 yd   1,760 yd = 1 mi

To measure something small, like a brick, use inches. To measure something bigger, like the length of a city block, use feet or yards. To measure something even bigger, like the distance across a city, use miles.

Liter-ally Liters

Write the amount shown in each beaker.
Then answer the questions.

GEOMETRY AND
MEASUREMENT

Liquid volume

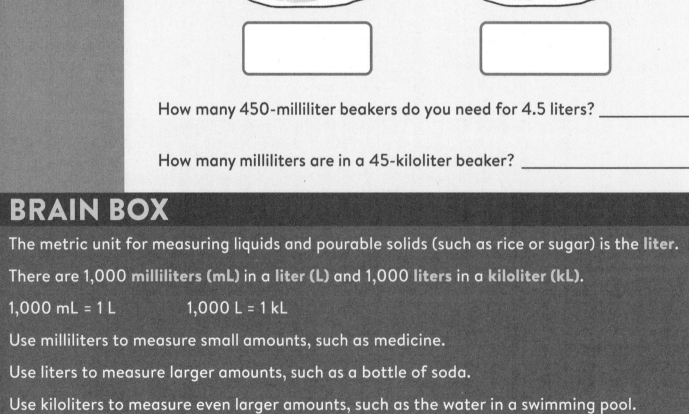

How many 450-milliliter beakers do you need for 4.5 liters? _____

How many milliliters are in a 45-kiloliter beaker? _____

BRAIN BOX

The metric unit for measuring liquids and pourable solids (such as rice or sugar) is the **liter**.

There are 1,000 **milliliters (mL)** in a **liter (L)** and 1,000 **liters** in a **kiloliter (kL)**.

1,000 mL = 1 L   1,000 L = 1 kL

Use milliliters to measure small amounts, such as medicine.

Use liters to measure larger amounts, such as a bottle of soda.

Use kiloliters to measure even larger amounts, such as the water in a swimming pool.

Care for a Cup?

Solve the word problems.

The oatmeal recipe calls for 4 cups of milk. How many pints is that? ....

Liquid volume

How many quarts is that? ....

You have 1 quart of buttermilk. You need 2 cups of buttermilk to make 1 loaf of soda bread. How many loaves of soda bread can you make? ....

There are 8 students and 2 gallons of chocolate milk. How many cups should each student get? ....

You need 1 cup of orange juice. What fraction of a quart do you need? ....

The recipe calls for $\frac{1}{4}$ cup of cream. What fraction of a pint do you need? ....

BRAIN BOX

The US customary unit for measuring liquids and pourable solids is the **cup**.

There are 2 cups in a **pint (pt)**, 4 cups in a **quart (qt)**, and 16 cups in a **gallon (gal)**.

2 cups = 1 pt

2 pt = 1 qt

4 qt = 1 gal

Such a Perfect Day

Fill in the blanks using the thermometer.

Water freezes at 0°C,
or _____ °F.

Hot chocolate tastes hot but
not scalding at 140°F,
or _____ °C.

A candle melts at 130°F,
or _____ °C.

A patient should call the doctor
if a fever reaches 104°F,
or about _____ °C.

If it were 20°C outside,
or about _____ °F,
most people would say it
was a perfect day.

41°F, or _____ °C,
would be a chilly day.

95°F, or about _____ °C,
would be a hot day.

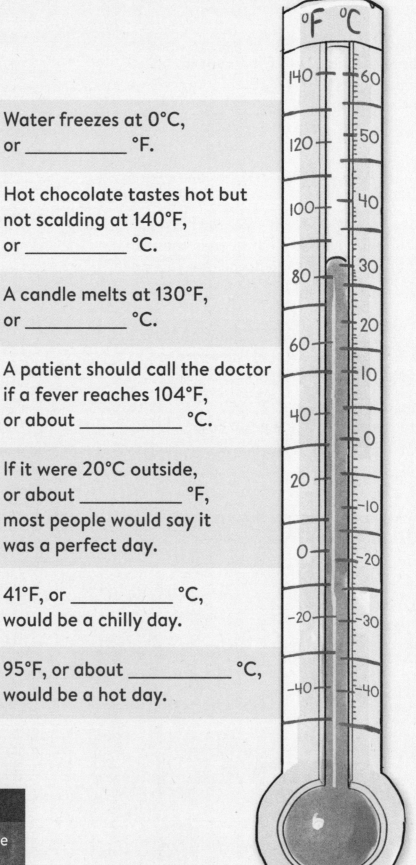

BRAIN BOX

The metric unit for temperature
is **degrees Celsius (°C)**. The US
customary unit for temperature
is **degrees Fahrenheit (°F)**.
0°C = 32°F

Time After Time

Answer the questions.

It took 2 hours and 15 minutes to plant all the vegetables in the school garden. If the students started planting at 10 a.m., what time did they finish? _____

The plane took off at 9:15 a.m. and landed at 1:30 p.m.
How much time did it spend in the air? _____

Max arrived at the library 1 hour and 45 minutes before it closed. If it closed at 9:00 p.m., when did he arrive? _____

The thunderstorm lasted from 11 p.m. to 2 a.m. How much time passed?
_____

The family began cooking dinner at 5:15 p.m. and finished at 5:45 p.m.
How long did it take? _____

Meseret eats breakfast at 7:30 a.m. Her school bus arrives 45 minutes after that. When does her school bus arrive? _____

The concert is scheduled to last for 2 hours and 30 minutes.
If it ends at 10:00 p.m., when does it begin? _____

BONUS! Javier can swim a lap in 30 seconds. How many laps can he swim from 4:00 p.m. to 4:05 p.m.? _____

BRAIN BOX

There is only one system for measuring time. There are 24 **hours (h.)** in a **day (d.)**, 60 **minutes (min.)** in an **hour (h.)**, and 60 **seconds (sec.)** in a **minute**. Seconds are divided into tenths of a second. In many countries, from 12:00 noon to 12:00 midnight, the time is designated **p.m.** From 12:00 midnight to 12:00 noon, the time is designated **a.m.**

To determine how much time has passed, first count the hours, then the minutes.

Example:
Hudson did his homework from 4:00 p.m. to 5:30 p.m.

4:00 p.m. to 5:00 p.m. is 1 hour.
5:00 p.m. to 5:30 p.m. is 30 minutes.
A total of 1 hour and 30 minutes passed.

Totally Triangular!

Draw 3 **isosceles triangles**. Turn the triangles into birthday hats.

Triangles

BRAIN BOX

A **triangle** is a closed figure with three sides.

In a **scalene triangle**, none of the three sides is the same length as the others.

In an **isosceles triangle**, two of the three sides are the same length.

In an **equilateral triangle**, all three sides are the same length.

Draw 3 **scalene triangles.** Turn them into race cars.

Triangles

Draw 3 **equilateral triangles.** Turn them into the roofs of houses.

Finding the Perfect Angle

Circle the **right angles.**

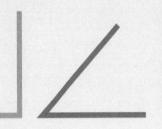

Circle the **acute angles.**

Circle the **obtuse angle.**

BRAIN BOX

An **angle** is formed where two line segments meet.

90°

A **right angle** is 90°.

An **acute angle** is less than 90°.

An **obtuse angle** is greater than 90°.

Every triangle has three angles.

When a triangle has one right angle it is a **right triangle.**

When all angles in a triangle are acute, it is an **acute triangle.**

When a triangle has one obtuse angle it is an **obtuse triangle.**

Aww, What Acute Angle

Circle the **acute triangles**.

Circle the **obtuse triangle**.

Circle the **right triangles**.

Clean Up!

Put away the **polygons**. Draw a line from the polygon to the box that it should go into based on its properties.

Polygons

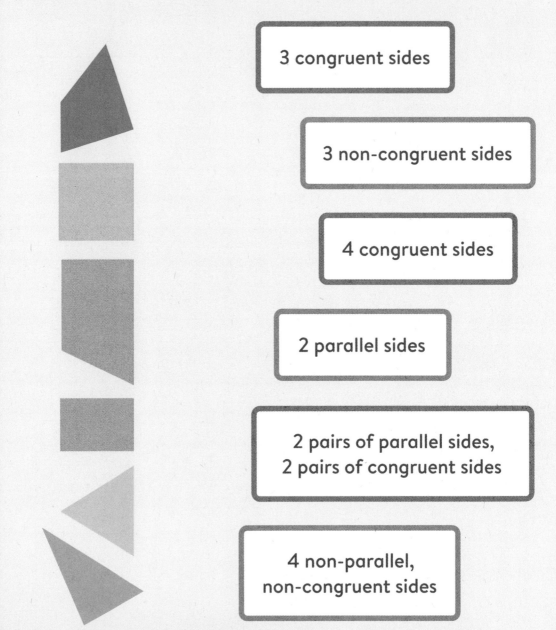

3 congruent sides

3 non-congruent sides

4 congruent sides

2 parallel sides

2 pairs of parallel sides, 2 pairs of congruent sides

4 non-parallel, non-congruent sides

BRAIN BOX

A **polygon** is a closed figure with several angles and three or more straight sides. A triangle, a square, and an octagon are just a few examples. Polygons are classified by their characteristics, or properties, like type of angles or sides they have. Polygons can have right, acute, or obtuse angles. Polygons can also be categorized by their number of sides, their number of **parallel** (non-intersecting) sides, or their number of **congruent** (same size) sides.

Four Sure

Read the definitions and study the quadrilateral classification chart. Then circle true (T) or false (F).

A **polygon** has 3 or more sides.

A **quadrilateral** has 4 sides.

A **parallelogram** has 2 pairs of parallel sides.

A **rhombus** has 2 pairs of parallel sides and 4 congruent sides.

A **rectangle** has 4 right angles.

A **square** has 4 right angles and 4 congruent sides.

A **trapezoid** has 1 pair of parallel sides.

A **kite** has no parallel sides but has 2 pairs of congruent sides.

Quadrilateral Classification Chart

parallelogram

trapezoid

other
(a quadrilateral
with no congruent
or parallel sides)

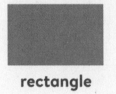

rectangle

rhombus

square

All squares are rectangles. **T** **F**

All rectangles are squares. **T** **F**

All rhombuses are parallelograms. **T** **F**

All parallelograms are rhombuses. **T** **F**

All quadrilaterals must have at least 1 pair of parallel sides. **T** **F**

All quadrilaterals are polygons. **T** **F**

All polygons are quadrilaterals. **T** **F**

Parallelograms and rectangles have 2 pairs of parallel sides. **T** **F**

A square and a rhombus both have right angles. **T** **F**

BRAIN BOX

A **quadrangle** or **quadrilateral** is a polygon with 4 sides. Quadrilaterals can be further classified based on their number of parallel sides, congruent sides, and right angles.

Fence or Tile?

Find the **perimeter** and **area** of each rectangle.

Perimeter and area of a rectangle

Perimeter _____

Area _____

5 inches

5 inches

Perimeter _____

Area _____

12 feet

10 feet

Perimeter _____

Area _____

6 centimeters

10 centimeters

Perimeter _____

Area _____

10 kilometers

5 kilometers

BRAIN BOX

The **perimeter** is the distance along the outside of a figure. If you want to build a backyard fence, you need to know the perimeter of the yard. You can find the perimeter by adding the lengths of the sides.

2 meters

2 meters

2 m + 2 m + 2 m + 2 m = 8 meters
Perimeter = 8 m

The **area** is the number of square units inside a figure. If you want to tile a floor, you need to know the area of the floor. You can find the area by multiplying length by width. The unit for measuring area is a square unit.

2 meters

2 meters

2 m × 2 m = 4 square meters
Area = 4 m²

Side by Side

Find the **perimeter** of each triangle.

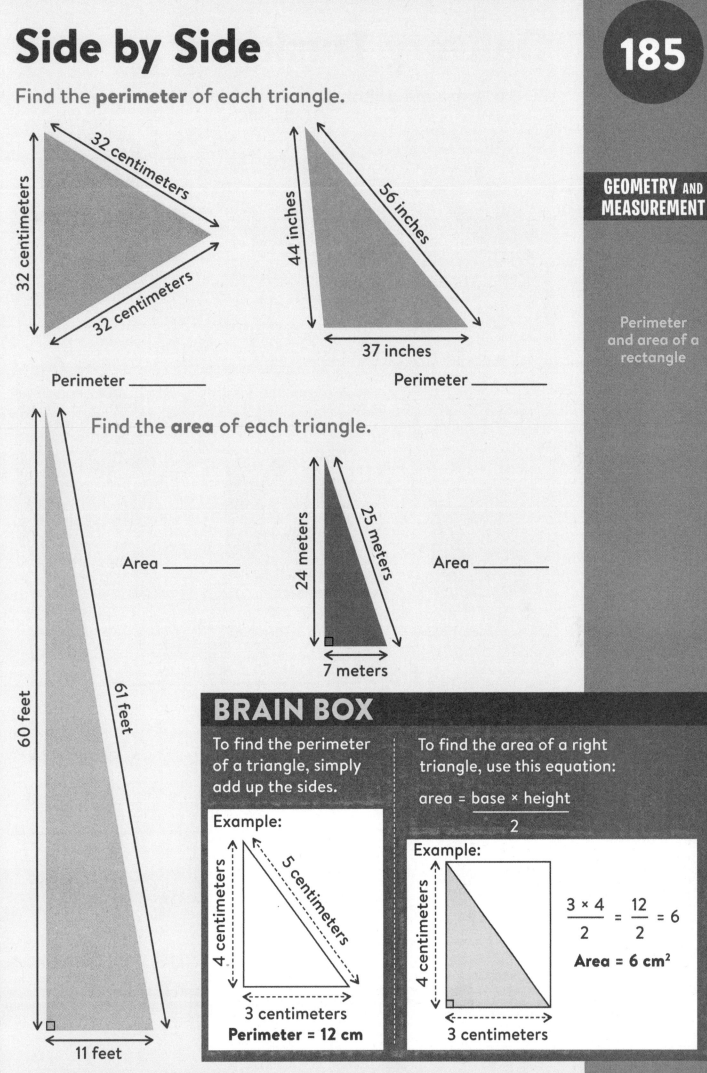

32 centimeters

32 centimeters

32 centimeters

56 inches

44 inches

37 inches

Perimeter _____

Perimeter _____

Perimeter and area of a rectangle

Find the **area** of each triangle.

60 feet

61 feet

11 feet

24 meters

25 meters

7 meters

Area _____

Area _____

BRAIN BOX

To find the perimeter of a triangle, simply add up the sides.

Example:

4 centimeters

5 centimeters

3 centimeters

Perimeter = 12 cm

To find the area of a right triangle, use this equation:

$$area = \frac{base \times height}{2}$$

Example:

4 centimeters

3 centimeters

$$\frac{3 \times 4}{2} = \frac{12}{2} = 6$$

Area = 6 cm²

Delivery Truck

Find the **volume** of each package.

Volume

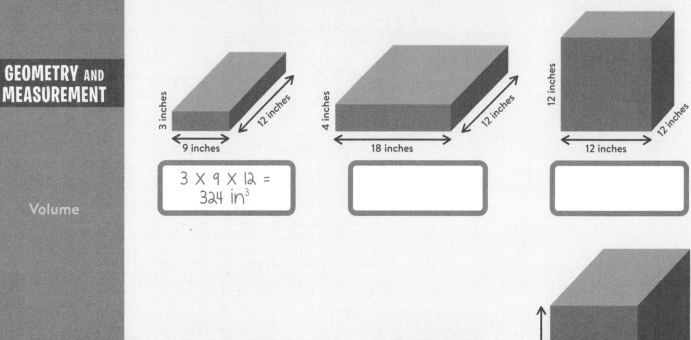

3 inches · 9 inches · 12 inches

$$3 \times 9 \times 12 = 324 \text{ in}^3$$

4 inches · 18 inches · 12 inches

12 inches · 12 inches · 12 inches

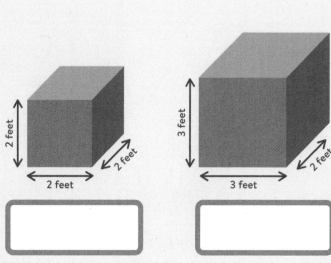

2 feet · 2 feet · 2 feet

3 feet · 3 feet · 2 feet

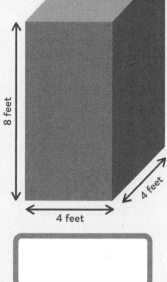

8 feet · 4 feet · 4 feet

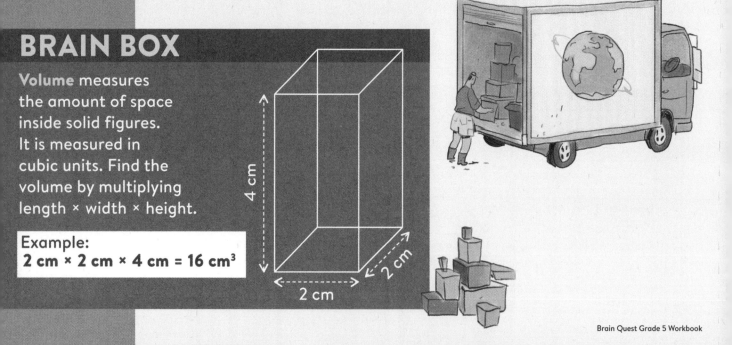

BRAIN BOX

Volume measures the amount of space inside solid figures. It is measured in cubic units. Find the volume by multiplying length × width × height.

Example:
2 cm × 2 cm × 4 cm = 16 cm³

4 cm · 2 cm · 2 cm

Ice Cold

Find the total volume.

2 ice cubes, each 3 × 3 × 3 cm

| 3 × 3 × 3 = 27 | cubic centimeters per ice cube |

| 27 + 27 = 54 | cubic centimeters for 2 ice cubes |

3 ice cubes, each 3 × 3 × 3 cm

| | cubic centimeters |

4 ice cubes, each 4 × 4 × 4 cm

| | cubic centimeters |

5 ice cubes, each 5 × 5 × 5 cm

| | cubic centimeters |

6 ice cubes, each 6 × 6 × 6 cm

| | cubic centimeters |

7 ice cubes, each 7 × 7 × 7 cm

| | cubic centimeters |

8 ice cubes, each 8 × 8 × 8 cm

| | cubic centimeters |

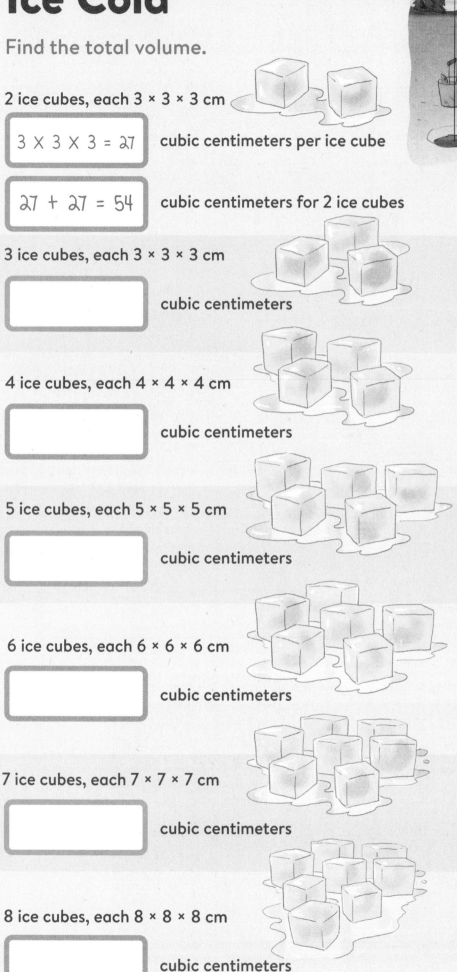

BRAIN BOX

Volume is additive. That means that the volume of two objects combined can be determined by adding them together.

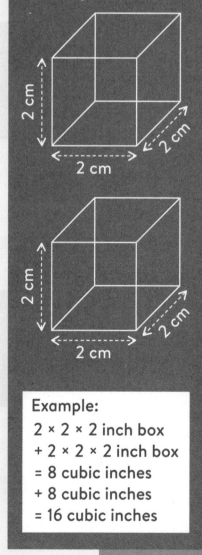

Example:
2 × 2 × 2 inch box
+ 2 × 2 × 2 inch box
= 8 cubic inches
+ 8 cubic inches
= 16 cubic inches

Mmm, Pi

Find the **circumference** of each pie.

Diameter and
circumference

4 inches

5 inches

6 inches

7 inches

BRAIN BOX

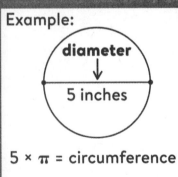

Example:

diameter
↓

5 inches

5 × π = circumference

5 × 3.14 = 15.7

The circumference of
the circle is 15.7 inches.

The length through the middle of a circle is the
diameter. The perimeter of a circle is called
the **circumference**. To find the circumference
of a circle, multiply the diameter by **pi (π)**.

Pi is a special number defined as the ratio of
the circumference of a circle to its diameter.

$$\pi = \frac{\text{circumference}}{\text{diameter}}$$

The decimal places of pi go on forever, but pi
is approximately 3.14.

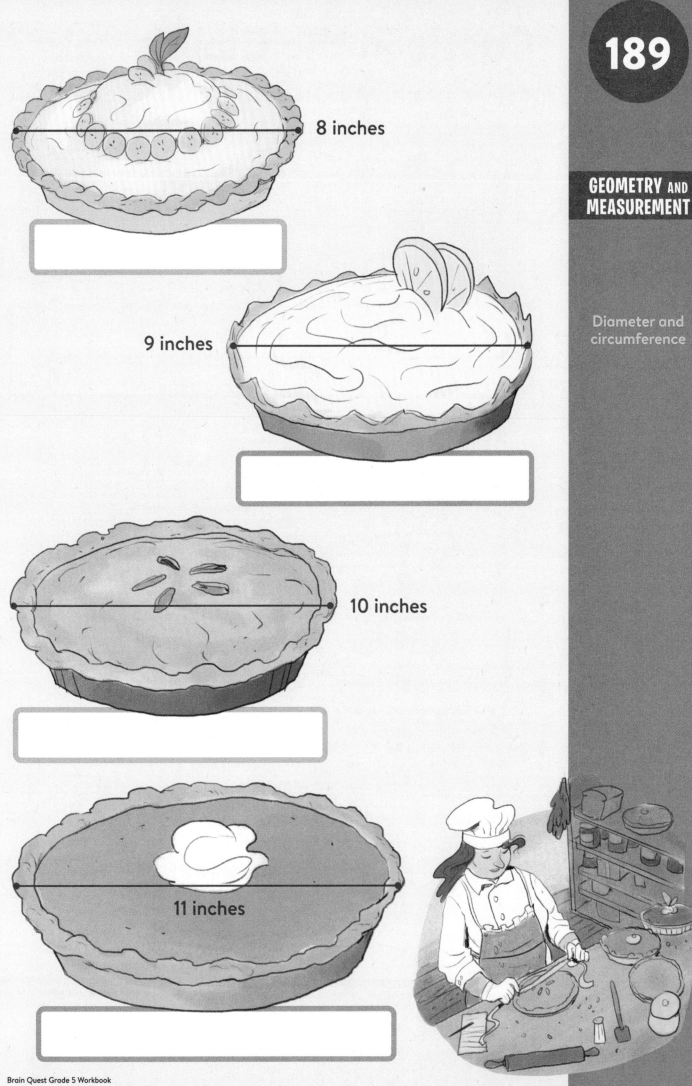

8 inches

9 inches

10 inches

11 inches

Castle in the Clouds

Find the **area** of the castle turrets.

Area of circles

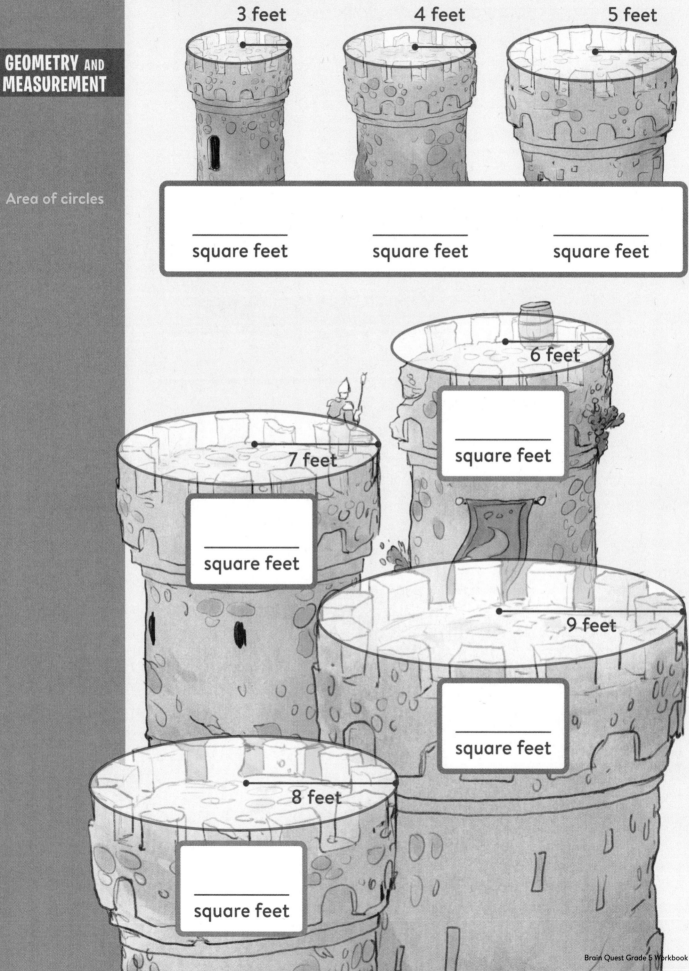

3 feet

4 feet

5 feet

_____
square feet

_____
square feet

_____
square feet

6 feet

7 feet

_____
square feet

_____
square feet

9 feet

_____
square feet

8 feet

_____
square feet

10 feet

_____
square feet

BRAIN BOX

The area of a circle is the product of the radius squared and pi. The **radius** (known as r) is half of the diameter. A squared number is a number times itself. Area = $\pi \times r^2$

radius ↓
5 inches

Example:
$3.14 \times 5 \times 5 = 3.14 \times 25 = 78.5 \text{ in}^2$

The area of the circle is 78.5 square inches.

Geometry and Measurement Crossword

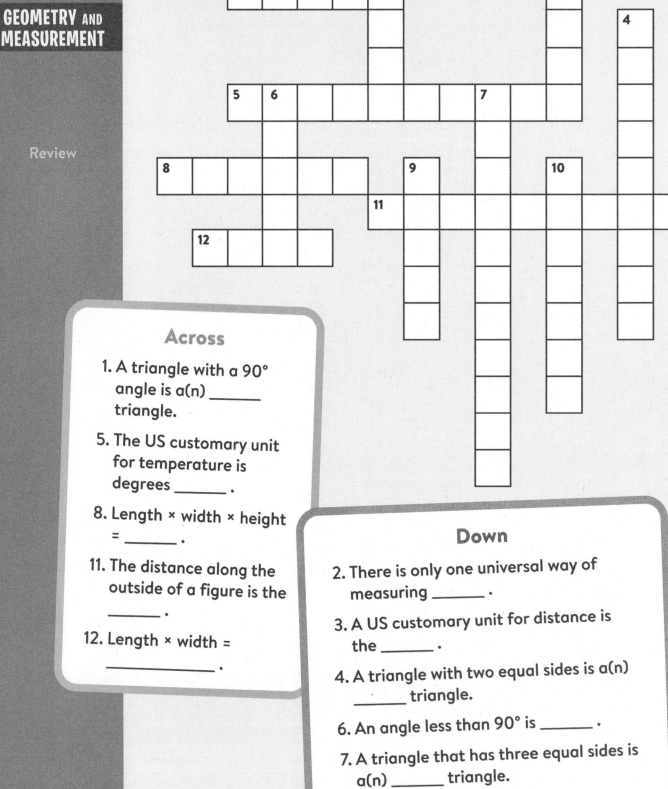

Across

1. A triangle with a 90° angle is a(n) _____ triangle.

5. The US customary unit for temperature is degrees _____ .

8. Length × width × height = _____ .

11. The distance along the outside of a figure is the _____ .

12. Length × width = _____ .

Down

2. There is only one universal way of measuring _____ .

3. A US customary unit for distance is the _____ .

4. A triangle with two equal sides is a(n) _____ triangle.

6. An angle less than 90° is _____ .

7. A triangle that has three equal sides is a(n) _____ triangle.

9. A metric unit for distance is the _____ .

10. A metric unit for measuring temperature is degrees _____ .

PROBABILITY AND DATA

Data is collected information like numbers, measurements, words, observations, and more. We use charts, tables, and graphs to help us compare and analyze data, find connections and patterns, and make predictions.

PARENTS Your child will explore and interpret different data using tables, scatterplots, graphs, charts, and more. Challenge your child to collect and chart their own data. Encourage them to graph the time spent on a frequent activity like practicing a sport or playing a musical instrument, and guide them to make observations from the data.

For additional resources, visit www.BrainQuest.com/grade5

Fro-Yo!

Chart the following **categorical data** by making tally marks on the graph on the following page.

Cameron's favorite frozen yogurt is lemon.

Marita's favorite is chocolate vanilla swirl.

Anika likes vanilla best.

Pete also prefers vanilla.

Elliot likes chocolate.

Carlos also likes chocolate.

Javantre prefers lemon.

Sophia likes vanilla.

John Paul's favorite is peanut butter.

Frank likes chocolate vanilla swirl the best.

Mae prefers vanilla.

Grace likes strawberry.

Categorical
data

Favorite Frozen Yogurt	Tally	Number
Chocolate		
Vanilla		
Chocolate vanilla swirl		
Lemon	I	
Peanut butter		
Strawberry		

BRAIN BOX

Categorical data is data sorted by characteristics. For example, frozen yogurt can be sorted by flavor.

When taking a survey about categorical data, you can use tally marks to show how many items are in each category.

Example:

Shoe Color	Tally	Number
Brown	IIII	4
Blue	III	3
Black	ⅢⅠ	5
White	II	2

Adventures in Babysitting

Use the **bar graph** to answer the questions on the next page.

Bar graphs

KEY	
monthly goal	
actual money made	

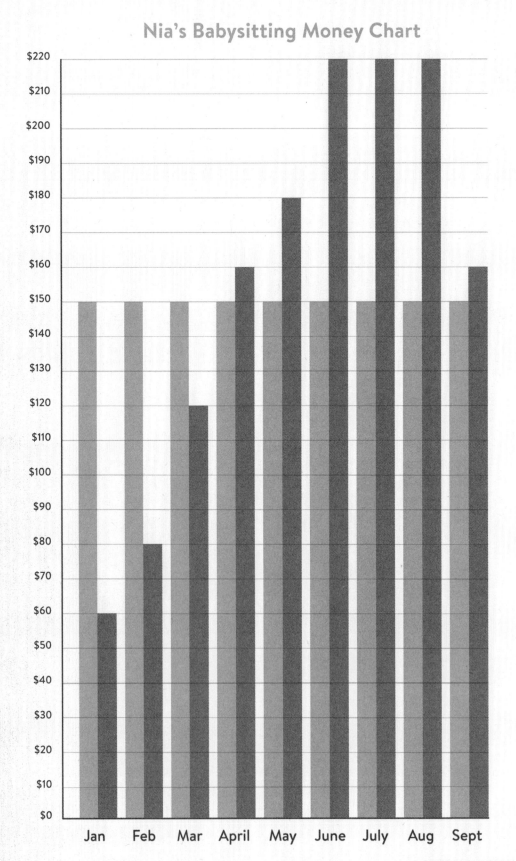

Nia's Babysitting Money Chart

BRAIN BOX

A **bar graph** is a picture, diagram, or drawing that shows how two or more things are related. Some graphs have a **key**. The key gives you information you need to understand the graph.

This graph shows that Nia hoped to make _____ every month for _____ months.

Nia fell short of her goal the months of _____ , _____ , and _____ .

Her goal was to make _____ total. She actually made _____ total.

The first month Nia exceeded her goal was _____ .

Nia made the most money over which three months? _____

Nia exceeded her goal in the months of _____ , _____ , _____ , _____ , _____ , and _____ .

If Nia's goal had been to make $190 per month, how many months would she have met or exceeded that goal? _____

Tomato, Tomahto

Fill in the **frequency table** to show how many tomatoes are on each plant.

Frequency tables

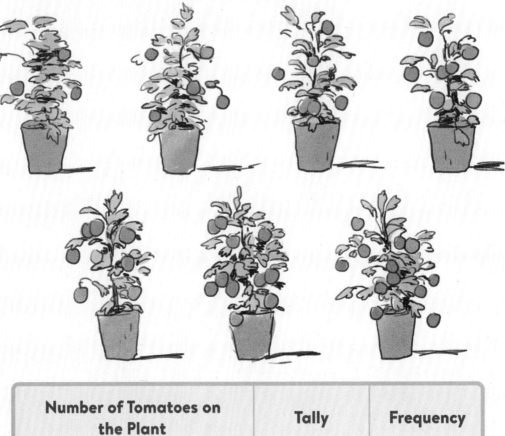

Number of Tomatoes on the Plant	Tally	Frequency
0–4		
5–9		
10–14		
15–19		

BRAIN BOX

A **frequency table** shows how often two or more things occur. It can be used for categorical or numerical data.

Example:

Number of Apples on a Tree	Tally	Frequency
100–109	⦀⦀	5
110–119	⦀⦀ II	7
120–129	⦀⦀ III	8
130–139	⦀⦀ I	6

Showtime

Make a **stem and leaf plot** to show how many people came to each performance of the fifth-grade musical.

Number of People Who Attended the Fifth-Grade Musical

Stem	Leaf

Stem and leaf plots

On Thursday evening, there were 88 people in the audience.

There were 92 people at the Saturday matinee.

32 people came to the Friday matinee.

Saturday evening, 95 people were in the audience.

Friday evening, 83 people came.

At the Sunday matinee, there were 44 people.

BRAIN BOX

A **stem and leaf plot** can be used to show which numbers occur in data. The "stem" on the left-hand side represents the tens digits. The "leaves" on the right-hand side represent the ones digits.

Example:

Money Spent on School Supplies by Each Student

Student 1 $52

Student 2 $64

Student 3 $68

Student 4 $71

Stem	Leaf
5	2
6	4,8
7	1

Note that there are two numbers in the leaf column next to the 6 stem. These numbers represent $64 and $68, respectively.

Temperature Rising

On the next page, make a **scatterplot** to show the relationship between the temperature and the number of people at the pool. Then answer the questions.

On the next page,

PROBABILITY AND DATA

Scatterplots

Saturday, June 1: 80°F, 50 people

Saturday, June 8: 85°F, 75 people

Saturday, June 15: 80°F, 75 people

Saturday, June 22: 90°F, 100 people

Saturday, June 29: 89°F, 100 people

Saturday, July 6: 94°F, 150 people

Saturday, July 13: 95°F, 150 people

Saturday, July 20: 100°F, 200 people

Saturday, July 27: 98°F, 200 people

BRAIN BOX

A **scatterplot** is a way to compare two sets of data.
A graph shows the relationship between the two sets.
In this example, each dot represents the time of sunset compared to when a family eats dinner. If the dots cluster around a straight line, the two sets are related.

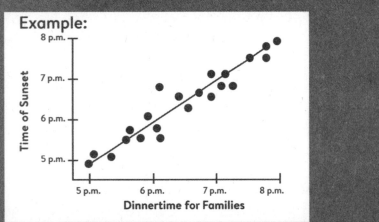

Because the dots are clustered around a line, dinnertime must be related to sunset time.

Scatterplot

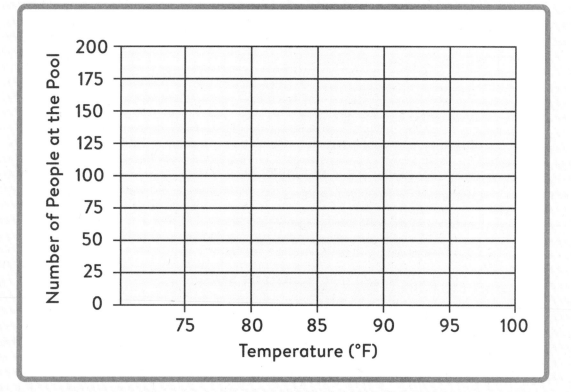

Do most of the dots cluster around a line? _____

What does that tell you about the two sets of data?

_____

_____

_____

Snack Bar Stats

Show the following data on the **line plot.**

Line plots

Customer 1 bought a cup of ice for $0.25.
Customer 2 bought a hot dog for $1.50.
Customer 3 bought nachos for $2.00.
Customer 4 bought a hot dog and chips for a total of $2.00.
Customer 5 bought a pack of gum for $0.50.
Customer 6 bought a soda and chips for a total of $1.50.
Customer 7 bought lemonade for $1.00.
Customer 8 bought a snow cone for $0.75.
Customer 9 bought a hot pretzel for $1.00.
Customer 10 bought 2 hot dogs for $3.00.

BRAIN BOX

Line plots (also called **dot plots**), can be used to show numerical data. A number line runs along the bottom of the graph. A dot represents how many times that number occurs.

Example:

Number of Pets Students Own

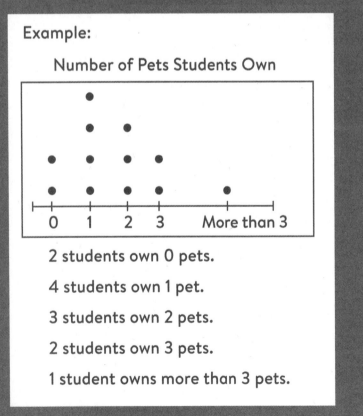

2 students own 0 pets.

4 students own 1 pet.

3 students own 2 pets.

2 students own 3 pets.

1 student owns more than 3 pets.

Line plots

Amount Spent by Customers at the Snack Bar

$0	$0.25	$0.50	$0.75	$1.00	$1.25	$1.50	$1.75	$2.00	$2.00+	

Coin Toss

Conduct the experiments and record your data.

Flip a coin 5 times.

Write a fraction representing how often you get heads.

Write a fraction representing how often you get tails.

Data
experiments

Flip a coin 8 times.

Write a fraction representing how often you get heads.

Write a fraction representing how often you get tails.

Flip a coin 10 times.

Write a fraction representing how often you get heads.

Write a fraction representing how often you get tails.

Ask someone else to flip a coin 10 times.

Write a fraction representing how often they get heads.

Write a fraction representing how often they get tails.

ALGEBRA

You're already good at algebraic thinking! You know how to identify and analyze patterns in shapes and numbers and to think flexibly about equations. Solving algebra problems is like looking for missing pieces of information to complete a puzzle.

PARENTS In this section, your child will practice pre-algebra skills with equations, number patterns, and the order of operations. Using graphs, they will model number patterns and relationships in various situations, including money earned selling lemonade and shoveling snow. Models such as these can demonstrate potential earnings, or other accomplishments, over time.

Go PEMDAS!

Write how to solve the problems using the order of operations, PEMDAS.

Order of operations

$4 \times (6 + 5)$ — Add 6 plus 5 and multiply the sum by 4.

$(2^2 + 4) - 3$

$(4 + 5) \div 3$

Use PEMDAS to solve the problems.

$(5 + 4) \div (1 + 2) = $ _____

$63 \div 3^2 = $ _____

$(7 + 7) \times 3 = $ _____

$111 - (4^2 + 12) = $ _____

$8^2 - 7 \times 2 = $ _____

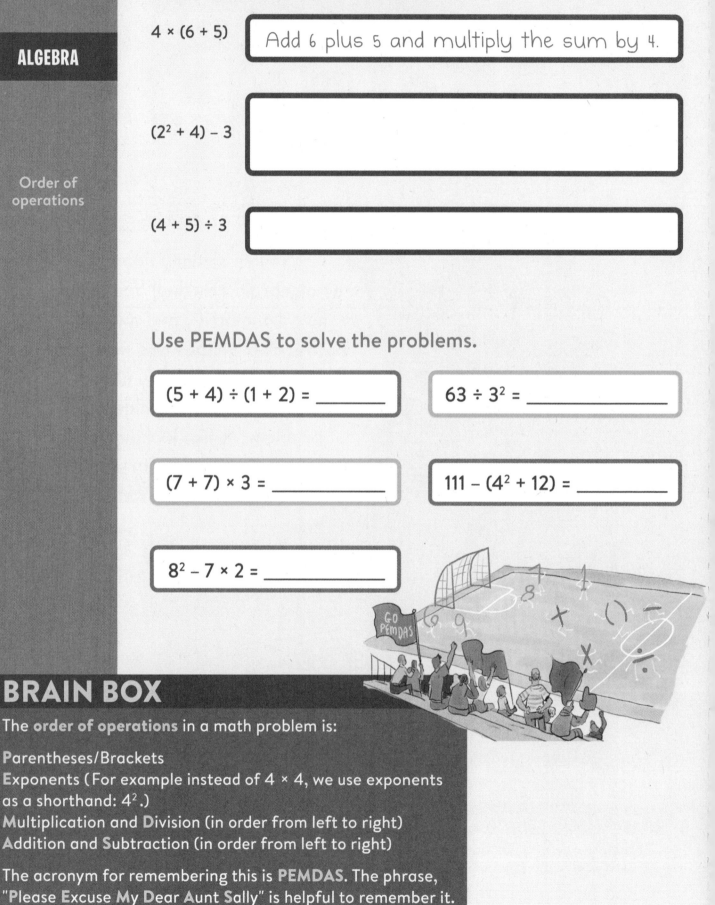

BRAIN BOX

The order of operations in a math problem is:

Parentheses/Brackets
Exponents (For example instead of 4×4, we use exponents as a shorthand: 4^2.)
Multiplication and Division (in order from left to right)
Addition and Subtraction (in order from left to right)

The acronym for remembering this is PEMDAS. The phrase, "Please Excuse My Dear Aunt Sally" is helpful to remember it.

Code Breaker

Explain the **pattern** of each number sequence.
Then compare the two patterns.

0, 3, 6, 9, 12   starting at 0, add 3.

0, 6, 12, 18, 24   starting at 0, add 6.

The numbers in the second sequence are 2 times
the corresponding numbers in the first sequence.

Patterns

0, 2, 4, 6, 8
0, 6, 12, 18, 24

0, 1, 2, 3, 4, 5
0, 5, 10, 15, 20, 25

BRAIN BOX

Numbers in
a sequence
can follow a
pattern. For
instance, the
numbers may
increase by 2.
The numbers
in a second
sequence of
numbers can
be compared
to the numbers
in the first
sequence. For
instance, the
numbers in
the second
sequence may
be double the
corresponding
numbers in
the first.

0, 1, 2, 3, 4, 5
0, 4, 8, 12, 16, 20

On the Grid

Write the number sequences as **coordinates**.
Then **graph** the coordinates.

0, 1, 2, 3, 4, 5
0, 3, 6, 9, 12, 15

(0,0) (1,3)

BRAIN BOX

The corresponding numbers of two sequences of numbers can be written as pairs, or **coordinates**.

0, 1, 2, 3, 4
0, 2, 4, 6, 8
can be paired and written as (0,0) (1,2) (2,4) (3,6) (4,8).

Then they can be **graphed** as points on a grid. The **x-axis** goes across. The **y-axis** goes up and down. The first number in the pair represents the **x coordinate**, and the second number represents the **y coordinate (x,y)**. To graph x, go across x number of squares. To graph y, go up y number of squares.

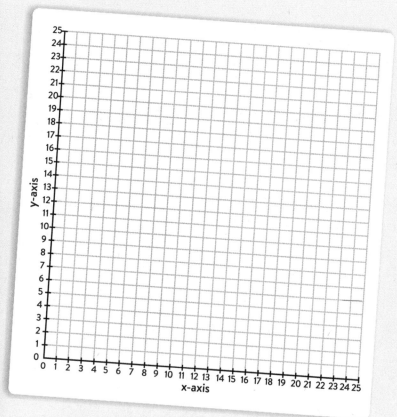

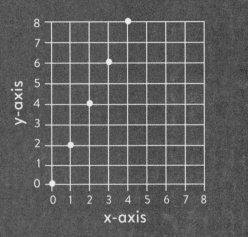

Notice that the points on the graph move up two squares for every one square they move over.

On the Grid II

Write the number sequences
as coordinates.
Graph the coordinates.

0, 2, 4, 6, 8

0, 6, 12, 18, 24

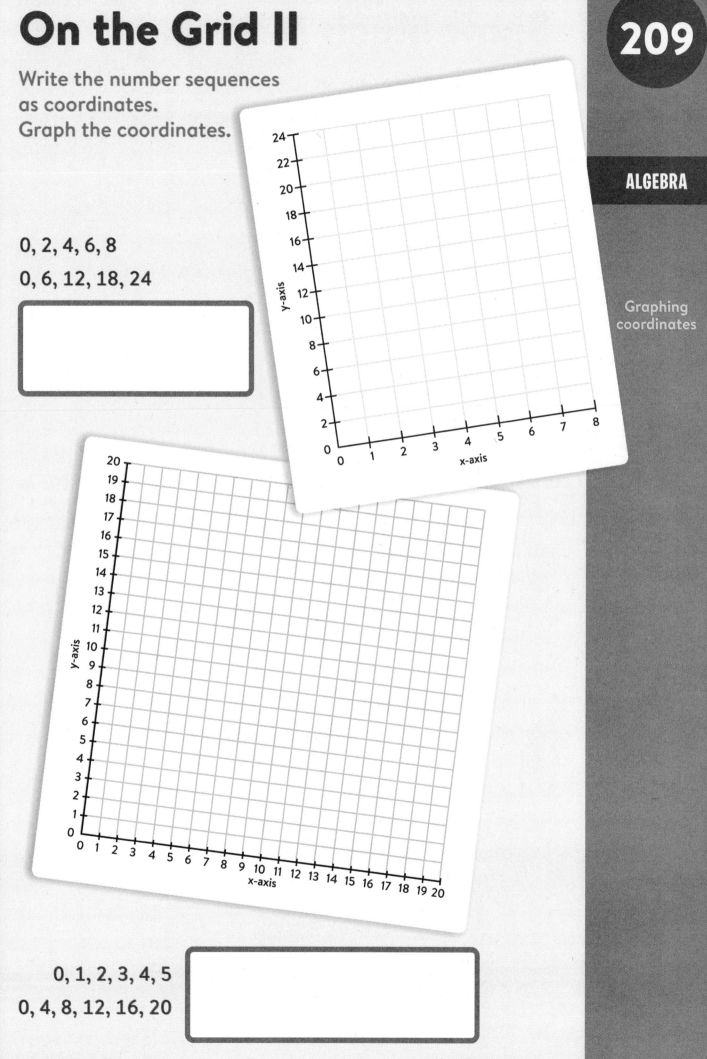

0, 1, 2, 3, 4, 5

0, 4, 8, 12, 16, 20

Snow Much Money

Graph the coordinates for the problems.

Leo makes $0.50 per lemonade he sells. Graph the relationship between the lemonades sold and money earned.

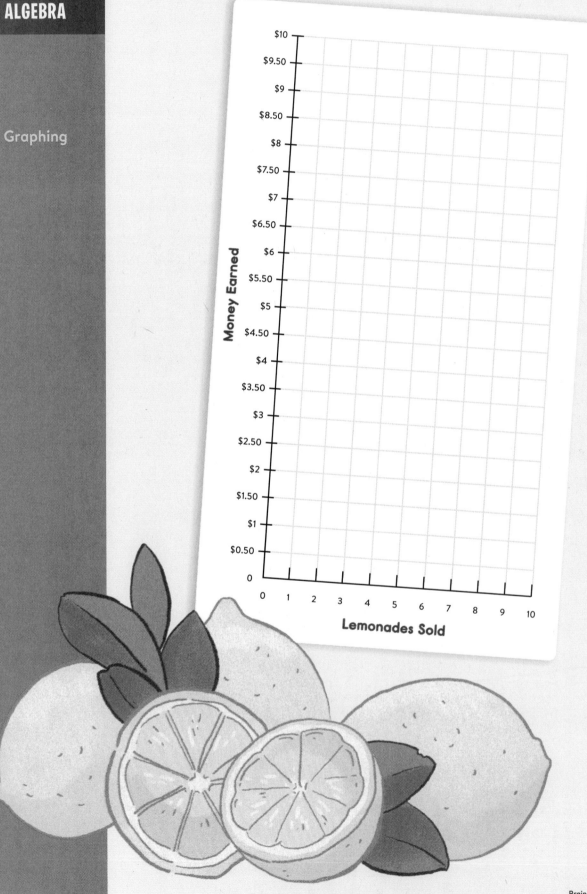

Maya earns $5 for every sidewalk she shovels. Graph the relationship between the sidewalks shoveled and the money earned.

ALGEBRA

Graphing

The Tortoise and the Hare

Answer the following questions based on the graphs.

How many hours would it take the tortoise to travel 1 mile? _____

How many miles would the tortoise have traveled in 8 hours? _____

How many hours would it take the tortoise to travel 3 miles? _____

How many miles would the tortoise have traveled in 16 hours? _____

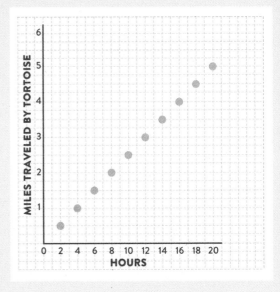

How many miles would the hare travel in 1 hour? _____

How many hours would it take the hare to travel 80 miles? _____

How many miles would the hare have traveled in 4 hours? _____

How many hours would it take the hare to travel 180 miles? _____

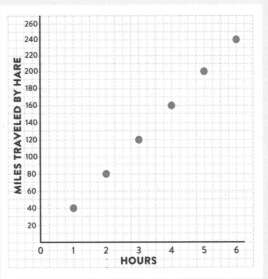

WORD PROBLEMS

If you complete three pages of this workbook each day, how many pages will you have completed at the end of one week? 3 pages per day x 7 days in a week = 21 reasons to be proud of yourself!

PARENTS In this section, your child will apply math skills practiced in previous sections to solve word problems. An important math process skill is making sense of problems and persevering in solving them. For challenging computations, refer back to earlier Brain Boxes for support.

For additional resources, visit www.BrainQuest.com/grade5

The Big Apple

Solve the word problems.

Use numerals to write "fifty-three billion one hundred twenty-seven million four hundred seventeen thousand five hundred six."

Sybil makes $270 per month babysitting. Each month she donates $25 to charity, spends $57 on school lunches, saves $125 for college, and the rest is spending money. How much spending money does she have each month?

Write the number 4,681 in expanded notation.

Write 2,000 + 400 + 60 + 8 in standard notation.

Aggie has 17 cupcakes and 7 friends at her party. Can the cupcakes be evenly divided among her friends?

Jack is selling 138 potatoes. Can he evenly divide them among 3 customers?

Mary is selling 135 apple fritters. Can she evenly divide them among 5 customers?

The Legend of Zero

Solve the word problems.

R. J. bought a dozen doughnuts for his Spanish club. There are 10 members in the club. If the doughnuts are divided evenly, how many should each member get? How many doughnuts are left over?

Joe starts out with 7 tickets. After playing games at the carnival, he has 10 times as many. How many tickets does he have now?

Frank makes $0.40 for each lemonade he sells. By the end of the day, he has sold 100 lemonades. How much money did he make?

How many zeroes does 70 billion have?

How many zeroes does 300 million have?

Write all the prime numbers between 1 and 10.

Party Treats

Solve the word problems.

Brendan baked 48 cupcakes for 10 guests. How many cupcakes were left over after they were divided evenly among the guests?

Maya baked 56 cookies for 15 guests. How many cookies were left over after they were divided evenly among the guests?

Ian made 38 fruit skewers for 8 guests. How many fruit skewers were left over after they were divided evenly among the guests?

Francie made 74 cake pops for 44 guests. How many cake pops were left over after they were divided evenly among the guests?

Ryan made 118 bags of trail mix for 52 guests. How many bags of trail mix were left over after they were divided evenly among the guests?

Animal Snackers

Solve the word problems.

7 bats eat an equal number of mosquitoes.
They eat 3,192 total. How many does each bat eat?

11 frogs eat an equal number of flies.
They eat 1,397 total. How many does each frog eat?

8 anteaters eat an equal number of ants.
They eat 7,168 total. How many does each anteater eat?

9 puffins eat an equal number of herring.
They eat 1,044 total. How many does each puffin eat?

6 squirrels eat an equal number of acorns.
They eat 2,064 total. How many does each squirrel eat?

3 koalas eat an equal number of eucalyptus leaves.
They eat 2,046 total. How many does each koala eat?

Hot Dog!

Solve the word problems.

Brady bought a used car for $8,460, which he paid for over 36 months. He paid the same amount each month. How much did he pay each month?

Sam owed $9,384 in student loans. She paid them off over 24 months. She paid the same amount each month. How much did she pay each month?

Grace's braces cost $5,786. Her parents paid for them over 22 months, and they paid the same amount each month. How much did they pay each month?

Calvin bought an oven for his restaurant for $4,788. He paid for it over 18 months, and he paid the same amount each month. How much did he pay each month?

Kara bought a hot dog stand for $5,064. She paid for it over 12 months, and she paid the same amount each month. How much did she pay each month?

Lunch Room Leftovers

Solve the word problems.

There were 386 fish sticks for 88 students. How many fish sticks were left over after each student got an equal number?

The school cook prepared 548 chicken nuggets for 96 students. How many chicken nuggets were left over after they were divided evenly among the students?

There were 853 apple slices for 79 students. How many apple slices were left over after each student got an equal number of slices?

There were 275 ounces of applesauce for 68 students. How many ounces were left over after each student got an equal amount?

There were 523 ounces of sloppy joe filling for 76 students. How many ounces were left over after each student got an equal amount?

Not Exactly

Solve the word problems.

The grocery store has 28 32-ounce bags of flour. Estimate (by rounding to the nearest 10) how many total ounces of flour the store has.

The store has 64 32-ounce cans of tomato sauce. Estimate (by rounding to the nearest 10) how many total ounces of tomato sauce the store has.

At the tournament, there are 28 teams, and each team has 14 players. Estimate (by rounding to the nearest 10) how many total players are at the tournament.

A ship contains 49 boxes filled with 68 tennis balls each. Estimate (by rounding to the nearest 10) how many total tennis balls the ship is carrying.

A box contains 34 candy bars with 82 peanuts each. Estimate (by rounding to the nearest 10) how many total peanuts are in all the candy bars.

Be Our Guest

Solve the word problems. Simplify if possible.

Mae had 8 pieces of rhubarb pie. She served 5 pieces to her guests. What fraction describes the amount of pie that remains?

[   ]

Liam had 24 chocolate drop cookies. His guests ate 18. What fraction describes the amount of cookies his guests ate?

[   ]

Kynthia ordered 2 large turkey club subs for her 6 guests. What fraction of a sub should each guest get?

[   ]

Brooks ordered 3 chocolate chip cookie cakes for his 12 guests. What fraction of a cookie cake should each guest get?

[   ]

Lucibell bought 2 gallons of rainbow sherbet for her 24 guests. What fraction of a gallon should each guest get?

[   ]

Sara fixed 3 large bowls of pimento cheese dip for her 72 guests. What fraction of a bowl should each guest get?

[   ]

School Supplies

Solve the word problems.

Dalen combined a box of pencils that was $\frac{3}{8}$ full with a box of pencils that was $\frac{1}{4}$ full. The boxes were equal in size. How full was the combined box?

Mary Ellen added a $\frac{3}{5}$ full box of markers to a $\frac{1}{4}$ full box of markers. The boxes were equal in size. How full was the combined box?

Justin's box of crayons was $\frac{3}{4}$ full. He gave half the crayons in the box to Daniel. How much remained in Justin's box?

Mrs. Layton found the box of glue sticks $\frac{2}{3}$ full. She took $\frac{1}{4}$ of the remaining glue sticks out of the box. How much of the box remained?

Mrs. Randolph borrowed a box of books from the library. She loaned $\frac{3}{5}$ to the students. How much of the box remained?

Maggie combined a $\frac{1}{6}$ full box of erasers with a $\frac{4}{5}$ full box. The boxes are equal in size. How full was the box now?

The Cooking Class

Solve the word problems.

Yura and Milo are taking a cooking class! Yura has $\frac{1}{2}$ cup of flour that she needs to divide into 4 bowls. How much flour should she put in each bowl?

Milo must divide 6 cups of blueberries into 3 equal parts for 3 different muffin recipes. How many blueberries will each muffin recipe get?

2 students in the class share $\frac{2}{3}$ of a cup of coconut when making homemade granola. How much of the coconut does each of them get?

5 students in the class shared $\frac{3}{4}$ of a canister of mixed nuts for breads each is making. How much of the canister did each student get?

Yura and Milo's cooking teacher takes $\frac{1}{4}$ of a bag of rice from the pantry and gives an equal amount to 4 different students. What fraction of the bag of rice did each student get?

Last week, all 16 students in the class made saag paneer. Paneer is a kind of cheese, and the students used 4 pounds of it while cooking. If all 16 shared the final dish, what amount of paneer did each person eat?

Dot Dot Dot

Solve the word problems.

The science student added 10.2 milliliters of lemon juice to 20.45 milliliters of milk. How much total liquid was there?

The scientist combined 3.4 milliliters of water and 2.1 milliliters of hydrogen peroxide. How much total liquid was there?

Which is greater: $\frac{4}{5}$ or 0.85?

What is the decimal equivalent of $\frac{3}{4}$?

How much money is 2 quarters, 2 dimes, 2 nickels, and 2 pennies?

What is the product of 43.5 and 0.87?

Tree House Refresh

Solve the word problems.

The Chan siblings are adding glass to the windows of their tree house. The windows are 18 inches wide and 24 inches high. How many square inches of glass do they need for each window?

The kids are carpeting the tree house. The floor is 8 feet wide by 10 feet long. How many square feet of carpeting do they need?

The kids are painting one interior wall with chalkboard paint. The wall is 8 feet wide and 7 feet tall. How many square feet do they need to paint?

The kids are adding a glow-in-the-dark wallpaper border. This will go along the top of the walls. Two of the walls are 8 feet across, and two are 10 feet across. How many feet of border do they need?

The kids are painting the outside of the tree house purple. Two walls are 8 feet × 7 feet, and two walls are 10 feet × 7 feet. How many square feet need to be painted altogether?

This and That

Solve the word problems.

What is the volume of a 12 × 12 × 12 centimeter cardboard box?

Maddie swam 30 laps. Each lap was 50 meters. How many kilometers did she swim?

The temperature on Monday was 89°F but dropped to 51°F overnight. What was the difference in temperature?

The diameter of the story-time circle is 10 feet. What is the circumference (using 3.14 as π)?

Mr. Tapko painted a circle with a 5-foot radius for a tetherball court. What is the area of the court (using 3.14 as π)?

Diona needed 32 cups of milk. How many gallons did she need?

SOCIAL STUDIES

In this section, we'll explore the United States! Along the way, we'll learn about significant people and events in history, culture, and technology.

PARENTS In this section, your child will apply reading, writing, and researching skills to new subjects while they expand their understanding of government, economics, geography, and history. Consider sharing your personal perspective about historical events or periods from your lifetime—you could also research the event or subject together to deepen your child's understanding.

Know Your States

Label the states on the US map that are missing their names. (Hint: turn the page for a list of state names.)

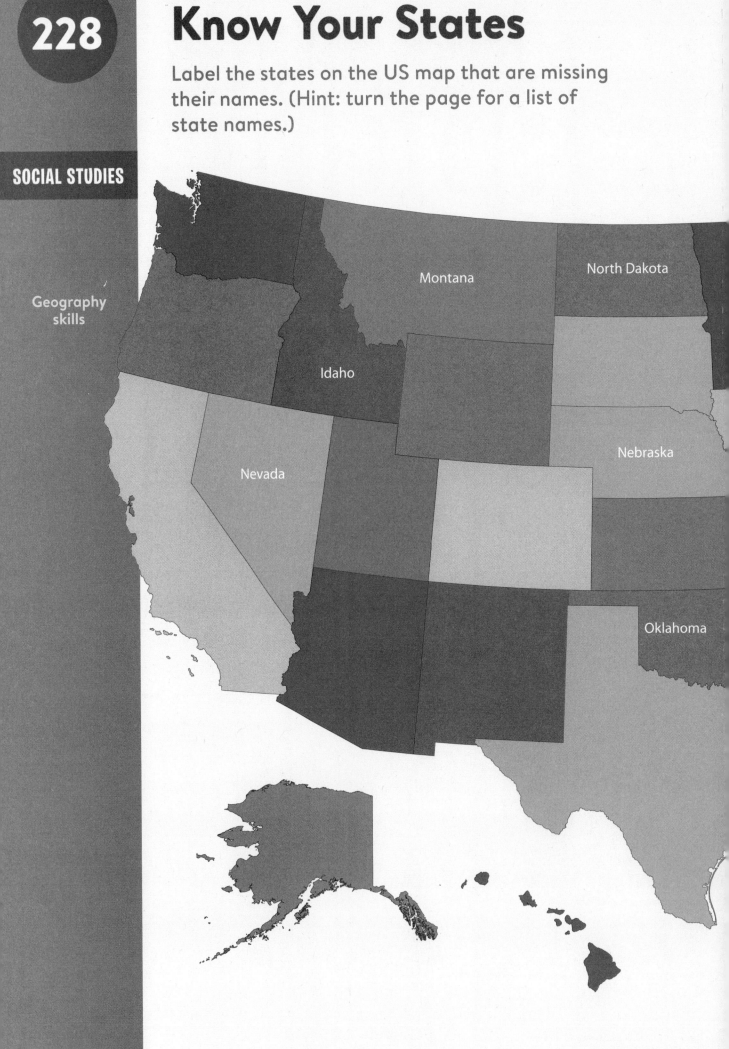

Geography skills

Montana

North Dakota

Idaho

Nevada

Nebraska

Oklahoma

Geography
skills

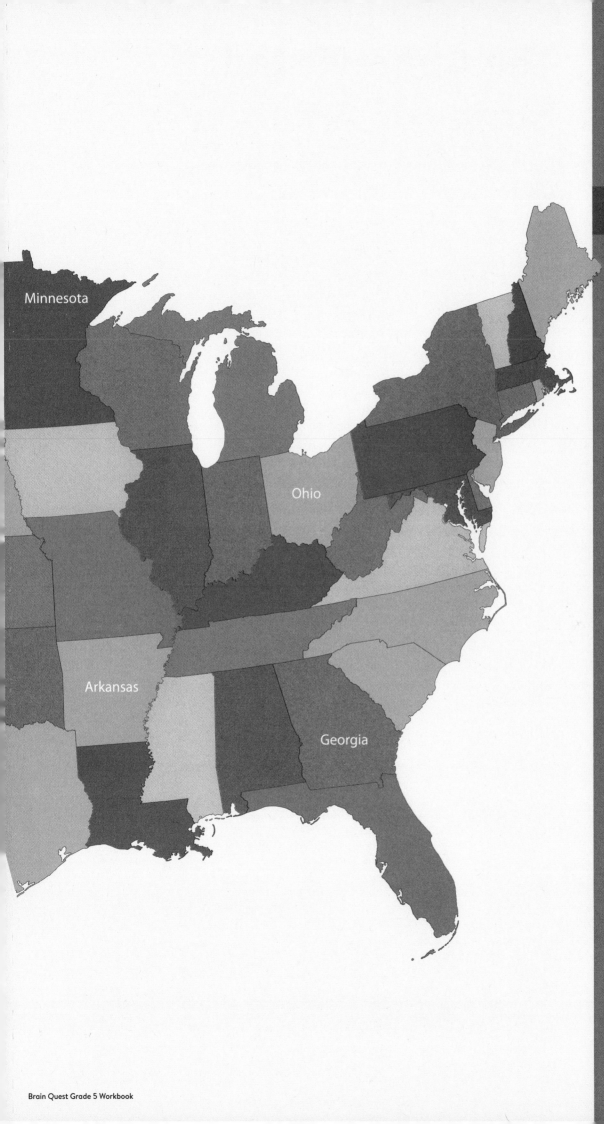

Minnesota

Ohio

Arkansas

Georgia

The Abbreviated States of America

Read the list of states and their abbreviations.
Then follow the directions below.

State
abbreviations

ALABAMA	AL	ILLINOIS	IL
ALASKA	AK	INDIANA	IN
ARIZONA	AZ	IOWA	IA
ARKANSAS	AR	KANSAS	KS
CALIFORNIA	CA	KENTUCKY	KY
COLORADO	CO	LOUISIANA	LA
CONNECTICUT	CT	MAINE	ME
DELAWARE	DE	MARYLAND	MD
FLORIDA	FL		
GEORGIA	GA		
HAWAI'I	HI		
IDAHO	ID		

HELLO MY NAME IS AL

Underline the abbreviations that
are the first two letters in the state's name.

Circle the abbreviations that are the first letters of the
two words that make up the state's name.

State abbreviations

MASSACHUSETTS — MA

MICHIGAN — MI

MINNESOTA — MN

MISSISSIPPI — MS

MISSOURI — MO

MONTANA — MT

NEBRASKA — NE

NEVADA — NV

NEW HAMPSHIRE — NH

NEW JERSEY — NJ

NEW MEXICO — NM

NEW YORK — NY

NORTH CAROLINA — NC

NORTH DAKOTA — ND

OHIO — OH

OKLAHOMA — OK

OREGON — OR

PENNSYLVANIA — PA

RHODE ISLAND — RI

SOUTH CAROLINA — SC

SOUTH DAKOTA — SD

TENNESSEE — TN

TEXAS — TX

UTAH — UT

VERMONT — VT

VIRGINIA — VA

WASHINGTON — WA

WEST VIRGINIA — WV

WISCONSIN — WI

WYOMING — WY

Put a star next to the abbreviations that are the first and last letters in the state's name.

Put a plus sign next to abbreviations that follow none of these patterns.

Bright Lights, Big Cities

Study the **political map** and answer the questions.

- ⭐ = State capital
- ☐ = Largest city in the state (in terms of population)
- ⭐ (boxed) = State capital + Largest city

Political maps

What is the largest city in Wisconsin?

Which city is both the capital and the largest city in Utah?

What is the capital of Alaska?

What is the largest city in Kansas?

What is the capital of Louisiana?

Is Memphis the capital, or the largest city in Tennessee?

What is the largest city in South Dakota?

Which city is both the capital and the largest city in Arkansas?

In which 17 states is the capital also the largest city?

_____   _____   _____

_____   _____   _____

_____   _____   _____

_____   _____   _____

_____   _____   _____

_____   _____   _____

Map labels

Maine
Vermont
Augusta
Burlington
Montpelier
Portland
Concord
New Hampshire
Manchester
Boston
Albany
Providence
Massachusetts
New York
Hartford
Rhode Island
Bridgeport
Newark
New York City
Michigan
Detroit
Pennsylvania
Connecticut
Lansing
Philadelphia
Trenton
Harrisburg
Baltimore
Wilmington
New Jersey
Indiana
Ohio
Annapolis
Dover
Columbus
West Virginia
Delaware
Indianapolis
Richmond
Maryland
Louisville
Charleston
Washington, D.C.
Frankfort
Virginia Beach
Virginia
Kentucky
Raleigh
North Carolina
Nashville
Charlotte
Tennessee
Columbia
Atlanta
South Carolina
Alabama
Birmingham
Georgia
Montgomery
Tallahassee
Jacksonville
Florida

BRAIN BOX

Political maps show government boundaries, such as state and country borders. They also show the location of cities, like state capitals.

Majestic Mountains

Study the **physical map** and answer the questions.

What mountain range spans Georgia to Maine?

From which state does the Mississippi River empty into the Gulf of Mexico?

Which states border Lake Michigan?

In which state is the Great Salt Lake located?

What body of water sits between Texas and Florida?

If you drive west through Kansas, does your elevation increase or decrease?

Physical maps

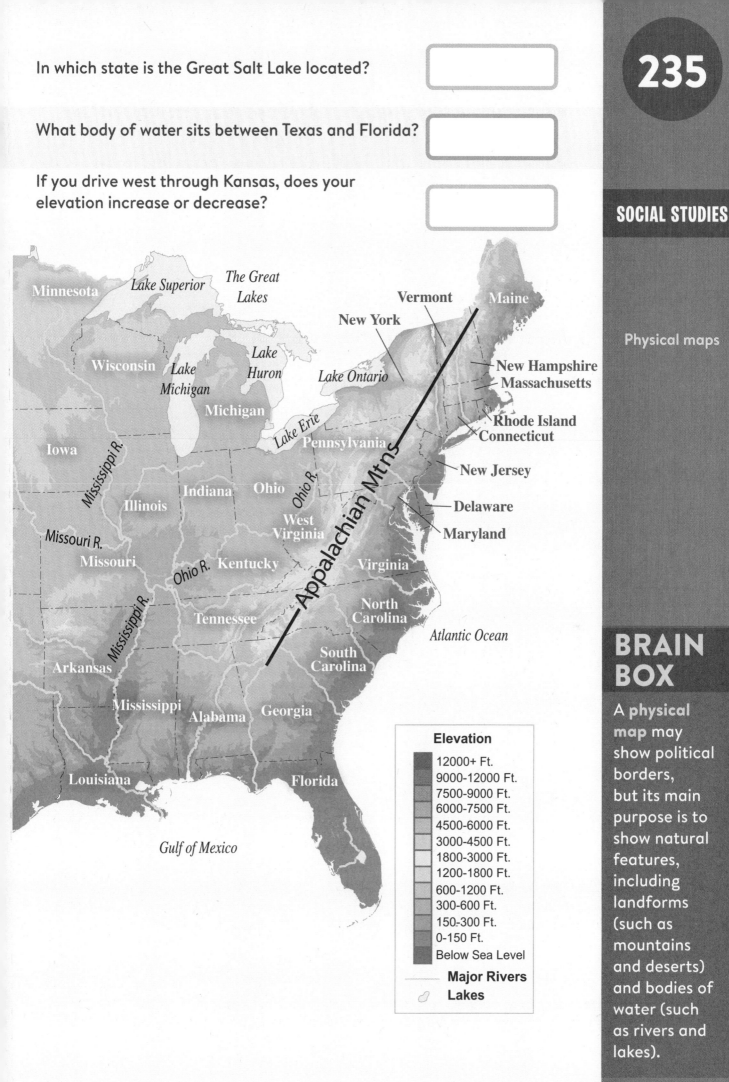

Elevation

12000+ Ft.
9000-12000 Ft.
7500-9000 Ft.
6000-7500 Ft.
4500-6000 Ft.
3000-4500 Ft.
1800-3000 Ft.
1200-1800 Ft.
600-1200 Ft.
300-600 Ft.
150-300 Ft.
0-150 Ft.
Below Sea Level

Major Rivers
Lakes

BRAIN BOX

A **physical map** may show political borders, but its main purpose is to show natural features, including landforms (such as mountains and deserts) and bodies of water (such as rivers and lakes).

Native Peoples Coast to Coast

For thousands of years before Europeans colonized the North American continent, **Indigenous people** (the original inhabitants of lands) lived in thriving societies, in all regions of the Americas.

Indigenous lands

Major Indigenous Societies Before 1492

Regions of the US

- Northwest Coast
- California
- Plateau
- Great Basin
- Southwest
- Great Plains
- Northeast
- Southeast

Indigenous lands

Each group had distinct customs, languages, diets, homes, and traditions. Use this map to answer the questions.

This Indigenous society, located in what is now New York State, lived in structures called longhouses.

_____

Name three Indigenous nations in the Southwest.

_____

Can the Lakota be found in the Great Plains or the southeast?

_____

The people of this Florida tribe call themselves the "Unconquered People," in reference to their nineteenth-century ancestors who avoided capture and forced relocation by the US government.

_____

On the map, this nation lives the farthest north on the west coast.

_____

 **On Your Own**

Indigenous people once inhabited every corner of the US. With the assistance of a parent or other trusted adult, do some research about the Indigenous people of your state or locality. Check out your local library for guidance and resources.

BRAIN BOX

Today, there are more than five hundred federally recognized American Indian and Alaska Native societies in the US. These diverse groups have languages, foods, clothes, and traditions that are as distinct from one another as they were before European colonization. The US government used forced relocation and other legal and cultural tactics to try and erase these diverse cultures, but Indigenous people have fought to preserve their languages, traditions, and history.

Jamestown, 1607

Read the story about the first permanent British colony in the Americas. Then, answer the questions.

The History of Jamestown

In 1607, 125 British colonists established Jamestown, the first permanent English colony in North America. The colonists were hired by a group of investors called the Virginia Company to create English colonies, exploit the land for natural resources, and search for gold and silver (which they never found).

This land was Tsenacomoco, a region home to dozens of Algonquin-speaking Indigenous nations who were politically united under one leader, Chief Powhatan. Approximately 14,000 people lived in villages across Tsenacomoco. They were skilled farmers, hunters, artisans, and warriors. They shared food and resources and formed a single, powerful military unit.

The British colonists built Jamestown on an uninhabited island in Tsenacomoco. It was uninhabited because it wasn't a good place to live. The nearby water wasn't safe to drink. The marshy land was hard to farm. It was infested with mosquitos that carried malaria, a deadly disease. Colonists quickly began dying from water-borne illnesses, malaria, and starvation. It is believed only 1 in 4 colonists survived Jamestown's early years.

Chief Powhatan was wary of the colonists, but he sent gifts of food and taught them how to grow maize. Even so, the colonists stole food, goods, and supplies from nearby villages. Fighting between the two groups escalated to war, and the English used vicious tactics, like burning down villages and killing their inhabitants, and kidnapping Powhatan's daughter Pocahontas, to weaken the powerful Powhatan Confederacy. The First Anglo-Powhatan War ended when Pocahontas married a settler named John Rolfe, beginning a short period of peace between the two groups.

Meanwhile, new English colonists kept arriving, and they got better at farming. John Rolfe was the first colonist to grow tobacco, a cash crop the Virginia Company sold for a huge profit. Jamestown began to grow in size and strength: English farms crowded out the people of Tsenacomoco, and their increasing population meant more people to fight resistance from the Powhatan Confederacy.

In time, and after many more wars, the English colonized all of Tsenacomoco, and Jamestown became part of a larger colony called Virginia.

When did the Jamestown colonists first arrive in Tsenacomoco?

_____

What were the Jamestown colonists hired to do?

_____

Jamestown

Write three facts about Tsenacomoco.

_____

_____

_____

Why did the original Jamestown settlers struggle to survive? Include at least two details.

_____

_____

_____

Why did war break out between the Jamestown settlers and the Powhatan Confederacy?

_____

Give two reasons that explain how the English colonists came to control the land that had once been ruled by Chief Powhatan.

_____

_____

The Originals

Use the clues under the map to fill in the names of the original **thirteen British colonies**.

Thirteen colonies

BRAIN BOX

In the 1500s, the French, Dutch, Spanish, and British began colonizing Indigenous land and establishing settlements in the Americas. In the early 1600s, the British took control, and established **thirteen colonies** along the eastern coast of North America. These colonies persisted until the end of the Revolutionary War in 1783, when they became the United States.

The southernmost colony is Georgia.

Maryland and Delaware share a peninsula.

Pennsylvania is the only colony that does not touch the Atlantic Ocean.

Rhode Island is nestled between Massachusetts and Connecticut.

A large island is part of New York.

New Jersey is below New York and above a peninsula.

Massachusetts has two land areas separated by New Hampshire.

Virginia is above North Carolina and South Carolina.

We the People

Read the preamble of the **US Constitution** and the definitions of some important vocabulary words. Then rewrite the preamble in your own words.

We the People of the United States, in Order to form a more perfect Union, establish Justice, insure domestic Tranquility, provide for the common defence, promote the general Welfare, and secure the Blessings of Liberty to ourselves and our Posterity, do ordain and establish this Constitution for the United States of America.

union: a country made up of states

justice: fairness and moral rightness

domestic: relating to a people's home country

tranquility: peace

welfare: health and happiness

liberty: freedom from unfair government rules

posterity: future generations

ordain: decree

establish: set up

BRAIN BOX

The **US Constitution** is the law of the land. Established in 1789, it describes the US system of government, including the three branches (executive, legislative, and judicial), and states' rights and responsibilities. It has been **amended**, or added to, 27 times. The first 10 amendments make up the **Bill of Rights**.

We the people,

_____

_____

_____

_____

_____

_____

_____

Revolutionary Players

Read the cards about the **Revolutionary War**.

Revolutionary
War

King George III

Claim to Fame: King of England for 59 years

Born: 1738

Died: 1820

Personal Fact: He and his wife, Charlotte, had fifteen children.

Role in the Revolution: Along with Parliament, he led the British in the war against the American colonists.

George Washington

Claim to Fame: First US President

Born: 1732

Died: 1799

Personal Fact: After the war, Washington wanted to return to farming but was talked into running for president.

Role in the Revolution: He was the commander in chief of the Continental Army.

BRAIN BOX

The **Revolutionary War** (or the **American Revolution** or the **US War of Independence**) lasted from 1775 to 1783 and ended with the thirteen North American colonies winning their independence from the British crown.

John Adams

Claim to Fame: Second US President

Born: 1735

Died: July 4, 1826

Personal Fact: His son, John Quincy Adams, became the sixth US president.

Role in the Revolution: He was a delegate to the Continental Congress and a leader in the American quest for independence.

Thomas Jefferson

Claim to Fame: Third US President

Born: 1743

Died: July 4, 1826

Personal Fact: He died within hours of his friend John Adams.

Role in the Revolution: He was a delegate to the Continental Congress and writer of the Declaration of Independence.

Mary Ludwig (aka Molly Pitcher)

Claim to Fame: Revolutionary War soldier

Born: 1754

Died: 1832

Personal Fact: She was nicknamed Molly Pitcher because she carried pitchers of water to the soldiers during the war.

Role in the Revolution: When her husband collapsed during the Battle of Monmouth, she fired his cannon in his place.

Abigail Adams

Claim to Fame: Second US First Lady

Born: 1744

Died: 1818

Personal Fact: She encouraged her husband, John Adams, to give women rights equal to those of men in the US Constitution.

Role in the Revolution: She advised her husband and interrogated Massachusetts women who remained loyal to the British crown.

Draw a line from each person to the statement that is true about him or her.

King George III	was the second US president
George Washington	fought at the Battle of Monmouth
John Adams	worked alongside Parliament to fight against the colonists
Thomas Jefferson	commanded the Continental Army
Mary Ludwig	questioned Massachusetts residents who remained loyal to the British crown
Abigail Adams	wrote the Declaration of Independence

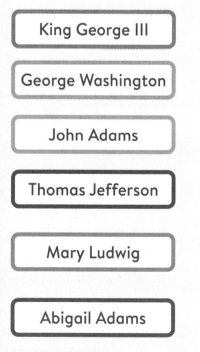

You Be the Judge

Read the summary of the **Bill of Rights.**

The Bill of Rights

Amendment I
The right to freedom of religion, freedom of speech, freedom of the press, and freedom to peaceably assemble

Amendment II
The right to bear arms as part of a well-regulated militia

Amendment III
The right not to be required to house soldiers

Amendment IV
The right not to be searched or to have your home or belongings searched without a warrant

Amendment V
The right to due process, which includes a grand jury for a capital crime, the right not to testify against oneself, and the right not to be tried twice for the same crime

Amendment VI
The right to a speedy and fair trial, including an attorney and an impartial jury

Amendment VII
The right to a trial by jury

Amendment VIII
The right not to be charged excessive bail or fines, or to suffer from cruel and unusual punishment

Amendment IX
The right to not be denied rights not listed in the Bill of Rights

Amendment X
The right of states to make and uphold laws not in the power of the federal government

BRAIN BOX

The first ten amendments to the US Constitution are collectively called the **Bill of Rights.** They grant basic rights and liberties to US citizens. Without the right to vote or own property at the time the Bill of Rights was written (in 1789), women, enslaved people, and Indigenous people were not protected by its guarantees.

Which amendment protects someone who wants to organize a rally to save endangered species? _____

Which amendment prevents the government from putting soldiers in someone's home during peaceful times (when there is no war)? _____

Which amendment prevents the government from passing a law saying that everyone must practice the same religion?

_____

Which amendment protects the right of a person accused of a crime to have a speedy trial? _____

Which amendment says that a police officer cannot search the trunk of someone's car without a warrant?

_____

Which amendment do you think is the most important? Why?

_____
_____
_____
_____
_____
_____
_____

The Cost of Expansion

Read the passage about **westward expansion** and answer the questions.

The term "Manifest Destiny" was coined by journalist John O'Sullivan in 1845. The idea was that the United States was destined by God to expand across the entire North American continent. The US used the idea of Manifest Destiny to justify violence against Indigenous people who were forced off their land in the process of expansion.

In 1803, the French government offered to sell the United States its claim to the Louisiana Territory. The land, extending from the Mississippi River to the Rocky Mountains, and from the Canadian border to the Gulf of Mexico, would double the area of the US. President Thomas Jefferson jumped at the offer: 827,000 square miles of land for $15 million—about 4 cents an acre. Dozens of Indigenous nations lived on the land. Nevertheless, white settlers moved west and began to make their homes there, and fifteen US states would eventually form from the new land.

Meanwhile, many Indigenous nations lived on valuable land in the southeast. Many Americans asked the US government to force Indigenous people off this land, so it would be available for white settlers to farm. Land speculators (people who bought land and sold it to settlers) were some of the strongest advocates of this because the sale of the valuable land would make a large profit. The US passed the Indian Removal Act of 1830, which made it legal for the government to force Indigenous nations east of the Mississippi River off their ancestral land and onto land in the west acquired in the Louisiana Purchase.

Under the administration of President Andrew Jackson, the US government forcibly removed Indigenous nations in the southeast—including the Cherokee, Choctaw, Muscogee (Creek), and the Chickasaw—and sent them to what was called "Indian Territory" in present-day Oklahoma. Indigenous people were forced to walk over 5,000 miles across nine states along a route now called the Trail of Tears. Many people died of starvation, sickness, and exhaustion along the way. Less than a quarter of the relocated Creek and Cherokee people survived the trip, and an estimated 100,000 Indigenous people died during these forced migrations. Their land was seized and sold to land speculators and white settlers for a profit.

What was the idea behind "Manifest Destiny"? _____

_____

How did the purchase of the Louisiana Territory affect the size of the United States? _____

_____

What did the Indian Removal Act of 1830 make it legal to do?

_____

_____

Why were land speculators some of the strongest supporters of removing Indigenous people from their land? _____

_____

What is the name for the forced migration of Indigenous people from their homes in the Southeast to Indian Territory west of the Mississippi River? _____

_____

Which Indigenous nations were most affected by the US government during this forced relocation? _____

_____

When the States Go Marching In

1.	Delaware	December 7, 1787
2.	Pennsylvania	December 12, 1787
3.	New Jersey	December 18, 1787
4.	Georgia	January 2, 1788
5.	Connecticut	January 9, 1788
6.	Massachusetts	February 6, 1788
7.	Maryland	April 28, 1788
8.	South Carolina	May 23, 1788
9.	New Hampshire	June 21, 1788
10.	Virginia	June 25, 1788
11.	New York	July 26, 1788
12.	North Carolina	November 21, 1789
13.	Rhode Island	May 29, 1790
14.	Vermont	March 4, 1791
15.	Kentucky	June 1, 1792

16.	Tennessee	June 1, 1796
17.	Ohio	March 1, 1803
18.	Louisiana	April 30, 1812
19.	Indiana	December 11, 1816
20.	Mississippi	December 10, 1817
21.	Illinois	December 3, 1818
22.	Alabama	December 14, 1819
23.	Maine	March 15, 1820
24.	Missouri	August 10, 1821
25.	Arkansas	June 15, 1836
26.	Michigan	January 26, 1837
27.	Florida	March 3, 1845
28.	Texas	December 29, 1845

Consult the order in which the states were admitted into the Union. Then label each state with the correct number. The first three have been done for you.

29. Iowa — December 28, 1846

30. Wisconsin — May 29, 1848

31. California — September 9, 1850

32. Minnesota — May 11, 1858

33. Oregon — February 14, 1859

34. Kansas — January 29, 1861

35. West Virginia — June 20, 1863

36. Nevada — October 31, 1864

37. Nebraska — March 1, 1867

38. Colorado — August 1, 1876

39. North Dakota — November 2, 1889

40. South Dakota — November 2, 1889

41. Montana — November 8, 1889

42. Washington — November 11, 1889

43. Idaho — July 3, 1890

44. Wyoming — July 10, 1890

45. Utah — January 4, 1896

46. Oklahoma — November 16, 1907

47. New Mexico — January 6, 1912

48. Arizona — February 14, 1912

49. Alaska — January 3, 1959

50. Hawai'i — August 21, 1959

249

SOCIAL STUDIES

Statehood

This Means War

Read the **Civil War** time line. Then answer the questions.

The Beginning of the Civil War

November 6, 1860
Abraham Lincoln becomes the sixteenth president of the United States. The new president opposes the expansion of slavery into new US territories, angering people in many states where slavery is legal.

December 20, 1860
In response to Lincoln's electoral victory, South Carolina legislators vote to secede from the Union.

January 9–February 1, 1861
Mississippi, Florida, Alabama, Georgia, Louisiana, and Texas also secede from the Union.

January 29, 1861
Kansas becomes the thirty-fourth state. It does not allow slavery.

February, 1861
The seceded states, now called the Confederate States of America, elect Jefferson Davis as their president.

April 12, 1861
The first shot of the Civil War is fired at Fort Sumter in Charleston Harbor, South Carolina.

April 15, 1861
Lincoln calls for 75,000 volunteers to enlist in the Union Army and fight the Confederate states.

April 17–May 20, 1861
Virginia, Arkansas, Tennessee, and North Carolina join the Confederate States of America.

April 19, 1861
Lincoln directs the Union army to cut off supplies from reaching Confederate ports.

April 21, 1861
Union troops from New York and Massachusetts defend Washington, DC, against the rebels.

May 24,1861
Union troops capture Alexandria, Virginia.

What does it mean to secede from the Union?

_____

Which state was the first to secede from the Union?

_____

Name all the states that seceded from the Union.

_____

Why did these states secede from the Union?

_____

Why did Lincoln call for volunteers to enlist in the
Union Army?

_____

What was the name of the government of the seceded states?

_____

Who was the president of the seceded states?

_____

Name three actions that the Union army took during the war.

_____

_____

Civil War

BRAIN BOX

The Union is another
term for the United
States. When a state
seceded from the Union,
it was withdrawing
from the United
States. The southern
states, which relied on
enslaved people for
free labor, seceded
because they feared
that, with President
Lincoln's election and
the growing power of
the northern states,
slavery would soon
be outlawed in the US.
During the Civil War,
the **Union army** was
referred to as the army
of the United States
(the states that did
not secede from the
Union). The **Confederate
army** fought for the
Confederate States of
America (the states that
seceded).

Immigration

Castle Garden

Read the excerpt from an article in the May 8, 1887, *Sun* newspaper about immigrants landing in **Castle Garden**.

Several hundred immigrants had just arrived by a German steamer, and were undergoing registration. The castle officials are not inclined to use unseemly haste in their work, and yet the formalities take very little time. Each immigrant, as he passed the clerk's desk, had to show his passport and tell whether he had any family, friends in this country, or money in his pocket. The vast majority of all immigrants answer these questions satisfactorily. That is, they have families and a little money, and they are able-bodied. In such case they are passed without further query. Able-bodied young men are passed if they have friends here who will agree to look out for them, even if they have no money. The reporter stood by the clerk during the registration. A young German presented his passport, and the name was transcribed upon the clerk's book. Then the questions:

"Have you any money?"

"No, sir." [Through an interpreter.]

"Friends in this city?"

"No, sir."

"Anywhere in the country?"

"No sir."

"What do you expect to do?"

"I am a baker, and I purpose to look for work here."

"How are you going to live until you find it?"

The young man hesitated, and the interpreter explained that he would have to satisfy the officials that he would not be compelled to resort to charity. He thereupon pulled from his trousers' pocket a large and heavy gold watch and laid it upon the clerk's desk.

"I was intending," he said, "to call on the German Consul and ask him to take it as surety for my board at some house he should recommend until such time as I should receive my first wages. It's mine by rights," he continued quickly: "you will find my father's name inscribed inside the case. It was his only legacy, and I would not sell it for anything."

He was held for further examination by the Commissioners, but was "allowed to land," as the saying is, when an officer of a Germany society agreed to assure the community that the young man would not become a charge upon it for a year.

BRAIN BOX

Before Ellis Island opened in 1892, **Castle Garden** was where immigrants arriving in New York City landed and were questioned before being allowed into the United States. Some would stay in New York; others moved on to other states.

Pretend you are an immigrant who has just arrived in New York City. Write a letter home to a friend. Include the following details:

- Your home country
- Your reason for immigrating to America
- What it was like at Castle Garden
- What you are doing for work
- How your family is doing
- What you like about America
- What you miss about home

_____

_____

_____

_____

_____

_____

_____

_____

_____

_____

_____

_____

_____

Castle Garden

Awesome Inventions and Innovations

Read the time line and use context clues
to fill in the blanks with the words below.

| Kevlar | air bag | plasma |

| heating system | Super Soaker | fire escape |

| life raft | windshield wiper |

Inventions

1882
Maria Beasley patents the _____ . Her invention saves many
lives, including more than seven hundred people aboard the *Titanic*.

1887
Anna Connelly invents the _____ . This helps ensure residents in multistory
buildings have a way to get out safely in case of an emergency, such as a fire.

1902
Mary Anderson invents the _____ after riding a streetcar on a snowy day
and observing the streetcar's driver repeatedly clean off the windshield by hand.

1919
Alice H. Parker patents a natural gas _____ with individually controlled
burners, a forerunner of the "zone heating" we have in buildings today.

1938
Dr. Charles Drew, called the "Father of the Blood Bank," develops a system that
allows _____ to be preserved and stored for longer periods of time.

1952
After an accident on a country road, John W. Hetrick wonders if a safety feature
could inflate in a car to protect passengers in the event of a collision. Later the same
year he files a patent for a "safety cushion," one of the most important developments
in auto safety: the _____ .

1965
Chemist Stephanie Kwolek invents _____, a fiber stronger than steel
that is most famous for being used in police protective vests.

1982
While at home working on an idea for an improved heat pump, NASA engineer Lonnie
Johnson winds up accidentally inventing the _____, which goes on to
become one of the bestselling toys of all time.

The Three Branches

Read the paragraph and study the diagram. Then fill in the blanks with the correct branch of government.

The writers of the Constitution wanted a system of government that didn't give any one person or group too much power. So they separated the power into three branches of government. The legislative branch (Congress) is in charge of making the laws. The executive branch (the president) leads the country and makes sure laws are obeyed. The judicial branch (the Supreme Court) interprets laws and decides whether certain laws are unconstitutional.

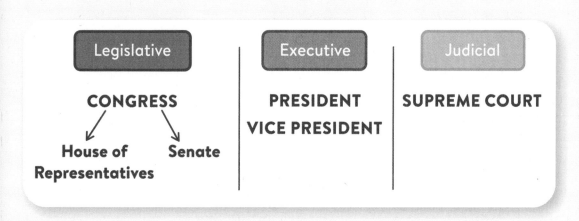

Legislative	Executive	Judicial
CONGRESS	**PRESIDENT**	**SUPREME COURT**
House of Representatives ← → Senate	**VICE PRESIDENT**	

Congress, the _____ branch, passes a law requiring power plants to reduce their carbon dioxide emissions.

The president, as the _____ branch, directs the Environmental Protection Agency (EPA) to enforce the new carbon dioxide reduction law.

The Supreme Court, acting as the the _____ branch, rules that this law can be enforced by the EPA because carbon dioxide emissions are a threat to human health.

Stars and Stripes

Read about the American flag.

The first American flag, created in 1777, had thirteen stars and thirteen stripes, one of each for each of the states. When Vermont and Kentucky became states in 1795, two more stars and two more stripes were added.

However, as more states joined the union, it became clear that if a stripe were added for each one, the flag would soon become crowded with too many stripes. Instead, Congress decided the flag should go back to having thirteen stripes, but that a new star would be added for each state. In 1912, Arizona and New Mexico became the forty-seventh and forty-eighth states. The flag was almost complete. Finally, in 1959, Alaska and Hawai'i also joined the Union, bringing the number of stars up to fifty. Will more stars ever be added? It is possible that Puerto Rico, whose residents are already US citizens, will one day become a state and have the flag's fifty-first star.

Based on what you learned in the paragraph, match the flags to the right year.

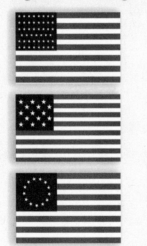

1795

1912

1777

Draw a picture of today's American flag, including the correct number of stars and stripes.

I Pledge Allegiance . . .

Read the facts below. Then, complete the time line.

Facts about the Pledge of Allegiance

The Pledge of Allegiance was written by Francis J. Bellamy in 1892.

The owner of the magazine *Youth's Companion* asked Bellamy to write the pledge to increase patriotism among kids.

The magazine also published directions for saluting the flag during the pledge. At the time, people held their right arm out straight toward the flag.

During World War II, Americans decided the straight-arm salute was too similar to Germany's Nazi salute. In 1942, Congress changed the salute to the hand-over-heart gesture we use today.

In 1954, with President Dwight D. Eisenhower's support, the words "under God" were added after "one nation."

American symbols

Ask a trusted adult before you go online.

1892

_____

1942

_____

1954

_____

Write the Pledge of Allegiance from memory.

_____
_____
_____
_____
_____
_____
_____
_____
_____

BRAIN BOX

If you don't know the **Pledge of Allegiance**, go to the website USA.gov and search for "Pledge of Allegiance."

A Monumental Vacation

Read about the national monuments.

The White House
Construction began on the official residence of the president in 1792. It was built by a workforce of free and enslaved laborers. That house burned during the War of 1812 but was rebuilt in 1817. President Theodore Roosevelt renovated the house in 1902, adding the West Wing, where the president's Oval Office is located. Roosevelt also named the residence the White House. Today, the White House has 132 rooms, including 35 bathrooms and 3 kitchens.

The Statue of Liberty
The Statue of Liberty was a gift from the people of France as a tribute to the United States' freedom. Sculpted by Auguste Bartholdi, it was unveiled in 1886. For immigrants arriving on nearby Ellis Island, the statue was a symbol of welcome after weeks at sea. In 1903, a poem by Emma Lazarus was added to the base of the statue.

The Lincoln Memorial
Completed in 1922, the Lincoln Memorial symbolizes President Lincoln's belief in the freedom of all people. Its thirty-six columns represent the thirty-six states that made up the United States when Lincoln died. Located in a chamber of the memorial is a statue of Lincoln sitting. It is 19 feet tall and weighs 175 tons (including the pedestal). The Gettysburg Address is engraved on the south wall of the monument.

Vermilion Cliffs National Monument
Mother Nature is the sculptor of this national monument in northern Arizona, on land once inhabited by the Ancestral Pueblo people. Elevation levels in Vermilion Cliffs' 280,000 acres range from 3,100 to 7,100 feet, with a variety of formations, including plateaus, cliffs, canyons, and buttes (tall, steep rock towers with flat tops). The colorful swirls of red-and-white sandstone in the formation known as "the Wave" get their color from the iron within the rocks.

Choose one national monument that you would like to visit. It can be one from the facing page or any other monument. Research it online and write four facts about it below.

1. _____

2. _____

3. _____

4. _____

Write a postcard to a friend, describing your visit to one monument.

_____
_____
_____
_____
_____
_____
_____
_____
_____
_____

PLACE
STAMP
HERE

MADE IN U. S. A

POST CARD

_____
_____
_____

SOCIAL STUDIES

National monuments

Ask a trusted adult before you go online.

Federal, State, or Local?

Read about different levels of government.

Federal, state, and local government

In the US, the authority to make laws and policies is divided among federal, state, and local governments. Powers that are not held by the federal government are divided between state and local governments. Power is shared so that neither the federal government nor the states have too much power. It is also shared because it is thought that some decisions and services are better handled at the state and local level.

The federal government makes policies that affect all the country's residents, such as the price of a US postage stamp, what US currency will look like, or what treaties the US has with other countries. State governments have jurisdiction (power to make laws) over issues that affect all the residents of a state, such as the specific requirements for obtaining a drivers' license in that state. Towns, cities, or counties regulate local issues, such as the speed limits on local roads.

Taxes, or financial charges, are collected from citizens by all levels of government. The federal government collects taxes for many reasons, including maintaining natural resources such as national parks. Local governments, for example, generally fund their city or town's emergency services, recreation centers, and public libraries using money from taxes.

Decide which level of government would have the power and responsibility to address each of the issues below. Then write either **federal**, **state**, or **local** on the line next to each.

Federal, state, and local government

Printing $5 bills _____

Setting the opening hours for the community pool _____

Issuing driver's licenses and license plates _____

Hiring the fire chief for the town fire department _____

Holding the election of a governor _____

Building a county public library _____

Funding national parks _____

Talking to leaders of other countries _____

Setting the speed limit on residential roads _____

Raising the price of postage stamps _____

Social Studies Crossword

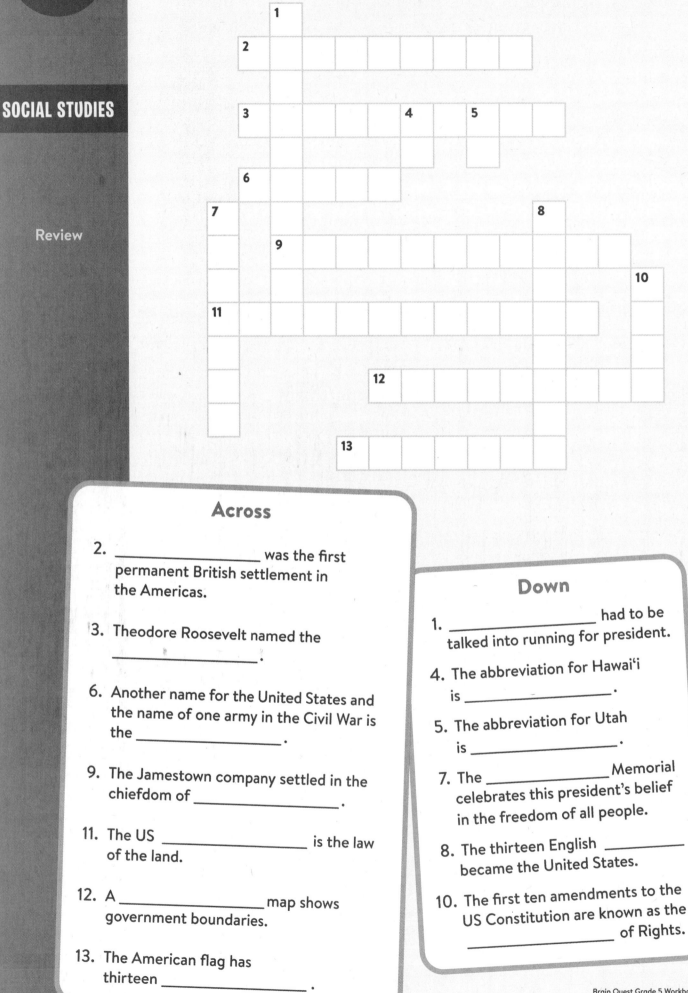

Across

2. _____ was the first permanent British settlement in the Americas.

3. Theodore Roosevelt named the _____.

6. Another name for the United States and the name of one army in the Civil War is the _____.

9. The Jamestown company settled in the chiefdom of _____.

11. The US _____ is the law of the land.

12. A _____ map shows government boundaries.

13. The American flag has thirteen _____.

Down

1. _____ had to be talked into running for president.

4. The abbreviation for Hawai'i is _____.

5. The abbreviation for Utah is _____.

7. The _____ Memorial celebrates this president's belief in the freedom of all people.

8. The thirteen English _____ became the United States.

10. The first ten amendments to the US Constitution are known as the _____ of Rights.

SCIENCE

From microscopic cells to the center of Earth, and from biomes to alternative energy sources, this section explores science topics big and small. Science is all about being curious, asking questions, and finding answers. What are you curious about?

PARENTS Your child will explore aspects of life, physical, earth, and space sciences in this section, building a foundation in preparation for middle and high school biology, chemistry, and physics classes. Encourage your child to think like a scientist by welcoming questions about anything—from the microscopic to the interstellar—and then seeking opportunities for further learning and exploration.

Classified Information

Read the **animal classification** chart and bullet points.

Animal Classification

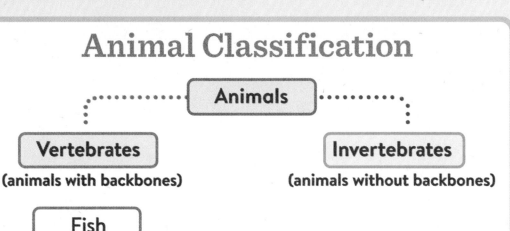

Vertebrates
(animals with backbones)

Invertebrates
(animals without backbones)

Fish

- live in water
- breathe using gills
- most are cold-blooded

Amphibians

- spend time on land and in water
- use gills to breathe for part or all of their lives
- do not have scales
- most go through metamorphosis
- are cold-blooded

Reptiles

- have scales
- breathe with lungs
- most lay eggs
- most are cold-blooded

Birds

- have feathers
- have wings (but not all fly)
- lay eggs
- are warm-blooded

Mammals

- produce milk to feed their babies
- have hair or fur
- most give birth (as opposed to laying eggs)
- are warm-blooded

Brain Quest Grade 5 Workbook

BRAIN BOX

Animals are **classified** by their relationships to each other. They are first divided into **vertebrates** and **invertebrates**. Vertebrates are more closely related to each other than to invertebrates. Vertebrates are further divided into fish, amphibians, reptiles, birds, and mammals. In each category, animals share certain characteristics. For example, all birds have feathers and lay eggs.

Answer the questions about vertebrates.

Life science

In a puddle, you find an animal with gills swimming along. Explain why this could be either a fish or an amphibian.

_____

_____

You see a creature that spends most of its time in the water. It has a bill shaped like the bill of a duck, has flippers, and lays eggs. It also has fur. Explain why this animal could be a mammal.

_____

_____

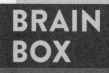

An animal spends most of its time in the water. It has a layer of fat under its skin. The animal is covered with feathers but doesn't fly. Explain why this animal is a bird.

_____

_____

An animal looks like a big fish, but you see that it comes to the surface of the water frequently to take breaths. It has only a few hairs on its head. Underwater, it can be seen feeding milk to its young. Explain why this animal is a mammal.

_____

_____

_____

_____

_____

_____

_____

BRAIN BOX

When classifying animals, pay attention to characteristics that all animals in that category have, and characteristics that only most of them have. For instance, all mammals have hair and feed milk to their young, but not all mammals give birth. A few lay eggs.

Life Cycles

Read about the **life cycles** of a frog and a moth, then answer the questions.

American Bullfrog Life Cycle

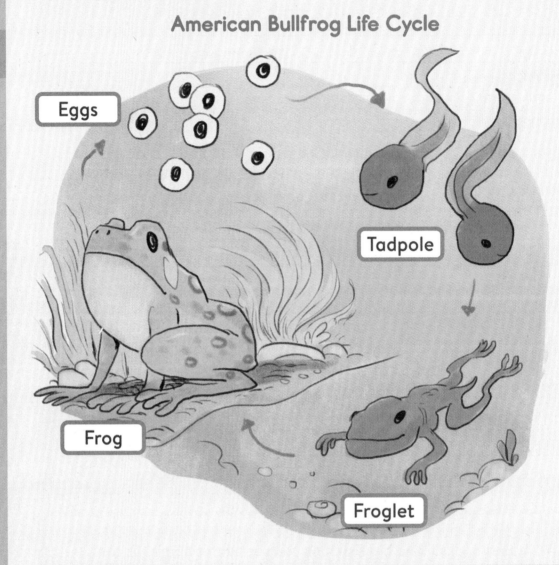

Eggs

Tadpole

Frog

Froglet

A female frog lays several unfertilized eggs in water, and a male frog fertilizes them.

After about four days, tadpoles hatch out of the eggs. The legless tadpoles live exclusively in the water and breathe through gills.

After about three weeks, the tadpoles sprout legs and arms but still have tails. They are froglets.

Gradually, the froglets outgrow their tails and become frogs. Five years after hatching, the frogs are ready to have tadpoles.

Silkworm Moth Life Cycle

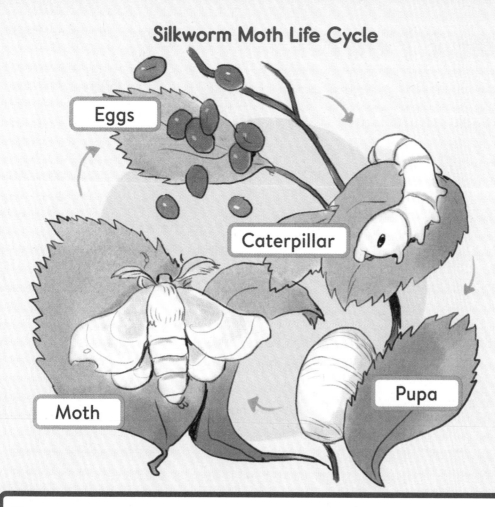

Eggs

Caterpillar

Pupa

Moth

The male and female silkworm mate, and the female lays several fertilized eggs on milkweed leaves.

Caterpillars hatch from the eggs and eat the milkweed. They grow bigger and bigger.

Next, the caterpillars spin cocoons out of silk. Inside the cocoons, they become pupas. This is when they transform from caterpillars into moths.

The new adult moths eat their way out of their cocoons. The whole process occurs in a matter of weeks, and now the moths are ready to lay eggs that will become caterpillars.

List three things that are similar about a frog's and a moth's life cycle.

_____

_____

List three things that are different about a frog's and a moth's life cycle.

_____

_____

BRAIN BOX

A **life cycle** describes an animal's stages of development from the egg stage to maturity, when it can have babies. Some insects and amphibians go through **metamorphosis.** That means that the young animals transform so that, as adults, they look and act completely different. For instance, a tadpole looks like and lives like a fish until it becomes a full-grown frog. A caterpillar is flightless until it transforms into a moth.

Neat Feet

Read about the **adaptations** and **characteristics** different animal feet have. Then answer the questions.

webbed feet

Animals that live in the water have webbed feet, which help them swim faster or farther to catch prey.

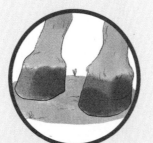

solid hooves

Prey animals that live in grasslands have solid hooves, which are built for speed. This allows hooved animals to escape predators.

talons

Birds of prey have talons in order to grab their prey and hold on to it as they fly to a safe place to eat it.

paws

Paws can be used for climbing trees to find food. The claws on paws can be used to dig for food or to grasp prey.

BRAIN BOX

Adaptations are traits, such as having feet instead of flippers, that help animals survive in their environment. Specific traits, called **characteristics**, are better suited to certain environments than to others.

Explain why ducks have webbed feet.

_____

Why are solid hooves helpful to horses?

_____

Why do eagles have talons?

_____

Why does a bear have paws?

_____

The Food Web

Read the article about **food webs**.

Food Webs

A food web is a model of intersecting food chains that show the connection between decomposers, producers, and consumers. Since most living things can eat and be eaten by lots of different animals, a simple food chain that shows one organism eating another doesn't give you a complete picture.

Organisms that make their own food, like plants, are called **producers**. Organisms that do not make their own food, like animals, are called **consumers** because they consume (eat) other living things. **Decomposers** are organisms, like bacteria, fungi (mushrooms), termites, and earthworms, that feed on and break down the organic material of dead animals and plants, which turns them into nutrients that nourish the soil. Decomposers are very important to food webs; without them, the nutrients that help producers grow (such as carbon, nitrogen, and phosphorus) would not get recycled into the soil.

A food web shows all of the food chains in one ecosystem. Label each organism as a producer, consumer, or decomposer using the letters P, C, or D.

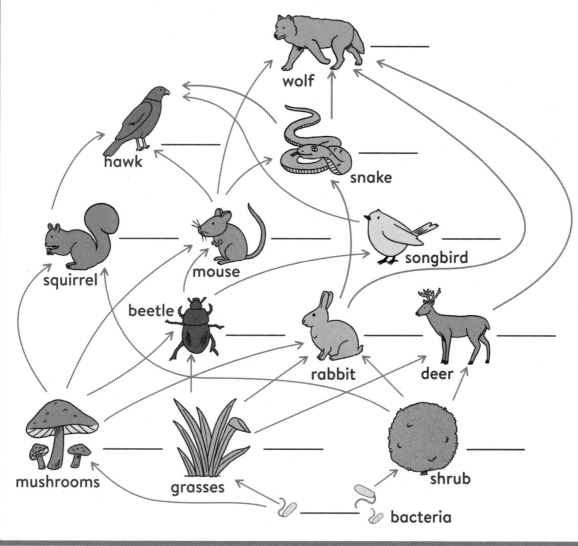

Biomes

Read the text and answer the questions.

A biome contains plants and animals that are adapted to life in that specific habitat. There are five main biomes: aquatic, desert, forest, grassland, and tundra. Grasslands exist around the world; they are called prairies in America and savannas in Africa.

Grasslands are full of grasses, which grazing animals eat. Because grasslands have few trees, and therefore few places to hide from predators, large grazing animals must be able to run away from danger. The hooved feet and long legs of grazers like horses and antelopes make them fast. Even American bison, which weigh 2 tons, can run 35 miles per hour.

Prairie plants also feed smaller animals, including insects. Insects, in turn, pollinate the plants. They also decompose dead plants and animals, returning nutrients to the soil and feeding the grass.

The climate in grasslands is extreme. Weeks can pass with no rain, followed by a thunderstorm. For this reason, grassland grasses have deep roots that store water. In temperate grasslands like the American prairie, temperatures are very hot in the summer and very cold in the winter. Animals like bison are adapted to these extremes: they have thick coats during the winter, which they shed in the spring.

BRAIN BOX

Biomes are types of land or water environments that have similar climates, plants, and animals no matter where they are in the world. Major biomes include grasslands, forests, deserts, wetlands, and aquatic biomes.

How have large grassland animals adapted to there being few hiding places from predators?

_____

What are two ways that insects help grassland plants grow?

_____

How are grassland grasses adapted to dry spells?

_____

How are bison adapted to the hot and cold extremes of the prairie?

_____

Cells

Using the clues, label the parts of the **animal cell**.

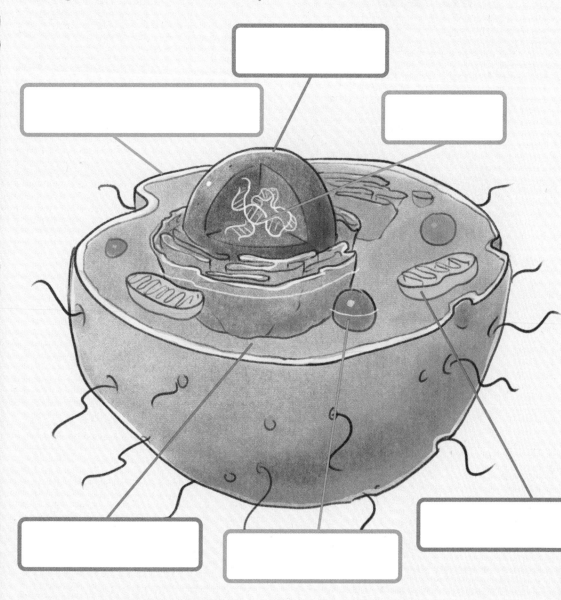

The **cell membrane** is the outer layer of the cell. It holds the cell together, but allows material to pass in and out.

In the middle of the cell, the **nucleus** controls the cell so that the cell carries out its function.

The nucleus contains **DNA**, which looks like a twisted ladder.

The **cytoplasm** lies between the cell membrane and the cell's nucleus.

The cytoplasm contains oval-shaped **mitochondria**, which produce chemical energy for the cell, and sac-shaped **vacuoles**, which store water and remove waste from the cell.

BRAIN BOX

Cells are the building blocks of all living things. They have various functions. For instance, cells can make up muscles or an organ. Multiple cells that have the same function form **tissue**.

Journey to the Center of the Earth

Using the clues, label the Earth's layers with words from below.

Even though the **inner core** is over 9,000° Fahrenheit, it is solid because the intense pressure of the rest of the planet prevents the iron center of Earth from melting.

The **crust** is the rocky, outermost layer of a planet. There are two types of crust on Earth: continental and oceanic.

The **mantle** is a mostly solid layer between the outer core and the crust. It makes up 84% of Earth's total volume!

The **outer core** is above the inner core and is the only true liquid layer. It is mostly composed of liquid iron and nickel.

BRAIN BOX

Earth is divided into four main layers—the **inner core, outer core, mantle, and crust.**

Rock It!

Read about the three kinds of rocks. Then choose the correct category for each type of rock.

> Igneous rocks form when molten (hot, liquid) rock cools and hardens. This occurs after a volcano erupts.

> Sedimentary rocks form when sediment piles up and then hardens. The sediment can include rock, sand, shells, and bones.

> Metamorphic rocks form when existing rocks are heated and put under pressure. Rocks buried deep in the Earth's crust are under pressure because of the weight of the Earth above them. They are also exposed to heat from the magma in the asthenosphere.

Limestone forms as plants, shells, and animal bones settle on the ocean floor. Over time, they harden to become rock. Limestone is:

an igneous rock   a sedimentary rock   a metamorphic rock

Marble is limestone that was heated and put under pressure. It is:

an igneous rock   a sedimentary rock   a metamorphic rock

Pumice is a lightweight rock ejected from volcanoes. It is:

an igneous rock   a sedimentary rock   a metamorphic rock

Sandstone forms when layers of sand harden over time to form rock. Sandstone is:

an igneous rock   a sedimentary rock   a metamorphic rock

Consider the Alternative

Match the descriptions of **alternative energy sources** to the correct illustrations.

Hydroelectric power comes from river water flowing through large dams. It supplies 16 percent of the world's energy.

Nuclear energy comes from splitting an atom at a nuclear power plant. Nuclear power supplies 8 percent of electricity in the United States.

BRAIN BOX

Fossil fuels are fuels created by ancient plants and animals. They include oil, gasoline, coal, and natural gas. When burned, they produce **energy**. However, these fuels release dangerous levels of carbon dioxide into the air. **Alternative energy sources** like wind and solar energy do not release carbon dioxide into the air.

Wind currently produces less than 3 percent of electricity in the United States. Wind power is produced by turbines, which look like giant fans.

Solar energy is captured by solar panels. In Hawai'i, more than 17 percent of the state's electricity comes from solar power.

Biofuels are an alternative to gasoline. They are made from recently living things such as switchgrass or algae.

Landforms

Read about the forces that create **landforms**.

Erosion is the wearing away of land by wind, water, or ice. Deposition is the flip side of erosion. Sediment that is scraped off the land by wind, water, or ice is then deposited somewhere else, building up the land in that location.

Plate tectonics refer to the movements of the Earth's lithosphere. The lithosphere is made up of large plates of rock, which fit together like puzzle pieces. These plates float on the semi-magma asthenosphere beneath the lithosphere. The plates can crash into each other, forming mountains, or pull away from each other, causing the land to spread out. These effects occur over very long periods of time.

A rise in sea level can swallow areas of land, leaving islands or peninsulas. A drop in sea level can expose land, causing an island to become part of another land mass.

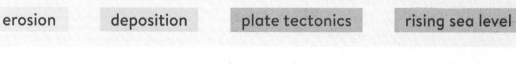

Circle the force that created each landform.

During the last ice age, glaciers extended into what is now the northern United States. They cut deep valleys through the land. When the glaciers melted, the water filled these valleys and formed the Great Lakes.

erosion   deposition   plate tectonics   rising sea level

Because ice-age glaciers eroded the land, they contained a great deal of sediment, pebbles, and even large boulders. When the glaciers melted, they released the sediment and rocks. In many places, boulders now stand alone in otherwise empty fields. These are called glacial erratics.

erosion   deposition   plate tectonics   rising sea level

During the last ice age, England and Ireland were part of mainland Europe. As the glaciers melted, sea levels rose worldwide, inundating some of the land so that Ireland and England became islands.

erosion   deposition   plate tectonics   rising sea level

250 million years ago, the continents were in a different place. Africa collided with North America. This squeezed the land, causing it to rise up and form the Appalachian Mountains.

erosion   deposition   plate tectonics   rising sea level

BRAIN BOX

A **landform** is any naturally occurring feature on land. Mountains, valleys, canyons, peninsulas, and sand dunes are all landforms. Landforms can be caused by many factors, including **erosion**, the wearing away of land, and **deposition**, the building up of sediment.

Chemistry Lab

Use the definitions to fill in the blanks below.

atom the smallest particle of an element that can exist while still being that element. Everything that is a solid, a liquid, or a gas is made up of atoms.

atomic number the number of protons in an atom's nucleus. An element always has the same atomic number.

element a chemical substance made up of one type of atom.

molecule two or more atoms bonded together.

compound a chemical substance made from two or more elements, chemically bonded in a set ratio. For instance, water (H_2O) has two hydrogen atoms for every one oxygen atom. Compounds can only be separated by chemical methods.

bond the attraction between atoms that results in two or more elements forming a compound.

mixture two or more elements or compounds mixed but not chemically bonded together. They can be separated by physical methods, such as occurs when large particles are filtered out.

BRAIN BOX

Chemistry is the study of the **elements** and **compounds** that make up all things. Chemists explore how elements and compounds react to one another and to chemical changes, such as heating.

Calcium has twenty protons in its nucleus. Its _____ is 20.

Josie performed an experiment on muddy lake water. She attached a coffee filter to a jar and poured the lake water over the filter. The filter caught some of the mud so that the water in the jar was clearer than the water in the bucket. This means that the muddy water was a _____, not a compound.

Sodium and chlorine form a _____ and thereby become the compound sodium chloride, or salt.

Gold exists as an _____ in nature. It is made up of one type of atom and not bonded to another substance.

Carbon dioxide is a _____ that has a ratio of one carbon _____ for every two oxygen atoms.

Light

Read about **light**. Then circle true or false.

What Is Light?

Light is a form of energy. It moves in waves that have different wavelengths. The different wavelengths are what give things their color. Substances absorb some wavelengths of light and reflect others. We see the wavelengths that are reflected. For instance, plants are green because their chlorophyll absorbs blue and red wavelengths and reflects green wavelengths.

Light is composed of a stream of particles called photons. Light travels in a straight line until it strikes an object. At that point, the object reflects the light. Light can be seen at its source and also where it is reflected from something. For instance, the sun can be seen (though it shouldn't be viewed directly) because it is a source of light. The moon can be seen because it reflects sunlight. Everything on Earth can be seen by day, because everything reflects sunlight. In pitch darkness, on the other hand, nothing can be seen because light is not being reflected.

Objects that are transparent, such as glass, allow light to pass through. Light can also be bent. This is called refraction. It happens when light passes from one substance to another, such as from air to water. This is why if you stand over water and see a fish, it appears to be a few inches away from where it really is. The light that you see reflecting off the fish is bent.

The colors that we see are the wavelengths that have been absorbed by objects.　　TRUE　　FALSE

The moon can be seen because it is a source of light.　　TRUE　　FALSE

In pitch darkness, objects cannot be seen because they are not reflecting light.　　TRUE　　FALSE

If something is transparent, it allows no light to pass through.　　TRUE　　FALSE

Refraction is when light is bent as it passes from one substance to another.　　TRUE　　FALSE

Investigate, Learn . . . Repeat!

Read about an investigation and answer the questions.

What do you do if you're curious about something? You investigate! One focus of science, technology, engineering, and math (STEM) is to identify problems and find solutions for them.

Follow these steps to determine which of two paper airplane types flies the farthest:

1 **Plan an investigation that produces data and evidence.**
Use two sheets of the same kind of paper and follow the directions below to make Plane 1 and Plane 2. The paper is the controlled variable because it is the same for both planes. The airplane designs are the independent variables, because they are what changes.

2 **Plan what methods and tools you will use to collect this data.**
Decide where and how to conduct your investigation. Will you test your designs inside or outside? What tool will you use to measure distance flown?

location: _____

measurement tool:_____

measurement unit:_____

3 **Conduct your investigation.**
Fly each type of design three times under the same conditions. Record the distances on the top of the next page.

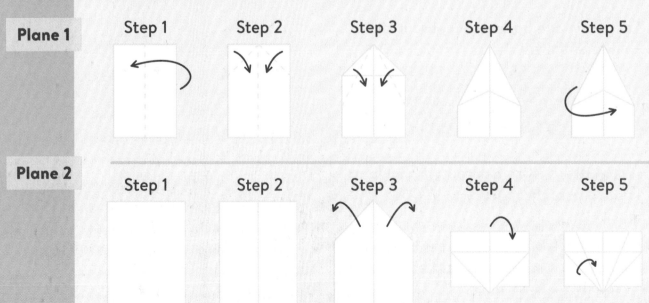

Plane 1 — Step 1, Step 2, Step 3, Step 4, Step 5

Plane 2 — Step 1, Step 2, Step 3, Step 4, Step 5

	Flight 1	Flight 2	Flight 3
Plane 1			
Plane 2			

4 **Make observations and/or measurements, and record your data.**
What did you learn from your initial investigation?
Does one airplane design consistently fly farther
than the other? Record your analysis here:

_____

_____

_____

Investigation

5 **Make predictions about what might happen if you were to change one of your variables.**
What would happen if you used a heavier paper to make the planes?
What if you flew the planes outside instead of inside? Record your
predictions:

_____

_____

_____

6 **Decide on next steps.**
Do you want to change one variable and run the investigation
again? Do you want to try a third airplane design? Write your next
steps:

_____

_____

_____

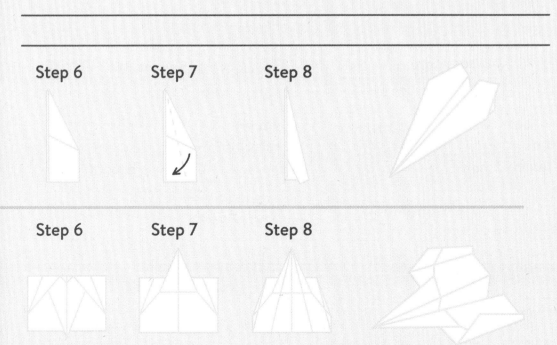

Step 6   Step 7   Step 8

Step 6   Step 7   Step 8

BRAIN BOX

When you carry out an **investigation**, you conduct an experiment to answer a question. A **variable** is something in your experiment you can control to test your question. You make a **prediction** about what might happen if you change your variable. **Evidence** is data that either proves or disproves your prediction.

Science Crossword

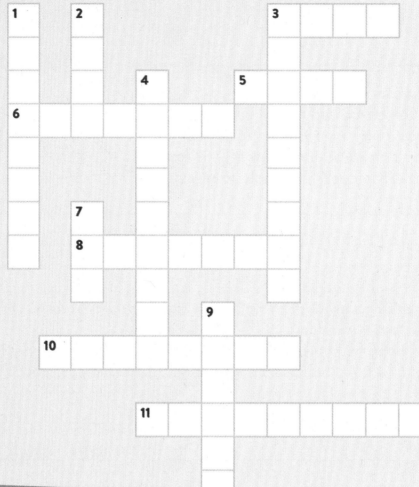

Across

3. The _____ is the building block of all living things.

5. The _____ is the smallest unit of an element.

6. A(n) _____ is a substance that always has the same atomic number.

8. The central part of a cell or an atom is called a(n) _____ . It holds the cell's genetic material.

10. A(n) _____ is a naturally occurring feature of land.

11. Each color of light has its own _____ . Substances absorb or reflect them.

Down

1. A(n) _____ is two or more atoms bonded together.

2. The innermost layer of Earth is the _____ .

3. _____ is located between the nucleus and the cell membrane.

4. We see light when it is _____ off objects.

7. _____ is a substance that is shaped like a twisted ladder and is located in a nucleus.

9. In the grasslands, many prey animals have solid _____ to escape predators.

TECHNOLOGY

In computing, it's more than just wires that complete a connection—the programs must also be mistake-free for the computer to understand them. Let's practice finding mistakes and clearing paths to make our systems connect.

PARENTS In this section, your child will practice connecting concepts to one another. They will learn to troubleshoot technology problems in a systematic way and understand how computer commands work together to accomplish a task.

For additional resources, visit www.BrainQuest.com/grade5

Go with the Flow (Chart)

The computer program below changes words spoken into a microphone into text on screen.

The steps in this flowchart are in the wrong order. Put each step in the right order so the flow of information works correctly.

Programming and algorithms

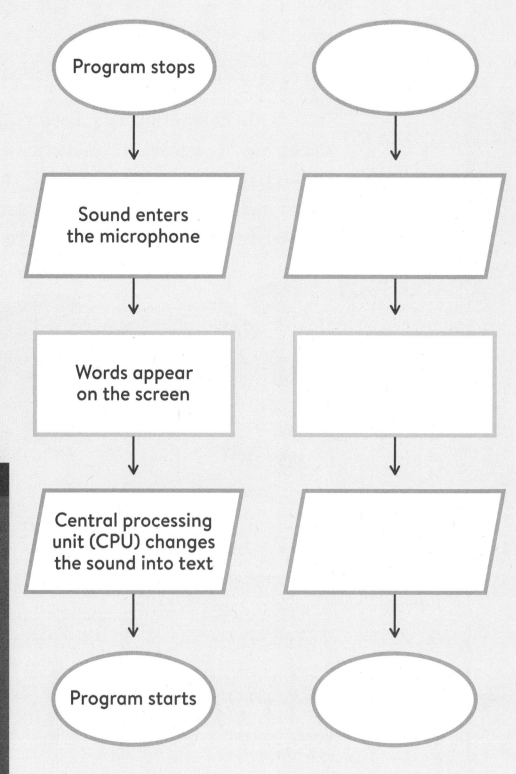

- Program stops
- Sound enters the microphone
- Words appear on the screen
- Central processing unit (CPU) changes the sound into text
- Program starts

BRAIN BOX

Programmers use **flowcharts** to model the flow of information through a computer system.

Each step in a computer program is represented by a brief description of the step inside a shape. Arrows point in the direction of information flow.

The steps of a new math game are listed below. Draw the shape around each step to indicate a start or stop, input, output, and processor.

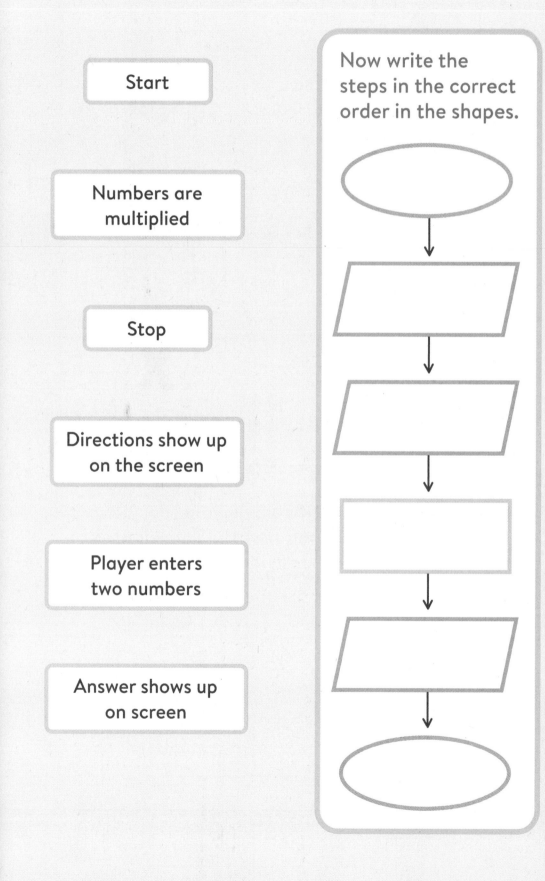

Start

Numbers are multiplied

Stop

Directions show up on the screen

Player enters two numbers

Answer shows up on screen

Now write the steps in the correct order in the shapes.

BRAIN BOX

Fully functioning computer systems have three parts. **Input** is information taken in by the computer. A **processor** takes the input and changes, or processes, it to create **output**—what the user sees or hears.

Flowcharts indicate these parts with different shapes: an **oval** for the start or stop of information flow, a **rectangle** for a processor, and a **parallelogram** for input or output.

Coordinates

Screen Time

Every square in a grid has coordinates. Use the **coordinates** to answer questions about the grids.

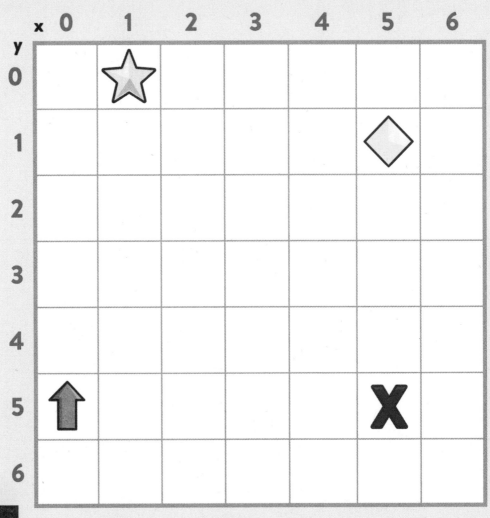

BRAIN BOX

Programmers code the position of graphics and text using the **screen coordinate system.**

These coordinates mimic a computer grid, which always starts at point 0,0 in the top left corner.

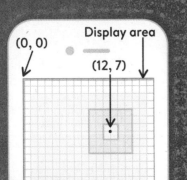

A square can be identified by giving the column number and the row number. The coordinates of the square with the star in it are: (1,0)

Write the coordinates for the other symbols.

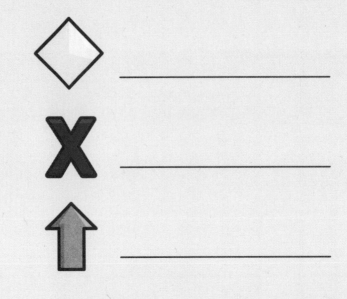

Write the coordinates of the boxes that should be colored in to make each rectangle.

Coordinates

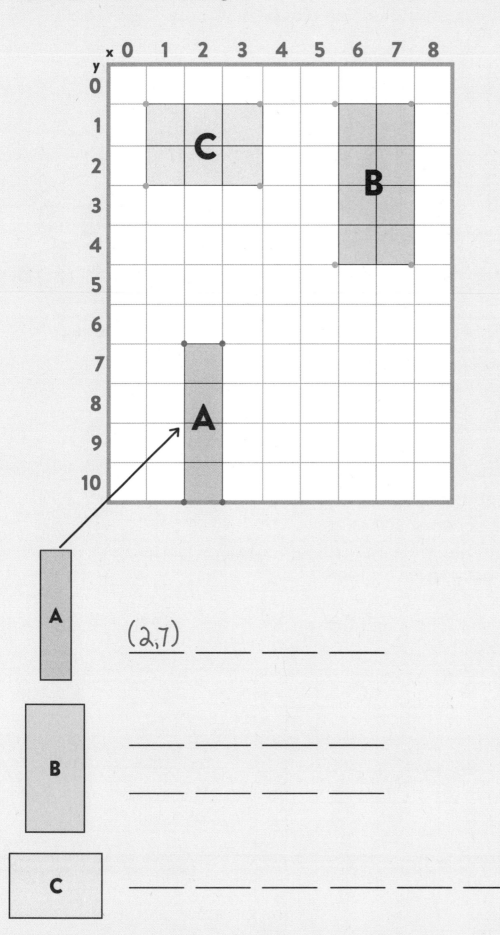

A $(2,7)$ ____ ____ ____

B ____ ____ ____ ____

____ ____ ____ ____

C ____ ____ ____ ____ ____ ____

Brain Quest Grade 5 Workbook

Pixel Party

To get pictures to appear on a computer, the computer reads directions written with numbers. These numbers tell the computer which **pixels** to color in.

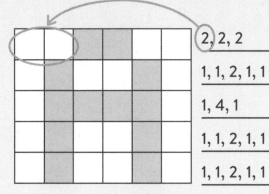

2, 2, 2 ___

1, 1, 2, 1, 1 ___

1, 4, 1 ___

1, 1, 2, 1, 1 ___

1, 1, 2, 1, 1 ___

The pixels create the letter A.

Look at the first row of numbers. The numbers match the shading of the squares: 2 white, 2 shaded, 2 white

QUICK FACT:
The computer will start every line with a white square unless it's told otherwise. If 0 is the first number, there are 0 white squares, and the next value represents the number of shaded squares.

Color the squares using the code. What letter do you see? Remember: the first number represents white squares, so count that many white squares and leave them blank.

1, 3, 1 ___

0, 1, 4 ___

0, 1, 4 ___

0, 1, 4 ___

1, 3, 1 ___

What picture does this make?

2, 4, 2 ___

1, 1, 4, 1, 1 ___

0, 1, 1, 1, 2, 1, 1, 1 ___

0, 1, 6, 1 ___

0, 1, 1, 1, 2, 1, 1, 1 ___

0, 1, 2, 2, 2, 1 ___

1, 1, 4, 1, 1 ___

2, 4, 2 ___

Write the code for the picture in the grid.

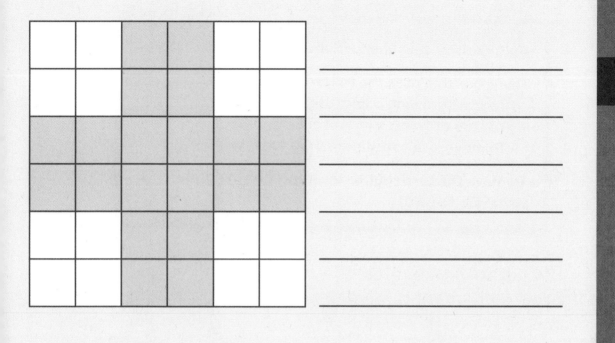

_____

_____

_____

_____

_____

_____

Design your own picture and then write the code.

_____

_____

_____

_____

_____

_____

_____

Ready, Set, Draw

Learn how to tell the turtlebot sprite what to draw!

An algorithm tells the turtlebot which shape to draw.

This algorithm uses the following commands:
- To start drawing a line, use: Start Draw
- To stop drawing a line, use: Stop Draw
- To move, use coordinates: Go to (x, y)

To move the turtlebot to the center of the grid, write: Go to (0,0)

The **algorithm** to make the turtlebot draw a diamond is missing coordinates.

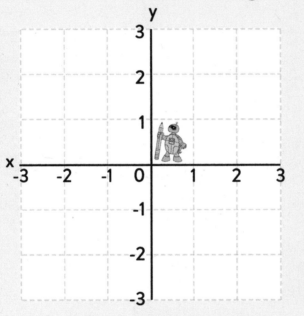

Fill in the missing coordinates, then draw the diamond.

1. Go to (3,0)

2. Start Draw

3. Go to (0,3)

4. Go to (-3,0)

5. Go to _____

6. Go to _____

7. Stop Draw

Write directions to make the turtlebot draw the shapes shown in the grids.

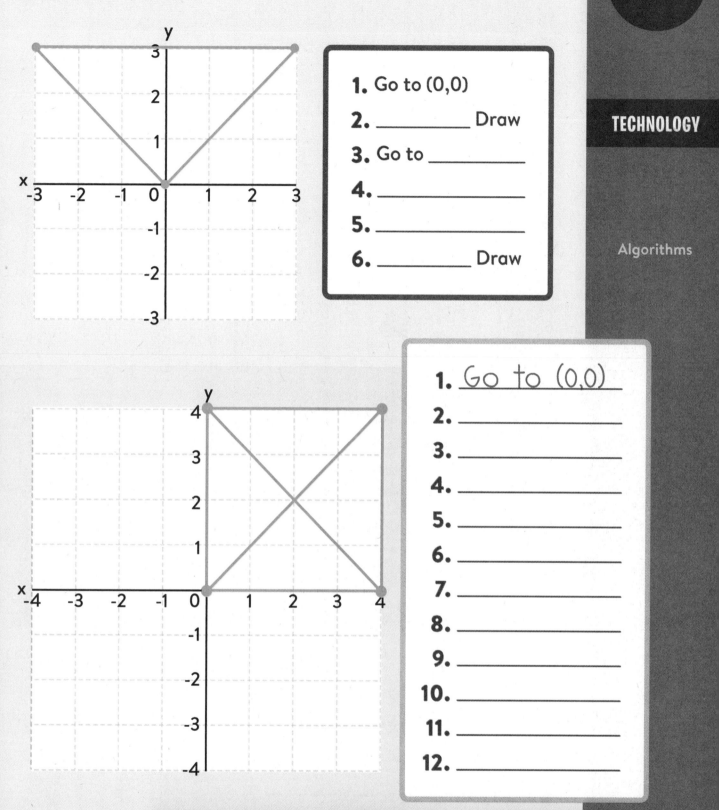

1. Go to (0,0)
2. _____ Draw
3. Go to _____
4. _____
5. _____
6. _____ Draw

Algorithms

1. <u>Go to (0,0)</u>
2. _____
3. _____
4. _____
5. _____
6. _____
7. _____
8. _____
9. _____
10. _____
11. _____
12. _____

BRAIN BOX

Programmers tell a sprite where to go by setting its position using commands. **Setting** the sprite's position assigns it coordinates on a grid so that it appears in a specific place onscreen.

The x coordinate goes first and makes the sprite move left and right. The y coordinate goes second and makes the sprite move up and down.

Debugging

No More Bugs!

The algorithm below should make the claw go to the ladybug, drop down on to the ladybug, come back up, and move to the star. But it's not working!

Draw the path on the grid using the commands.

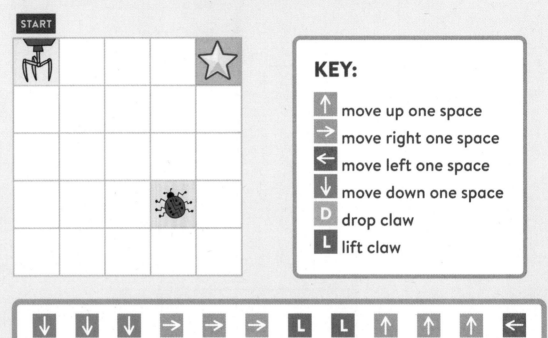

KEY:

↑ move up one space
→ move right one space
← move left one space
↓ move down one space
D drop claw
L lift claw

↓ ↓ ↓ → → → L L ↑ ↑ ↑ ←

Debug the algorithm by finding the mistakes and fixing them. Rewrite the code on the lines below.

1. move down one space
2. _____
3. _____
4. _____
5. _____
6. _____
7. _____
8. _____
9. _____
10. _____
11. _____
12. _____

BRAIN BOX

Debugging is the process of finding and fixing mistakes when writing code. When debugging it's important to take a systematic approach—to go step by step—until you find the error.

Programmers use loops to make the computer repeat a command more than once. Follow the directions in the algorithm to draw the path on the grid. Find and circle the bugs.

| → loop 3 times | ↓ | D | L | ↓ loop 3 times | → |

START

Rewrite the algorithm correctly so that the claw picks up the ladybug, then moves to the star.

1.

4.

2.

5.

3.

6.

Accessibility

Make It Accessible

Everyone should be able to use technology, but sometimes hardware or software does not work for all. In each example, circle which program would help the user solve their problem.

Satsuki, who speaks only Japanese, would like to send an email to Mateo, who speaks both English and Spanish. What could Satsuki use to help her communicate with Mateo?

A A program that translates text in one language to another

B A program that can read Japanese words out loud

Justine is reading directions for an online science experiment. Even though she is wearing glasses, the text is too small for her to see it clearly. Which program would be better to use?

A A program that can read text out loud

B A program that will do the science experiment for her

BRAIN BOX

When technology is **accessible**, people with different levels of learning, ability, and experience can use it.

Max's aunt is driving him to the museum. She would like to use the GPS on her phone to get directions and still drive the car safely. Which program would be better to use?

A A program that adds captions to the screen

B A program that can respond to the user's voice

To Use or Not to Use

Read the sentences below. Match what each person should do in order to **cite** the source. Not all answers will be used. Some answers may be used more than once.

Include the title and author of the book	Include quotation marks around a direct quote
Include a summary of the content in the video	Include the name of the person who took the video, and the date it was taken
No citation is needed	
Include the source of the picture and its photographer	Include the title and the artist of the song

Attribution and citing sources

Ari uses video clips from the news as part of a presentation to their class.

_____

_____

_____

Tarique searches for photos from NASA.gov to use in a report about space.

_____

_____

_____

BRAIN BOX

The internet is full of information. If this information is reused, in a school report, for example, it's important to **cite** the source so others understand where the information came from.

A student changes the lyrics to a pop song and uses the song in a presentation.

_____

_____

_____

Translation Tools

ASCII assigns each letter of the alphabet its own code. Computers use the code to display the matching letter.

ASCII ALPHABET

A	1000001	N	1001110
B	1000010	O	1001111
C	1000011	P	1010000
D	1000100	Q	1010001
E	1000101	R	1010010
F	1000110	S	1010011
G	1000111	T	1010100
H	1001000	U	1010101
I	1001001	V	1010110
J	1001010	W	1010111
K	1001011	X	1011000
L	1001100	Y	1011001
M	1001101	Z	1011010

BRAIN BOX

Some computers use code that's called American Standard Code for Information Interchange, or ASCII. It's a binary code made of two different symbols: 0 and 1.

Can you translate the words using the ASCII alphabet key?

1000010   1010010   1000001   1001001   1001110

_____

1010001   1010101   1000101   1010011   1010100

_____

ANSWER KEY

Some problems have only one answer. Some problems have many answers. Turn the page to check your work.

SPELLING and VOCABULARY

pg. 8

com, combine
ob, oblong
sub, submerge
sub, subheading
com, companion
ob, obnoxious
com, comrade
ob, obstruct
sub, subway
sub, subplot

pg. 9

inadequate: unacceptable
disadvantage: a situation that puts one behind others
inaccurate: incorrect or inexact
untimely: happening at an inconvenient time

pg. 10

adaptable
breakable
comfortable
desirable
distinguishable
inflatable
lovable
notable
believable
Four words ending in able:
adorable
bearable
memorable
preferable
(Answers may vary.)

pg. 11

Hey, Charlie,
I just heard the horrable news that your cupcakes were stolen. That's terrable! I hope there is tangable evidence pointing to whoever is responsable! I always felt comfortable leaving my food unattended, but not after this unbearible event. I guess none of us is invincable. We are all susceptable to thievery. The sad thing is: The cupcakes probably had incredable frosting.

Sincerely,
Your lovible dog, Junior

P.S. Please excuse the crumbs.

horrible, terrible, tangible,
responsible, comfortable,
unbearable, invincible, susceptible,
incredible, lovable

pg. 12

collision
nation
duration
division
persuasion
editions
addition
revision
decision
ambition

pg. 13

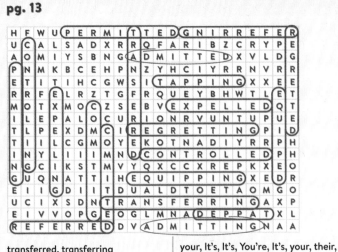

transferred, transferring
controlled, controlling
equipped, equipping
permitted, permitting

referred, referring
expelled, expelling
regretted, regretting
tapped, tapping
committed, committing

pg. 14

interesting, no
forgetting, yes
appearing, no
treating, no
stopping, yes
acting, no
explaining, no
exiting, no
beginning, yes
editing, no

pg. 15

signaled
criticized
criminal
electricity
financial
authenticity
residential
publicity
circumstantial
influential

pg. 16

āt
it
it
āt
it

Both
Meaning
Meaning
Both
Both

pg. 17

batter; bank; novel; bluff; cobbler;
loom; hail; crane; patient; peer

pg. 18

I love you're hat! Its so cute!
I didn't know you went to Silver Beach this summer! Its my favorite place!
Your so photogenic!
Did you ever get ice cream at Mimi's? Its across the street from the beach.
Where did you're family buy they're great sunglasses?
My cousins live in that town. We stayed at they're house last year.
Kaitlyn, I played beach volleyball with you're cousins. Their cool.
Let's all meet up next summer if your around when I am.

your, It's, It's, You're, It's, your, their, their, your, They're, you're

pg. 19

(Answers will vary.)
Although
In addition
For instance
Similarly
However
Moreover
Therefore

pg. 21

perilous: risky
throng: a large crowd
surged: moved powerfully
lofty: tall
dazzled: amazed by
fulfilled: achieved
assert: to demand acceptance of
scarcely: barely
satisfactory: acceptable
tamely: without force or power

pg. 23

tele   geology
meter   claustrophobia
photo   ambivalent
ambi
amphi
aero
anti
audi
logy, astro
phobia

pg. 25

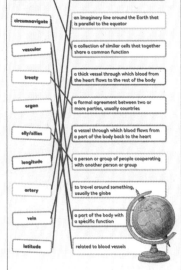

tissue — a collection of similar cells that together share a common function
circumnavigate — to travel around something, usually the globe
vascular — related to blood vessels
treaty — a formal agreement between two or more parties, usually countries
organ — a part of the body with a specific function
ally/allies — a person or group of people cooperating with another person or group
longitude — an imaginary line around the Earth that is perpendicular to the equator
artery — a thick vessel through which blood from the heart flows to the rest of the body
vein — a vessel through which blood flows from a part of the body back to the heart
latitude — an imaginary line around the Earth that is parallel to the equator

pg. 27

long a
a noun
Answers will vary: The two sides parleyed in an attempt to make peace.
loot
interjection
stop
Answers will vary: friend, comrade
noun
avast

pg. 28

the whole nine yards
cool as a cucumber
apple of my eye
bee's knees
piece of cake
have a cow
pie in the sky
dressed to the nines
bell the cat
in a pickle

pg. 29

it is a tragedy; h
lit up the room; h
a million; h
like maniacs; s
blind as bats; s
hungry as bears; s
a gift from heaven; m, h
as big as a house; s
time flew by; h
as cute as buttons; s

pg. 31

Practice makes perfect.
A stitch in time saves nine.
Actions speak louder than words.
The early bird gets the worm.
No man is an island.
Rome wasn't built in a day.
If it ain't broke, don't fix it.
You can catch more flies with honey than with vinegar.
Don't look a gift horse in the mouth.
Fortune favors the bold.

pg. 32

LANGUAGE ARTS

pg. 34

above the door
at sundown
under the blanket
outside the strike zone
with the eye patch
toward the shipwreck
along the shore
against a rip current
Behind the mountain
During the Little Ice Age

pg. 35

under the chair; beneath the blanket; beside the plant; behind the curtain; in the cage
Over the river
through the wood
To grandfather's house
Through the white and drifted snow

pg. 36

Wow! Ouch!
Uh-oh! Well
Stop Yikes
Hey Zoinks
Oops! Yum

pg. 37

and unless
or Although
but if
so yet or but
because while

pg. 38

and
but also
or
nor
as
but
or
Neither a borrower nor a lender be.
Either you are with us or you are against us.

pg. 39

will have hiked
has been
has studied
had graduated
have practiced
has watched
will have solved
had suctioned
had entered
have volunteered

pg. 40

pg. 41

The longest River in the world is the nile river.

However, the amazon river is the largest river by volume.

From its base, which is far below sea level, to its summit, mauna kea is the tallest mountain in the world.

Measuring from sea level to summit, Mount Everest is the highest Mountain.

With an average temperature of 93°F, the Danakil Desert in ethiopia is the world's hottest Desert.

The highest temperature on earth—134°F—was recorded in Death Valley, california.

The record was set on july 10, 1913.

Only two us states have never surpassed 100°F: Alaska and hawai'i.

The lowest temperature ever—negative 136°F—was recorded in antarctica.

The coldest town in the world is oymyakon, Russia, where the average temperature is negative 58°F.

pg. 42

pg. 43

Living with Lions

What if your neighbors were lions? That is true for the San people of the Kalahari Desert. The San are hunters and gatherers. They work, play, and eat outside. They also share their land with lions. Usually, the San are able to avoid the lions. Lions generally hunt at night, and the San hunt and gather during the day. The San still sometimes encounter lions by day. In that case, the people calmly walk away from the lions. The lions usually walk away, too.*

At night, lions can be heard roaring, and they sometimes visit the people's camps. The San tell the lions in a stern voice to go away. If the lions do not leave, the people wave flaming branches at the giant cats. This does not hurt the lions, but it scares them off. What about when the San are sleeping? They sleep in shelters made of grass and sticks, so the lions are unable to attack them from behind. This is the lions' preferred method of attack. Therefore, the lions tend to leave the San alone even when they are sleeping.

The San are afraid of the lions, and it's easy to see why. A lion can easily kill a person. In some situations, groups of lions have been known to attack people. The lions that live with the San rarely attack. By avoiding the lions by day, confronting them with fire in the evening, and sleeping in shelters at night, the San have managed to stay safe. As for the lions, they have learned not to see people as easy prey. For both the San and the lions, being neighbors is a way of life.

*Note: Use of a comma before and after *too* varies. There are 19 commas including a comma before *too*.

pg. 45

Giana and her friend Rose were taking turns going off the high and low diving boards. Giana did a flip off the low dive after Rose did one off the high dive. Now it was Giana's turn to do a flip off the high dive. But she was scared.

"Let's both jump instead of doing a flip," said Giana. "I'll jump off the high dive, and then you jump off the low."

"Why? Are you scared to do a flip off the high dive?" asked Rose.

"No," said Gianna.

"It's okay if you're scared," said Rose. "I won't make fun of you. I promise."

"Okay," said Giana. "I'm scared."

"What are you afraid of?" asked Rose.

"I'm afraid of doing a belly flop," said Giana.

"How about you jump this time, but while you're in midair, you picture yourself doing a flip," said Rose. "Then maybe you'll be ready to do a flip next time."

Giana jumped off the high dive, closed her eyes, and pictured herself doing a flip.

Rose asked, "So are you ready to do a flip this time?"

"I think so," Giana said.

Giana jumped, flipped, and landed on her belly, but it didn't hurt too much.

Now it was Rose's turn to flip off the high dive. She hesitated. "Now I'm scared I'm going to land on my belly," she said, backing away from the edge.

pg. 46

police officers' coffee
doctors' stethoscopes
pilots' airplanes
ducks' pond

children's ice creams
referees' whistles
babies' bottles
bears' berries
ants' crumbs

pg. 47

Dear Diary, ¶ Today, I went to the Centennial Exposition—the first World's Fair ever to be held in America. And to think, it was held right here in Philadelphia! President Ulysses S. Grant, the emperor of Brazil, and pretty much everybody in Philadelphia were there—not to mention folks who traveled from far and wide. ¶ I can't describe all the exhibits, but I'll tell you the highlights. There was tomato ketchup. Very tasty! I also tasted root beer made with sixteen roots and berries. Not only was it delicious, the poster said it is also good for your blood. I'm feeling healthier already! ¶ Second best to the food and drinks was the telephone. This device allows you to talk to your friend without either of you ever leaving home! It was made by Alexander Graham Bell. ¶ Not everything at the World's Fair was American, of course. The Italian exhibition had statues of men, women, and children. They looked so real! ¶ As for the British, they brought bicycles. These are machines with two wheels—a giant one in front and a tiny one in back. The man demonstrating how they worked sped downhill and appeared to be flying! When the wheel hit a tree root, he really did go flying through the air, over the bicycle, and onto the grass. I wonder if I will ever be so brave as to ride a bike. ¶ As I write, my mind is full of possibilities. I feel like the world must be full of such things as bicycles. I hope to see them all!

pg. 48

(Answers will vary.)

If a rat can squeeze through a hole the size of a quarter, then the rat could have come in through this hole in the floor.

Did you know dolphins gossip? They chat about good places to find food.

Most monarch butterflies live for only eight weeks, but the generation that migrates to Mexico each fall lives eight months.

The bats under the bridge hunt mosquitoes at night.

When ants find crumbs, they notify the other ants in the nest.

pg. 49

(Answers will vary.)

Modern jelly was invented in the Middle Ages, but peanut butter as we know it today wasn't invented until 1895.

At first, peanut butter was served at fancy parties, and it was not served with jelly, but with pimientos or watercress.

Then a businessperson began to sell peanut butter in jars, and it became affordable for families.

In 1928, sliced bread began being sold, and that helped kids make their own sandwiches.

Peanut butter and jelly sandwiches have been popular ever since, but peanut butter also goes with bananas, apples, or bacon on sandwiches.

Many children are allergic to peanuts, so some schools do not allow peanut butter in the lunchroom.

pg. 50

Capitalize proper nouns. Do not capitalize the names of animals. Do not capitalize words like mother when they are not used as proper names.

READING

pg. 52

(Answers may vary.)
Ten-thousand-year-old heart-shaped drawings have been found in caves.
A heart shape appears on an old coin from Cyrene.
The heart from the coin represents the silphium seed.
There are heart-shaped flowers called bleeding hearts.
Greeks and Aztecs believed the heart contained the human soul.

pg. 53

(Answers may vary.)
First Paragraph
Main idea: The Sami live in Norway, Sweden, Finland, and Russia.
Supporting detail: They have their own language, style of clothing, and way of making a living.

Second Paragraph
Main idea: The Sami are reindeer herders.
First supporting detail: They follow their reindeer across the Arctic as the reindeer migrate.
Second supporting detail: They sleep in cone-shaped tents.

Third Paragraph
Main idea: The reindeer are the Sami's livelihood.
First supporting detail: They have traditionally eaten the meat.
Second supporting detail: Today, they sell the reindeer meat.

Fourth Paragraph
Main idea: The way of life is changing for the Sami.
First supporting detail: They must build fences.
Second supporting detail: Many have jobs other than reindeer herding.

pg. 54

Montana, Wyoming, Colorado, New Mexico, North Dakota, South Dakota, Nebraska, Kansas, Oklahoma, Texas, Minnesota, Iowa, Missouri, Arkansas, and Louisiana
the Mississippi River
the eastern half
the Gulf of Mexico
No

pg. 55

increase
17,063,353
66,573,715
1900
The data through 1860 does not include captive Africans who were forcibly taken to the US.

pg. 56

apps
9%
11%
purple
60%

pg. 57

False, coal forms from trees and other woody plants
True
True
False, coal is formed by swamp plants
False, the decomposing plants first become peat
False, it takes millions of years

pg. 59

August 27–29, 1776
France promised financial support to the US war effort.
"Give me liberty or give me death!"
April 19, 1775
December 25–26, 1776 and February 27, 1782
financially
1,400
the British
September 3, 1783
nearly one year

pg. 60

$20,000
the Green Team
through a recycling drive and business sponsorships
It is going to save the school money and teach the students about renewable energy.
(Answers may vary.)
"We thought the biggest impact our club could have would be to help our school switch to clean energy."
Magda Kita

pg. 61

four
Step 4 because onions are optional
one
a knife, a cutting board or plate, a bowl, a mixing spoon or a fork
mash
squeeze

pg. 63

A. machine base 1; B. motor 2; C. shaver 3; D. shaver lid 4; E. bowl 5

pg. 64

(Answers may vary.)
Opinion: The school needs to turn off lights and electronic devices at night.
Supporting Evidence:
Lights and other electronic devices are seen to be left on overnight.
Wasting energy wastes money.
The Seattle School District saved money by turning off beverage machine lights at night.
If all American workers turned off their computers at night, they would save $2.8 billion dollars altogether.

pg. 65

fact
fact
opinion
fact
fact
fact
fact
fact
opinion
opinion

pgs. 66–67

chronological order
comparing and contrasting
chronological order
comparing and contrasting

pg. 69

79 CE
They did not know the mountain was an active volcano.
through Pliny's letters
He was afraid he and his companions would be trampled by the crowd.

Those who fled Herculaneum and Pompeii right away survived.
The surges of gases and ash were the deadliest effect of the volcano.
The people were terrified to see their town buried in ashes.
Pliny's letters would survive for thousands of years.
Men and women were shrieking and yelling.
There was a risk of being trampled as people fled.
A dark cloud spread over the land.

In some places, the temperature during the eruption reached 570°F.

pg. 71

(Answers may vary.)
Over the years, explorers have found connections to other cave systems in the area.
Mammoth Cave was created by the erosion of limestone by water.
Animal species in Mammoth Cave have adapted over time to live in the dark, subterranean (below ground) environment.
About 130 species of animals make their homes in the caves.
Tours of varying lengths, distances, and level of difficulty are available.
Visitors can also fish, hike, camp, and go canoeing in the national park.

pg. 72

(Answers may vary.)
The river was wide and muddy.
The jungle was gloomy and dense.
The trees grew close to each other, and high ferns with sticky leaves grew between them.
The father ate three tangerines.
He put on his rubber boots.
The swamp was as deep as his boot tops.
He got stuck in the oozy, mucky mud.
He unpacked his compass and figured out the direction he should walk.
The sticky leaves of the ferns caught the father's hair, and he kept tripping over roots and rotten logs.
He tried to run, but he tripped over more roots.

pg. 73

C
A

pg. 75

close
loving
hard-working
considerate
appreciative
joyful

(Answers may vary.)
The noise woke up his sister Kate.
He wanted to wish his sister a happy birthday.
They joked and laughed together.
They have never owned beds.
They did not eat food from fancy restaurants.
understanding
happy

pg. 77

Pea wants to be left in its pod.
The prince wants to find a real princess.
It's told from the point of view of the pea.
Pea thinks the queen should write a letter to the princess's kingdom to see if she is really a princess.
She thinks, "Let's drag Pea into this mess and make its life miserable!"
Pea says that it slept terribly, and the queen thinks that the princess has said it.

pgs. 78–79

mystery; science fiction; fantasy; historical fiction; realistic fiction

pgs. 80–81

actions
words
actions

both
actions
regretful

actions
bothered; actions

words
helped
"I'm sorry for pushing you"

pg. 82

A
C
B
B

pg. 83

noon
bees
November
alliteration

pg. 84

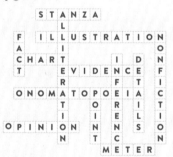

WRITING

pg. 86

persuades
entertains
informs
informs
connects to the human experience

pg. 87

plan
brainstorm
write
research
revise
proofread

pg. 102

The Nazca peoples
The Nazca Lines
southern Peru
around 200 BCE to 600 CE
We don't know. The lines might depict constellations, or be part of a ritual to ask for rain.

pg. 111

Narwhals are the most interesting animals on Earth.

(Answers may vary.)
Males usually have a giant tooth that grows through their upper lip. This tooth can grow up to ten feet long.
Narwhals can live up to fifty years.
Narwhals change color as they get older.

pg. 113

R
U
R
U
R
R

pg. 114

Related:
- Black holes are areas in space where a large amount of matter is compressed into a small area.
- The gravitational field around a black hole is so strong that not even light can get out.
- Like most galaxies, the Milky Way has a supermassive black hole at its center.
- NASA uses tools like telescopes and satellites to gather information about black holes.

Unrelated:
- Neptune is the planet in our solar system with the fastest winds.
- Gravity on Mars is about one-third as strong as gravity on Earth.
- The average surface temperature on Venus is about 900 degrees Fahrenheit.

pg. 119

The hive:
Honeybees live in a hive.
Hives are usually in hollow trees.
Eighty thousand bees can live in a hive.

Workers, queens, and drones:
Female bees known as workers find food, build the hive, clean, care for the baby bees, and make honey.
The queen's only job is to lay eggs.
Drones (male bees) mate with the queen.

How and why bees make honey:
Bees drink nectar from flowers.
Back in the hive, the bees regurgitate the nectar into the honeycomb.
The water in the nectar evaporates. Honey is left behind.
Bees eat honey in the winter when there are no flowers.

Bee stings:
Bees sting to defend themselves or the hive.
Their stingers are barbed.
The stinger is attached to a venom sac inside the bee.
When the bee stings someone, the venom sac detaches from the bee and kills the bee.
The sting hurts because of the venom.

pg. 120

Capybaras

Capybaras are the world's largest Rodents. They live in the rain forests and savannas of central america and south america. Weighing 75 to 100 pounds, they are the size of a large dog. The giant rodents are ~~are~~ semiaquatic. They cool off in the water, graze on aquatic plants, and also use water for protection. predators capybara include jaguars, anacondas, and caimans. If a predator threatens a, it dives underwater. A capybara can hold its breath underwater for 5 minutes!

Capybaras live in groups of 3 to 30. Together, they their defend territory. Capybaras communicate through scent and sound. They bark to warn each other of trouble. A male's scent indicates his social status and whether ~~whether~~ he is ready to mate.

The closest relatives to capybaras are guinea pigs. Like guinea pigs, capybaras are easily domesticated. In some places, they are now raised on ranches. Some people even keep them as pets.

MATH SKILLS

pg. 122

3,275
999,999,999,999
77,777
500,223
33,000
800,400,200
45,453,892
703
922,003
202,000,002

703
3,275
33,000
77,777
500,223
922,003
45,453,892
202,000,002
800,400,200
999,999,999,999

pg. 123

⑧,432	thousands
46⑧	ones
⑤85	tens
8③2	hundreds
1,2⑦8	ones
4⑧9	tens
⑧73,322	hundred thousands
5,⑧10	hundreds
⑧0,100	ten thousands

Answers will vary: 38; 86; 813; 8,452; 85,603; 845,317

pg. 124

1,246 = 1,000 + 200 + 40 + 6
2,357 = 2,000 + 300 + 50 + 7
3,467 = 3,000 + 400 + 60 + 7
4,578 = 4,000 + 500 + 70 + 8
5,689 = 5,000 + 600 + 80 + 9
6,790 = 6,000 + 700 + 90 + 0
4,219 = 4,000 + 200 + 10 + 9
3,652 = 3,000 + 600 + 50 + 2
5,342 = 5,000 + 300 + 40 + 2
9,243 = 9,000 + 200 + 40 + 3

91,837
46,546
74,359
88,201
29,812
32,784
23,195

pg. 125

10
1,000
100,000
1,000
10
10
100

pg. 126

100
10,000
10
100
1,000
100
10
1,000

pg. 127

pg. 128

20
② ⑩
② ⑤
$2 \cdot 2 \cdot 5 = 20$

32
② ⑯
② ⑧
② ④
② ②
$2 \cdot 2 \cdot 2 \cdot 2 \cdot 2 = 32$

27
⑨ ③
③ ③
$3 \cdot 3 \cdot 3 = 27$

MULTIPLICATION AND DIVISION

pg. 130

5 + 5 + 5 + 5 = 20
4 × 5 = 20

8 + 8 + 8 = 24
3 × 8 = 24

3 + 3 + 3 + 3 = 12
4 × 3 = 12

6 + 6 + 6 = 18
3 × 6 = 18

pg. 131

1 × 12 = 12
2 × 6 = 12
3 × 4 = 12

1 × 14 = 14
2 × 7 = 14

1 × 15 = 15
3 × 5 = 15

1 × 16 = 16
2 × 8 = 16
4 × 4 = 16

1 × 18 = 18
2 × 9 = 18
3 × 6 = 18

pgs. 132–133

6 × 6 = 36
6 × 12 = 72
3 × 7 = 21
4 × 6 = 24
6 × 6 = 36
8 × 9 = 72
4 × 9 = 36
8 × 3 = 24

pg. 134

774	3,492	7,326
294	4,851	1,872
1,476	5,608	2,776
		2,395

pg. 135

315	2,508	2,451
1,240	5,103	7,328
3,612	5,747	3,714
4,640		

pgs. 136–137

56,700	22,344
22,776	13,230
	24,318
72,890	20,608
26,077	52,762
9,750	

pgs. 138–139

17,081	36,288
9,215	31,832
81,432	36,801
34,047	23,958
57,218	42,054

pg. 140

Divide 20 basketball players into 4 teams of 5.

$20 \div 4 = 5$

Divide 9 lacrosse players into 3 teams of 3.

$9 \div 3 = 3$

Divide 28 gymnasts into 7 teams of 4.

$28 \div 7 = 4$

Divide 24 wrestlers into 6 teams of 4.

$24 \div 6 = 4$

Divide 18 soccer players into 6 teams of 3.

$18 \div 6 = 3$

Divide 32 football players into 4 teams of 8.

$32 \div 4 = 8$

pg. 141

$121 \div 11 = \boxed{11}$
$56 \div 7 = \boxed{8}$
$43 \div 6 = \boxed{7 \text{ R}1}$
$63 \div 9 = \boxed{7}$
$66 \div 8 = \boxed{8 \text{ R}2}$
$81 \div 9 = \boxed{9}$
$49 \div 7 = \boxed{7}$

pgs. 142–143

73 R5
53
91 R2
81 R2
47
247

pgs. 144–145

219
213
28
168
184
212

pg. 146

45 R5	64
87 R2	56
82 R7	26
	251

pg. 147

469	381	
153	147	211
166	132	
108		

pg. 148

$40 \times 40 = 1{,}600$
$40 \times 80 = 3{,}200$
$40 \times 80 = 3{,}200$
$80 \times 30 = 2{,}400$
$90 \times 30 = 2{,}700$
$50 \times 100 = 5{,}000$

$6{,}800 \div 20 = 340$
$8{,}800 \div 40 = 220$

FRACTIONS AND DECIMALS

pg. 150

$\frac{2}{6}$
$\frac{7}{10}$
$\frac{4}{12}$ (or $\frac{1}{3}$)
$\frac{1}{4}$
$\frac{12}{15}$ (or $\frac{4}{5}$)
$\frac{2}{8}$ (or $\frac{1}{4}$)

pg. 151

$\frac{1}{5}$
$\frac{2}{3}$
$\frac{1}{2}$

pg. 152

$\frac{8}{64}$ or $\frac{1}{8}$
$\frac{9}{81}$ or $\frac{1}{9}$
$\frac{4}{36}$ or $\frac{1}{9}$
$\frac{6}{12}$ or $\frac{1}{2}$
$\frac{9}{45}$ or $\frac{1}{5}$
$\frac{6}{24}$ or $\frac{1}{4}$

pg. 153

$9\frac{5}{7}$
$3\frac{1}{3}$
$10\frac{5}{11}$
$7\frac{3}{4}$
$2\frac{1}{11}$
$6\frac{1}{2}$

pg. 154

$\frac{1}{2}$
$1\frac{2}{5}$
$3\frac{3}{7}$
$1\frac{2}{3}$
$1\frac{4}{11}$
$\frac{2}{5}$
$1\frac{5}{7}$
$\frac{1}{3}$

pg. 155

$\frac{1}{3} + \frac{2}{3}$

$\frac{4}{8} - \frac{1}{8}$

$\frac{4}{5} + \frac{3}{5}$

$\frac{3}{4} + \frac{1}{4}$

pg. 156

$\frac{39}{8}$
$\frac{25}{8}$
$\frac{17}{6}$
$\frac{25}{3}$
$\frac{15}{4}$
$\frac{17}{5}$
$\frac{13}{2}$

pg. 157

$\frac{7}{10}$
$\frac{3}{10}$
$\frac{1}{4}$
$\frac{8}{15}$
$\frac{5}{12}$
$\frac{27}{40}$
$\frac{21}{64}$
$\frac{3}{7}$
$\frac{1}{3}$

pg. 158

$\frac{1}{2}$
$\frac{3}{10}$
$\frac{1}{3}$
$\frac{5}{44}$
$\frac{7}{16}$
$\frac{1}{4}$
$\frac{3}{5}$

pg. 159

$\frac{1}{2}$
$\frac{5}{6}$
$1\frac{5}{7}$
$1\frac{1}{5}$
$\frac{15}{28}$
$\frac{9}{10}$
$1\frac{1}{5}$
$\frac{8}{15}$
$1\frac{3}{32}$

pg. 160

$9\frac{3}{5}$
$\frac{1}{6}$
$\frac{1}{32}$
$10\frac{1}{2}$
$\frac{6}{35}$
27
$12\frac{6}{7}$
$\frac{9}{20}$
$3\frac{3}{4}$

pg. 161

$\frac{1}{2} \cdot 5 = \frac{1}{10}$ $\frac{1}{3} \cdot 3 = \frac{1}{9}$

$4 \div \frac{1}{2} = \boxed{8}$

$5 \div \frac{1}{3} = \boxed{15}$

$6 \div \frac{1}{4} = \boxed{24}$

pg. 162

$1\frac{1}{2}$
$\frac{7}{8}$
$\frac{13}{14}$
$\frac{9}{10}$
$1\frac{5}{9}$
$\frac{7}{16}$
$1\frac{1}{4}$
$1\frac{1}{10}$
$1\frac{1}{3}$

pg. 163

   0.11
0.7   0.461
0.57

9/10   63/1000
777/1000   323/1000
17/100

pg. 164

   0.28
0.5   0.58
0.65   0.8
0.12
0.34
0.6

pg. 165

0.1, 0.312, 0.78
0.006, 0.095, 0.856
0.32, 0.5, 0.613
0.18, 0.454, 0.54
0.19, 0.41, 0.62
0.13, 0.37, 0.4
0.014, 0.11, 0.42
0.09, 0.53, 0.867
0.02, 0.29, 0.523

pg. 166

=
<
<
=
>
>
>
>
>

pg. 167

40.731	820.2088	13
146.554	0.8918	15.14
184.26	13.403	
175.98		

pg. 168

\$0.98	$\boxed{\$1.10}$	\$0.42
$\boxed{\$1.50}$	\$0.71	$\boxed{\$1.00}$

pg. 169

0.25912
1.0125
24.624
13.76544
706.32
5,926.272
0.1344
37.83432
1.74
122.4496

pg. 170

	47.19	21 2/3
0.09894	77/96	$1\frac{1}{4}$
9/10	2 1/12	6

GEOMETRY AND MEASUREMENT

pg. 172

centimeters
meters
kilometers
meters
centimeters
kilometers

3
4,000
5
50
500

pg. 173

inches
feet/yards
inches
feet/yards
miles
miles

24	3,520	
4	2	300

pg. 174

100 mL   250 mL
300 mL   450 mL

10 beakers
45,000,000 mL

pg. 175

2 pints
1 quart
2 loaves
4 cups
$\frac{1}{4}$ quart
$\frac{1}{8}$ pint

pg. 176

32
60
54
40
68
5
35

pg. 177

12:15 p.m.
4 hours, 15 minutes
7:15 p.m.
3 hours
30 minutes
8:15 a.m.
7:30 p.m.
10 laps

pg. 180

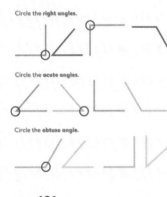

Circle the **right angles**.

Circle the **acute angles**.

Circle the **obtuse angle**.

pg. 181

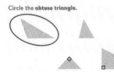

Circle the **acute triangles**.

Circle the **obtuse triangle**.

Circle the **right triangles**.

pg. 182

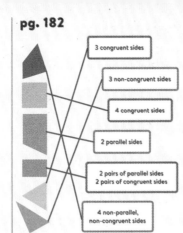

3 congruent sides
3 non-congruent sides
4 congruent sides
2 parallel sides
2 pairs of parallel sides
2 pairs of congruent sides
4 non-parallel, non-congruent sides

pg. 183

True
False
True
False
False
True
False
True
False

pg. 184

20 inches, 25 square inches
44 feet, 120 square feet
32 centimeters, 60 square centimeters
30 kilometers, 50 square kilometers

pg. 185

96 centimeters
330 square feet
137 inches
84 square meters

pg. 186

864 cubic inches
1,728 cubic inches
8 cubic feet
18 cubic feet
128 cubic feet

pg. 187

81
256
625
1,296
2,401
4,096

pg. 188

15.7
21.98
12.56
18.84

pg. 189

25.12
28.26
31.4
34.54

pgs. 190–191

28.26
50.24
78.5

153.86	113.04
200.96	254.34

314

pg. 192

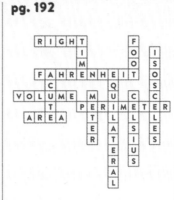

PROBABILITY AND DATA

pg. 195

Chocolate	II	2
Vanilla	IIII	4
Chocolate vanilla swirl	II	2
Lemon	II	2
Peanut butter	I	1
Strawberry	I	1

pg. 197

$150, 9
January, February, March
$1,350, $1,420
April
June, July, and August
April, May, June, July, August, and September
3

pg. 198

0–4	I	1
5–9	IIII	4
10–14	II	2
15–19	0	0

pg. 199

Stem	Leaf
3	2
4	4
8	3, 8
9	2, 5

pg. 201

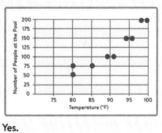

Yes.
The two sets of data are related.

pg. 203

Amount Spent by Customers at the Snack Bar

ALGEBRA

pg. 206

Square 2 and add that to 4.
Subtract 3 from the sum.
Add 4 plus 5. Divide the sum by 3.

3	7
42	83

50

pg. 207

Starting at 0, add 2.
Starting at 0, add 6.
The numbers in the second sequence are 3 times the corresponding numbers in the first.

Starting at 0, add 1.
Starting at 0, add 5.
The numbers in the second sequence are 5 times the corresponding numbers in the first.

Starting at 0, add 1.
Starting at 0, add 4.
The numbers in the second sequence are 4 times the corresponding numbers in the first.

pg. 208

(2,6) (3,9) (4,12) (5,15)

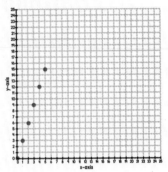

pg. 209

(0,0) (2,6) (4,12) (6,18) (8,24)

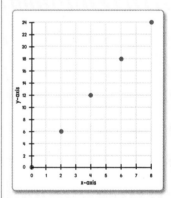

(0,0) (1,4) (2,8) (3,12) (4,16) (5,20)

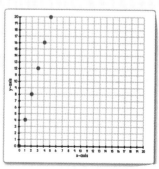

pgs. 210–211

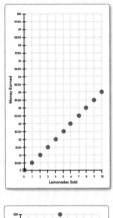

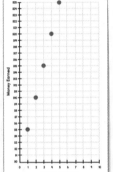

pg. 212

4
2
12
4

40
2
160
4.5

WORD PROBLEMS

pg. 214

53,127,417,506
$63
4,000+600+80+1
2,468
No
Yes
Yes

pg. 215

1, 2
70
$40
10
8
2,3,5,7

pg. 216

8
11
6
30
14

pg. 217

456
127
896
116
344
682

pg. 218

$235
$391
$263
$266
$422

pg. 219

34
68
63
3
67

pg. 220

900
1,800
300
3,500
2,400

pg. 221

$\frac{3}{8}$
$\frac{18}{24}$ or $\frac{3}{4}$
$\frac{2}{6}$ or $\frac{1}{3}$
$\frac{3}{12}$ or $\frac{1}{4}$
$\frac{2}{24}$ or $\frac{1}{12}$
$\frac{3}{72}$ or $\frac{1}{24}$

pg. 222

$\frac{5}{8}$
$\frac{17}{20}$
$\frac{3}{8}$
$\frac{5}{12}$
$\frac{2}{5}$
$\frac{29}{30}$

pg. 223

$\frac{1}{8}$ cup
2 cups
$\frac{2}{6} = \frac{1}{3}$ cup
$\frac{3}{20}$ of the canister
$\frac{1}{16}$ of the bag
$\frac{4}{16}$ or $\frac{1}{4}$ lb.

pg. 224

30.65 mL
5.5 mL
0.85
0.75
$0.82
37.845

pg. 225

432 square inches
80 square feet
56 square feet
36 feet
252 square feet

pg. 226

1,728 cubic centimeters
1.5 kilometers
38°F
31.4 feet
78.5 square feet
2 gallons

SOCIAL STUDIES

pgs. 228–229

pgs. 230–231

pg. 233

Milwaukee
Salt Lake City
Juneau
Wichita
Baton Rouge
Largest city
Sioux Falls
Little Rock

Arizona, Arkansas, Colorado, Georgia, Hawai'i, Idaho, Indiana, Iowa, Massachusetts, Mississippi, Ohio, Oklahoma, Rhode Island, South Carolina, Utah, West Virginia, Wyoming

pgs. 234–235

The Appalachian Mountains
Louisiana
Michigan, Wisconsin, Illinois, and Indiana
Utah
The Gulf of Mexico
Increase

pgs. 236–237

Haudenosaunee (Iriquois)
Apache, Navajo, Pueblo
Great Plains
Seminole
Chinook

pg. 239

1607
create English colonies, exploit the land for natural resources, and search for gold and silver

Any 3: Approximately 14,000 people lived there. There were dozens of groups and villages. All of the groups spoke Algonquin languages. It was home to skilled artisans, farmers, hunters, and warriors. They were ruled by Chief Powhatan.

The water wasn't safe to drink. The marshy land was hard to farm. Mosquitos on the land carried malaria, a deadly disease.

The colonists built on land that belonged to the people of Tsenacomoco, and they stole food, goods, and supplies from nearby villages.

The settler population grew and farms and settlements crowded out Indigenous people. The settler army grew stronger and able to compete with the Tsenacomoco warriors.

pg. 240

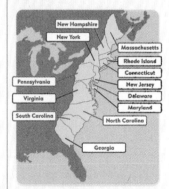

pg. 243

King George III worked alongside Parliament to fight against the colonists.
George Washington commanded the Continental Army.
John Adams was the second US president.
Thomas Jefferson wrote the Declaration of Independence.
Mary Ludwig fought at the Battle of Monmouth.
Abigail Adams questioned Massachusetts residents who remained loyal to the British crown.

pg. 245

Amendment I
Amendment III
Amendment I
Amendment VI
Amendment IV

pg. 247

The United States was destined by God to expand across the entire North American continent.
The United States doubled in size.
The US government could force Indigenous nations east of the Mississippi River off their ancestral land and onto land in the west.
They could make a large profit from buying and selling the land.
Trail of Tears
Muscogee (Creek) and Cherokee

pgs. 248–249

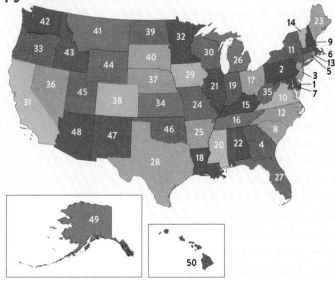

pg. 251

Seceding from the Union means to withdraw from the United States.
South Carolina
South Carolina, Mississippi, Florida, Alabama, Georgia, Louisiana, Texas, Virginia, Arkansas, Tennessee, North Carolina
When Lincoln was elected president, the Southern states feared that he would bring an end to slavery.
He needed troops to fight the Confederate states.
The Confederate States of America
Jefferson Davis
The Union Army cut off supplies from reaching Confederate ports, it defended Washington, DC, and it captured Alexandria, Virginia.

pg. 254

life raft
fire escape
windshield wiper
heating system
plasma
air bag
Kevlar
Super Soaker

pg. 255

legislative
executive
judicial

pg. 256

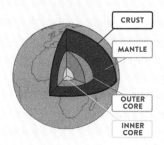

1795
1912
1777

pg. 257

1892: The Pledge of Allegiance was written by Francis J. Bellamy.
1942: Congress changed the salute to the hand-over-heart gesture.
1954: The words "under God" were added after "one nation."

I pledge allegiance to the flag of the United States of America, and to the republic for which it stands, one nation under God, indivisible, with liberty and justice for all.

pg. 261

federal
local
state
local
state
state
federal
federal
local
federal

pg 262

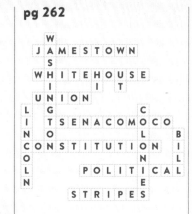

```
        W
  J A M E S T O W N
        S
  W H I T E H O U S E
        I        I T
  U N I O N
L     G            C
I     T S E N A C O M O C O
N     O            L     B
C O N S T I T U T I O N   I
O     O            N      L
L                  P O L I T I C A L
N                  E
      S T R I P E S
```

SCIENCE

pg. 265

Both fish and amphibians have gills.
Animals with fur are mammals.
Animals with feathers are birds.
Animals that feed their young milk are mammals. Mammals also have hair.

pg. 267

Similarities:
Both start out as eggs.
Both are very different as babies and adults.
Both lay several eggs at a time.

Differences:
Frogs lay their eggs in water, and silkworms lay their eggs on land.
Frogs transform from a tadpole to a frog without spinning a cocoon; silkworms spin cocoons.
It takes a frog five years to fully mature; it only takes a silkworm weeks.

pg. 268

Ducks have webbed feet so that they can swim better to catch prey.
Horses have hooves in order to run fast to escape predators.
Eagles have talons so that they can grab and hold on to prey.
Bears have paws so that they can climb trees, dig for food, and grasp prey.

pg. 269

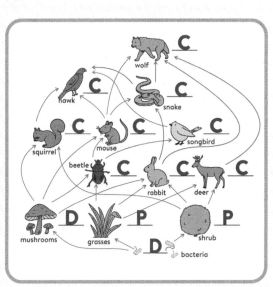

pg. 270

They've developed hooves so that they can quickly run away from predators.
Insects pollinate plants, and decompose dead plants and animals into soil, which feeds the grass.
Grassland grasses have deep roots that store water.
Bison grow a thick coat in winter and shed it in the spring

pg. 271

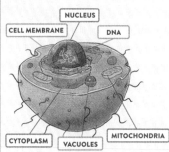

pg. 272

pg. 273

sedimentary
metamorphic
igneous
sedimentary

pg. 274

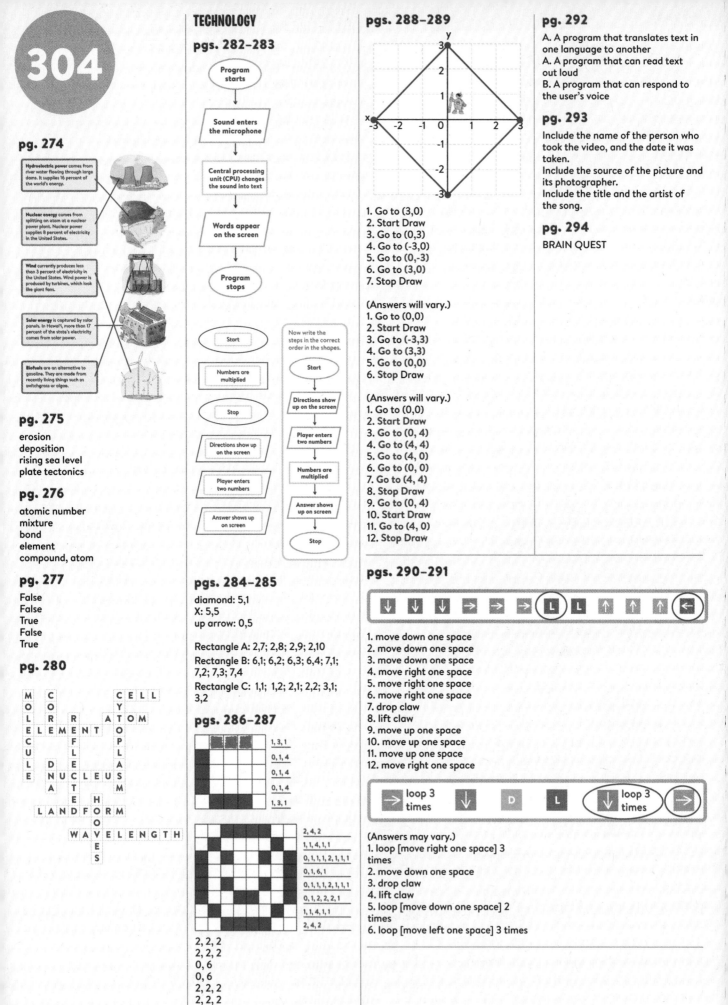

Hydroelectric power comes from river water flowing through large dams. It supplies 16 percent of the world's energy.

Nuclear energy comes from splitting an atom at a nuclear power plant. Nuclear power supplies 8 percent of electricity in the United States.

Wind currently produces less than 3 percent of electricity in the United States. Wind power is produced by turbines, which look like giant fans.

Solar energy is captured by solar panels. In Hawai'i, more than 17 percent of the state's electricity comes from solar power.

Biofuels are an alternative to gasoline. They are made from recently living things such as switchgrass or algae.

pg. 275

erosion
deposition
rising sea level
plate tectonics

pg. 276

atomic number
mixture
bond
element
compound, atom

pg. 277

False
False
True
False
True

pg. 280

Crossword:
MOLECULE
CORR
CELL
CYTOPLASM
ELEMENT · ATOM
RIFLE
D · E
NUCLEUS
A · TE · H
LANDFORM · HOOVES
WAVELENGTH
S

TECHNOLOGY

pgs. 282–283

Program starts
↓
Sound enters the microphone
↓
Central processing unit (CPU) changes the sound into text
↓
Words appear on the screen
↓
Program stops

Start
Numbers are multiplied
Stop
Directions show up on the screen
Player enters two numbers
Answer shows up on screen

Now write the steps in the correct order in the shapes.

Start
↓
Directions show up on the screen
↓
Player enters two numbers
↓
Numbers are multiplied
↓
Answer shows up on screen
↓
Stop

pgs. 284–285

diamond: 5,1
X: 5,5
up arrow: 0,5

Rectangle A: 2,7; 2,8; 2,9; 2,10
Rectangle B: 6,1; 6,2; 6,3; 6,4; 7,1; 7,2; 7,3; 7,4
Rectangle C: 1,1; 1,2; 2,1; 2,2; 3,1; 3,2

pgs. 286–287

1, 3, 1
0, 1, 4
0, 1, 4
0, 1, 4
1, 3, 1

2, 2, 2
2, 2, 2
0, 6
0, 6
2, 2, 2
2, 2, 2

2, 4, 2
1, 1, 4, 1, 1
0, 1, 1, 1, 2, 1, 1, 1
0, 1, 6, 1
0, 1, 1, 1, 2, 1, 1, 1
0, 1, 2, 2, 2, 1
1, 1, 4, 1, 1
2, 4, 2

pgs. 288–289

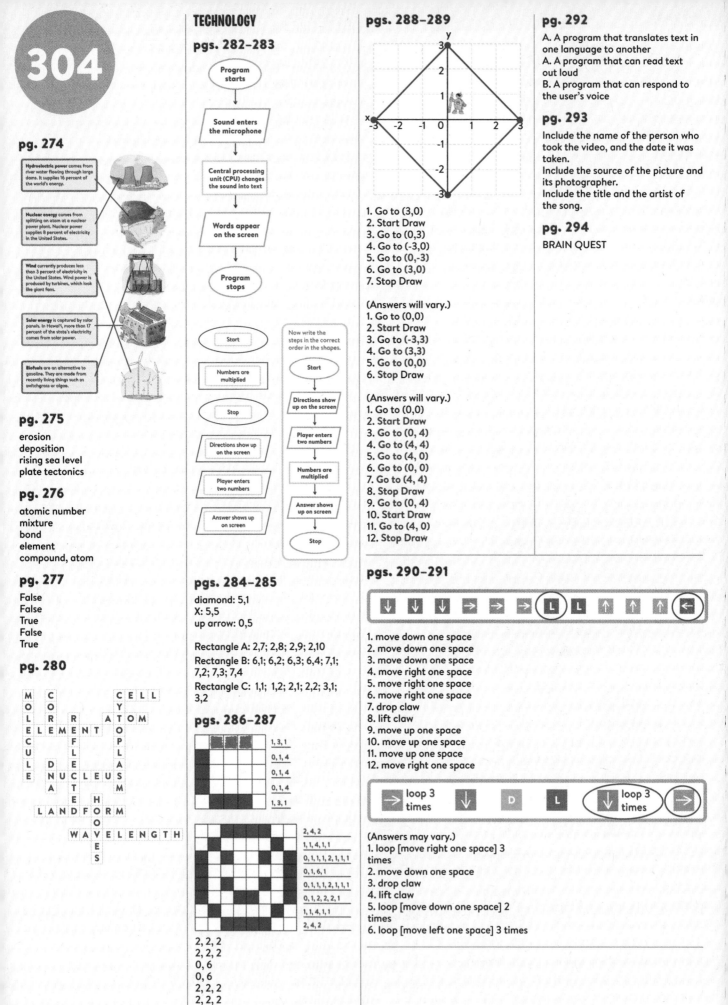

1. Go to (3,0)
2. Start Draw
3. Go to (0,3)
4. Go to (-3,0)
5. Go to (0,-3)
6. Go to (3,0)
7. Stop Draw

(Answers will vary.)
1. Go to (0,0)
2. Start Draw
3. Go to (-3,3)
4. Go to (3,3)
5. Go to (0,0)
6. Stop Draw

(Answers will vary.)
1. Go to (0,0)
2. Start Draw
3. Go to (0, 4)
4. Go to (4, 4)
5. Go to (4, 0)
6. Go to (0, 0)
7. Go to (4, 4)
8. Stop Draw
9. Go to (0, 4)
10. Start Draw
11. Go to (4, 0)
12. Stop Draw

pgs. 290–291

↓ ↓ ↓ → → → (L) L ↑ ↑ ↑ (←)

1. move down one space
2. move down one space
3. move down one space
4. move right one space
5. move right one space
6. move right one space
7. drop claw
8. lift claw
9. move up one space
10. move up one space
11. move up one space
12. move right one space

→ loop 3 times   ↓   D   L   (↓ loop 3 times)   (→)

(Answers may vary.)
1. loop [move right one space] 3 times
2. move down one space
3. drop claw
4. lift claw
5. loop [move down one space] 2 times
6. loop [move left one space] 3 times

pg. 292

A. A program that translates text in one language to another
A. A program that can read text out loud
B. A program that can respond to the user's voice

pg. 293

Include the name of the person who took the video, and the date it was taken.
Include the source of the picture and its photographer.
Include the title and the artist of the song.

pg. 294

BRAIN QUEST

BRAIN QUEST
EXTRAS

You finished the book! Time to make a Brain Quest Mini-Deck so you can play and learn wherever you go. Write your name on your certificate. Great work!

CONGRATULATIONS!

You've finished the Brain Quest Workbook!

All your hard work paid off! Cut out these SMART CARDS to make your own Brain Quest Mini-Deck.

You can play these anywhere— in the back of the car, at the park, or even the grocery store. Remember: It's fun to be smart!

QUESTIONS

ENGLISH
What is the suffix of *partition*?

SOCIAL STUDIES
The "shot heard round the world" started which war?

ENGLISH
What is the correct spelling: r–e–g–r–e–t–t–i–n–g or r–e–g–r–e–t–i–n–g?

MATH
How many equal sides does an isosceles triangle have?

BRAIN QUEST

QUESTIONS

ENGLISH
Does *purchase* mean <u>buy</u> or <u>count</u>?

MATH
What type of angle is greater than 90 degrees?

GEOGRAPHY
How many state names contain the word *new*?

MATH
In 3,565,287, what number is in the thousands place?

BRAIN QUEST

QUESTIONS

ENGLISH
Which part of *unfortunate* is the prefix?

MATH
How many sides does a quadrilateral have?

ENGLISH
Which means the opposite of *include*: e–m–i–t or o–m–i–t?

GEOGRAPHY
What state names start with the letter *I*?

BRAIN QUEST

QUESTIONS

ENGLISH
Which is correct? "Mari paid for <u>their</u>/<u>they're</u> ice cream."

SCIENCE
Mammalogy is the study of what?

GEOGRAPHY
What state has the southernmost tip?

MATH
What does *congruent* mean?

BRAIN QUEST

Brain Quest Mini-Deck

Card 1

ANSWERS

buy
(ENGLISH)

obtuse angle
(MATH)

4 state names (New Hampshire, New Jersey, New Mexico, New York)
(GEOGRAPHY)

5
3,565,287
(MATH)

BRAIN QUEST

Card 2

ANSWERS

-tion
(ENGLISH)

the Revolutionary War
(SOCIAL STUDIES)

r-e-g-r-e-t-t-i-n-g (regretting)
(ENGLISH)

2 equal sides
(MATH)

BRAIN QUEST

Card 3

ANSWERS

"Mari paid for their ice cream."
(ENGLISH)

mammals
(SCIENCE)

Hawai'i
(GEOGRAPHY)

the same size
(MATH)

BRAIN QUEST

Card 4

ANSWERS

un-
(ENGLISH)

4 sides
(MATH)

o-m-i-t (omit)
(ENGLISH)

Idaho, Illinois, Indiana, Iowa
(GEOGRAPHY)

BRAIN QUEST

QUESTIONS

ENGLISH Is *mean as a snake* a simile or a metaphor?

GEOGRAPHY What four states touch at their corners?

ENGLISH What does *the whole enchilada* mean?

MATH How many congruent sides does a rhombus have?

BRAIN QUEST

QUESTIONS

ENGLISH Which word is NOT a preposition: to, outside, is, after?

SCIENCE 4°C is warmer than 32°F. True or false?

ENGLISH What part of speech is "Oh, my!"?

MATH How many pairs of parallel sides does a trapezoid have?

BRAIN QUEST

QUESTIONS

ENGLISH What part of speech is *and*?

GEOGRAPHY What state has the longest ocean coastline?

ENGLISH Which is correct: "J.J. ate a hot dog." or "J.J. ate a Hot Dog."?

MATH Simplify $\frac{6}{15}$.

BRAIN QUEST

QUESTIONS

ENGLISH Which is correct? "Huck Finn rowed down the Mississippi river/River."

MATH The Cub Scouts bought 18 baseball tickets for $11.50 each. How much did they pay in all?

ENGLISH Rainbow sherbet is the most delicious sherbet. Fact or opinion?

MATH What is 56 × 1,000?

BRAIN QUEST

Brain Quest Mini-Deck

ANSWERS

ENGLISH
is

SCIENCE
true (4°C equals 39.2°F.)

ENGLISH
an interjection

MATH
1 pair

BRAIN QUEST

ANSWERS

ENGLISH
a simile

GEOGRAPHY
Arizona, Colorado, New Mexico, Utah

ENGLISH
the whole thing or everything

MATH
4 congruent sides

BRAIN QUEST

ANSWERS

ENGLISH
"Huck Finn rowed down the Mississippi River." (In this sentence *river* is part of a proper noun.)

MATH
$207
(11.50 × 18 = 207)

ENGLISH
opinion

MATH
56,000

BRAIN QUEST

ANSWERS

ENGLISH
a conjunction (A word that connects clauses and/or phrases in a sentence.)

GEOGRAPHY
Alaska

ENGLISH
"J.J. ate a hot dog." (Hot dog is not a proper noun.)

MATH
$\frac{2}{5}$ (Divide the numerator and denominator by 3. 3 is the greatest common multiple of 6 and 15.)

BRAIN QUEST

Brain Quest Mini-Deck

QUESTIONS

SOCIAL STUDIES Is a letter from an 1800s immigrant about Ellis Island an <u>eyewitness</u> or a <u>secondhand</u> account?

MATH Add $\frac{3}{8} + \frac{5}{16}$.

ENGLISH "I dove into the shark-infested water." Is this written in <u>first person</u> or <u>second person</u> point of view?

MATH Which is NOT a prime number: <u>7</u>, <u>17</u>, <u>87</u>?

BRAIN QUEST

QUESTIONS

ENGLISH What does the proofreading mark ¶ mean?

SOCIAL STUDIES In what year did the Revolutionary War begin?

ENGLISH Which is a synonym for *absurd*: <u>ridiculous</u> or <u>admirable</u>?

MATH What is $\frac{5}{8} - \frac{3}{8}$?

BRAIN QUEST

QUESTIONS

ENGLISH Is an *antagonist* an <u>opponent</u> or a <u>friend</u>?

SOCIAL STUDIES In what year did the Civil War begin?

SCIENCE At what temperature Fahrenheit does water boil?

MATH What is $10 \times \frac{1}{2}$?

BRAIN QUEST

QUESTIONS

ENGLISH "She blew out the candle and hid." Is this written in <u>first person</u> or <u>third person</u> point of view?

GEOGRAPHY What divide separates rivers that run into the Pacific Ocean from the Atlantic Ocean?

ENGLISH Does *abolish* mean to <u>end</u> or to <u>vote</u>?

MATH What is $3 \div \frac{1}{3}$?

BRAIN QUEST

Brain Quest Mini-Deck

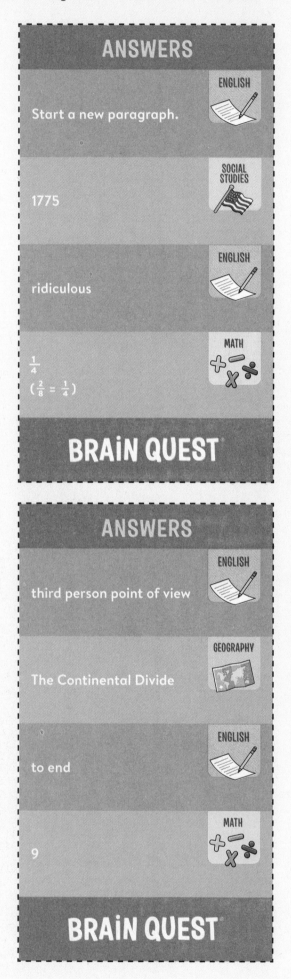

ANSWERS

ENGLISH
Start a new paragraph.

SOCIAL STUDIES
1775

ENGLISH
ridiculous

MATH
$\frac{1}{4}$
($\frac{2}{8} = \frac{1}{4}$)

BRAIN QUEST

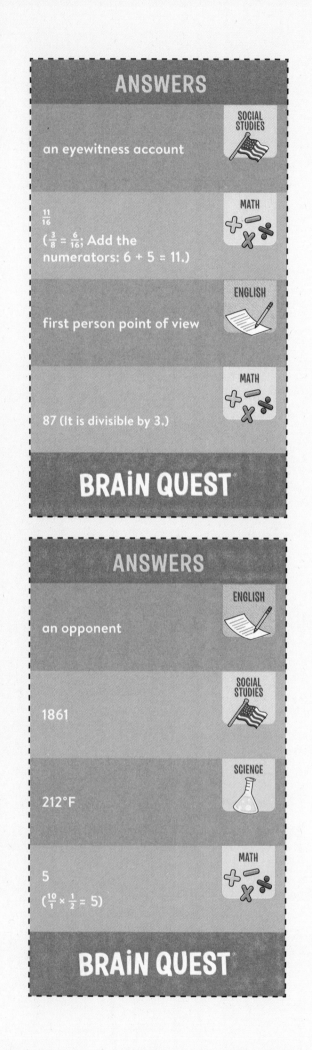

ANSWERS

SOCIAL STUDIES
an eyewitness account

MATH
$\frac{11}{16}$
($\frac{3}{8} = \frac{6}{16}$; Add the numerators: 6 + 5 = 11.)

ENGLISH
first person point of view

MATH
87 (It is divisible by 3.)

BRAIN QUEST

ANSWERS

ENGLISH
third person point of view

GEOGRAPHY
The Continental Divide

ENGLISH
to end

MATH
9

BRAIN QUEST

ANSWERS

ENGLISH
an opponent

SOCIAL STUDIES
1861

SCIENCE
212°F

MATH
5
($\frac{10}{1} \times \frac{1}{2} = 5$)

BRAIN QUEST

QUESTIONS

ENGLISH
Does *anxious* mean <u>worried</u> or <u>excited</u>?

MATH
What is $\frac{5}{7} \times \frac{5}{8}$?

SOCIAL STUDIES
Was the Plymouth Colony founded <u>before</u> or <u>after</u> the Jamestown Colony?

MATH
Simplify $\frac{8}{64}$.

BRAIN QUEST

QUESTIONS

ENGLISH
Which is an antonym for *bland*: <u>flavorful</u> or <u>unfashionable</u>?

MATH
How many cups are in a quart?

SOCIAL STUDIES
Who was the fourth US president?

MATH
Solve by cross canceling: $\frac{1}{2} \times \frac{2}{3} \times \frac{3}{4}$

BRAIN QUEST

QUESTIONS

ENGLISH
Is a concept an <u>idea</u> or an <u>argument</u>?

MATH
Marianna pays $62 per month for internet. How much does she pay in a year?

SOCIAL STUDIES
Which two US presidents had sons who also became presidents?

MATH
What is $\frac{3}{4} \div \frac{5}{8}$?

BRAIN QUEST

QUESTIONS

ENGLISH
Cold is to *frigid* as *hot* is to <u>sweltering</u> or <u>damp</u>.

MATH
If numbers are declining, are they getting <u>smaller</u> or <u>bigger</u>?

SCIENCE
When you eat a sweet potato, what part of the plant are you eating?

MATH
Which is greater: 0.15 or $\frac{1}{5}$?

BRAIN QUEST

Brain Quest Mini-Deck

ANSWERS

ENGLISH

flavorful

MATH

4 cups

SOCIAL STUDIES

James Madison

MATH

$\frac{1}{4}$

$(\frac{1}{2} \times \frac{1}{2} \times \frac{1}{4} = \frac{1}{4})$

BRAIN QUEST®

ANSWERS

ENGLISH

worried

MATH

$\frac{25}{56}$

SOCIAL STUDIES

after (Jamestown was the first permanant English colony in North America.)

MATH

$\frac{1}{8}$ (Divide both the numerator and denomenator by 8.)

BRAIN QUEST®

ANSWERS

ENGLISH

Cold is to *frigid* as *hot* is to <u>sweltering</u>.

MATH

smaller

SCIENCE

the root

MATH

$\frac{1}{5}$

$(\frac{1}{5} = 0.2)$

BRAIN QUEST®

ANSWERS

ENGLISH

an idea

MATH

$744
(62 \times 12 = 744)$

SOCIAL STUDIES

John Adams and George H. W. Bush

MATH

$1\frac{1}{5}$

$(\frac{3}{4} \times \frac{8}{5} = \frac{24}{20} = \frac{6}{5} = 1\frac{1}{5})$

BRAIN QUEST®

QUESTIONS

ENGLISH — Is a hardy plant <u>healthy</u> or <u>sick</u>?

MATH — How many degrees are in a circle?

ENGLISH — *Tiny* is to *miniature* as *huge* is to <u>immense</u> or <u>compact</u>.

MATH — What fraction of the months have 31 days?

BRAIN QUEST®

QUESTIONS

ENGLISH — Does *industrious* mean <u>boring</u> or <u>hardworking</u>?

MATH — Find the common denominator to solve $\frac{1}{8} + \frac{1}{2}$.

GEOGRAPHY — What is the fiftieth US state?

MATH — Change the decimal to a fraction: 0.45.

BRAIN QUEST®

QUESTIONS

ENGLISH — Does *pardon me* mean <u>help me</u> or <u>forgive me</u>?

MATH — It was sunny 28 days in August. What fraction of the month was sunny?

ENGLISH — *Die* is to *perish* as *live* is to <u>survive</u> or <u>falter</u>.

MATH — Change the fraction to a decimal: $\frac{3}{4}$.

BRAIN QUEST®

QUESTIONS

ENGLISH — *Sluggish* is to *fast* as *vivid* is to <u>bright</u> or <u>drab</u>.

MATH — What is 0.32 + 0.5?

ENGLISH — Is the opposite of *seldom* <u>rarely</u> or <u>often</u>?

MATH — Round 78 to the nearest 10.

BRAIN QUEST®

Brain Quest Mini-Deck

ANSWERS

ENGLISH

hardworking

MATH

$\frac{5}{8}$

$(\frac{1}{2} \times \frac{4}{4} = \frac{4}{8}; \frac{1}{8} + \frac{4}{8} = \frac{5}{8})$

GEOGRAPHY

Hawai'i

MATH

$\frac{9}{20}$

$(\frac{45}{100} = \frac{9}{20})$

BRAIN QUEST

ANSWERS

ENGLISH

healthy

MATH

360°

ENGLISH

immense

MATH

$\frac{7}{12}$

(January, March, May, July, August, October, and December.)

BRAIN QUEST

ANSWERS

ENGLISH

drab

MATH

0.82

ENGLISH

often

MATH

80

BRAIN QUEST

ANSWERS

ENGLISH

forgive me

MATH

$\frac{28}{31}$

ENGLISH

survive

MATH

0.75 (Multiply the numerator and the denominator by 25 to get 75/100. Then represent it as a decimal.)

BRAIN QUEST

QUESTIONS

ENGLISH Spell the word that sounds like *rain* but means *to rule*.

MATH What is 342 × 18?

SCIENCE Is magnesium sulphate ($MgSO_4$) an <u>element</u> or a <u>compound</u>?

MATH Mary worked from 7:01 a.m. to 8:03 p.m. How much time passed?

BRAIN QUEST

QUESTIONS

ENGLISH Spell the word that sounds like *team* but means *to be full of.*

MATH What is 420 ÷ 5?

ENGLISH Add a comma: "You toast the marshmallows and I'll break the chocolate bars in half."

MATH Find the numbers that are multiples of 7: <u>14</u>, <u>23</u>, <u>28</u>, <u>37</u>.

BRAIN QUEST

QUESTIONS

ENGLISH Does *gravy train* mean an <u>easy</u> way to make a living or a <u>dishonest</u> way to make a living?

MATH What is the perimeter of a square with 5-foot sides?

ENGLISH *Have swum* is in the perfect tense. True or false?

MATH Estimate the product by rounding the numbers 49 × 32 to the nearest 10.

BRAIN QUEST

QUESTIONS

ENGLISH Does *have a cow* mean to <u>spend too much money</u> or to <u>get upset</u>?

MATH What is the volume of a box that is 8 cm high, 100 cm long, and 50 cm wide?

ENGLISH Add a comma: "Text me later Kaitlyn!"

MATH What is pi (π) rounded to the nearest hundredth?

BRAIN QUEST

Brain Quest Mini-Deck

ANSWERS

ENGLISH
t–e–e–m (teem)

MATH
84

ENGLISH
"You toast the marshmallows, and I'll break the chocolate bars in half."

MATH
14, 28

BRAIN QUEST

ANSWERS

ENGLISH
to get upset

MATH
40,000 square centimeters or 400 square meters (8 × 100 × 50 = 40,000; 100 centimeters = 1 meter.)

ENGLISH
"Text me later, Kaitlyn!"

MATH
3.14

BRAIN QUEST

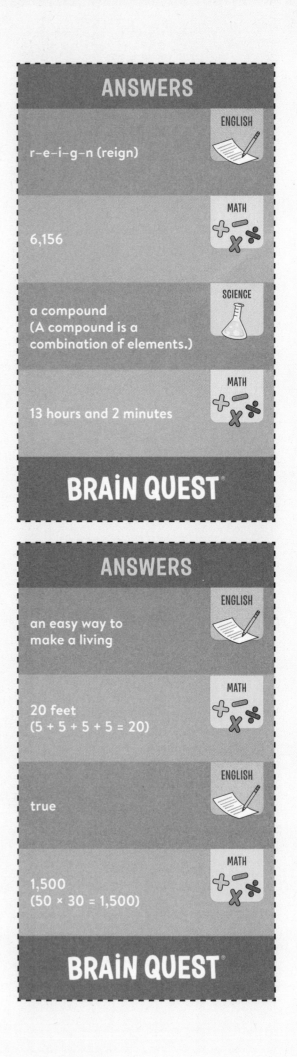

ANSWERS

ENGLISH
r–e–i–g–n (reign)

MATH
6,156

SCIENCE
a compound (A compound is a combination of elements.)

MATH
13 hours and 2 minutes

BRAIN QUEST

ANSWERS

ENGLISH
an easy way to make a living

MATH
20 feet (5 + 5 + 5 + 5 = 20)

ENGLISH
true

MATH
1,500 (50 × 30 = 1,500)

BRAIN QUEST

YOU DID IT!

CONGRATULATIONS!

You completed every activity in the Brain Quest Grade 5 Workbook. Cut out the certificate and write your name on it. Show your friends! Hang it on the wall! You should feel proud of your hard work.

CERTIFICATE OF ACHIEVEMENT

Earned by

_____

for completing all sections in the

BRAIN QUEST®
GRADE 5 WORKBOOK

It's fun to be smart!
From America's #1 Educational Bestseller

Available wherever children's books are sold, or visit brainquest.com.

workman

Brain Quest Grade 5 Workbook